Arrow Lakes Indian Chief James Bernard, 1904.
National Anthropological Archives,
Smithsonian Institution, 4NAAPPP0061.

"Before the coming of the white man, our resources on
this continent, if we could sum it up had a value we could
never put into figures and dollars. Our forests were full
of wild game; our valleys covered with tall grass; we had
camas, huckleberries and bitter-root, and wild flowers of
all kinds. When I walked out under the stars, the air was
filled with the perfume of the wild flowers. In those days,
the Indians were happy, and they danced day and night,
enjoying the wealth created by the Almighty God for the
Indian's use as long as he lived."

—Sinixt Chief James Bernard, addressing a
US congressional committee in the early 20th century

The
GEOGRAPHY
of
MEMORY

The
GEOGRAPHY
of
MEMORY

*Reclaiming the Cultural, Natural
and Spiritual History of the
Snʕayckstx (Sinixt) First People*

EILEEN DELEHANTY PEARKES

RMB

For information on purchasing bulk quantities of this book, or to obtain media excerpts or invite the author to speak at an event, please visit rmbooks.com and select the "Contact" tab.

RMB | Rocky Mountain Books Ltd.
rmbooks.com
@rmbooks
facebook.com/rmbooks

Cataloguing data available from Library and Archives Canada
ISBN 9781771605212 (paperback)
ISBN 9781771605229 (electronic)

Cover and interior design by LimeDesign
Cover photos courtesy of the Canadian Museum of History, 26616, and Mike Graeme

Printed and bound in China

We acknowledge the financial support of the Government of Canada through the Canada Book Fund and the Canada Council for the Arts, and of the province of British Columbia through the British Columbia Arts Council and the Book Publishing Tax Credit.

Disclaimer
The views expressed in this book are those of the author and do not necessarily reflect those of the publishing company, its staff, or its affiliates.

For those who have called out from the past
and for David Neil Delehanty, who taught me to listen

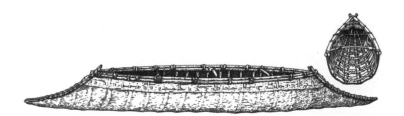

Contents

Foreword xi
Preface xiii

Introduction to the New Edition 1

1. Parting the Veil of Time 7

2. Rivers as Highways and Byways 28

3. Revelstoke to Fauquier · *Journey into the Heartland* 44

4. Fauquier to Castlegar · *Long Shadows in a Broad Valley* 69

5. Rossland to Omak, WA · *Following the Salmon* 92

6. Slocan Lake to Slocan Pool · *Land of the Living* 127

7. Bonnington Falls to the West Arm & Salmo
    Shifting Geographies 148

8. Spokane, WA, to Sinixt Territory
    Lines and Shaded Areas 170

9. Gathering It All In 200

Appendices 219
Notes 237
Contributor Bios 243
Selected Bibliography 245
Acknowledgements 249
Index 251

Foreword

SHELLY BOYD

Sinixt/Arrow Lakes Cultural Facilitator

I feel the weight of my ancestors as I introduce this book. I also feel their strength. I hear their voices. I cannot see them, but they are all around us. They are the mountains and waters of the upper Columbia. **Púti? kʷu? alá?** (we are still here), they whisper. If you stand still and open your ears and heart you can hear them, too.

We stand in a place and time where science often quells the spirit. This book is a paradox in how it uses science, history, archaeology and geography to invoke the spiritual truth of our ancestors.

As a people, we have internalized much of what has been done to us. This book is a medicine for the resulting generational trauma, and a true validation of our experience. Truth is a powerful tonic, but so often, it is bitter to swallow. I cried often reading this book, as I swallowed the bitterness, but that is how healing manifests itself. I cannot speak for the settler communities, but I suspect there is a different bitterness to swallow. Perhaps there is a different medicine, too.

Whatever the trauma and pain that both the Indigenous and settler communities have internalized, I do know that it will not heal with time if left ignored. It is our job to do what we can to keep from passing this trauma to the next generations. Truth is a powerful thing when we follow it and allow it to inspire and give direction to our lives. As I read these pages, I asked myself, "What is my responsibility going forward?" I believe this is a question we all should be asking ourselves.

My mother is one of the wisest people I have ever known. Once, we had a conversation about how I thought she should take on less responsibility and work that others should or could do as she aged into her beautiful years. She told me very sternly: "Shelly I don't *got* to do anything. I *get* to do these things." She went on to say that she may be old, but her arms still work, and she recognizes her abilities and the gift of being able to contribute to the greater good.

I have often observed individuals and government officials saying, "It is not our right to say anything [or often *do* anything] regarding Indigenous history, culture or the Canadian 'reconciliation' project." I say this not as a criticism to the settler culture but hopefully as an empowerment: As human beings, we cannot let fear or politeness keep us from doing the hard work of our generation. Settlers must not sit back and defer all the work of healing to us, the Indigenous People. We must all always remember that we possess the gifts and strength of our arms to do the work. To say the words, to listen and act on truth, as this book does. We must do these things even when we are afraid, because we love our children and those not yet here. Together, we must stop the generational trauma under which we *all* operate – Indigenous or settler.

Lim̓ lm̓ tx (thank you), Eileen, for your ability to stand still, your ability to listen. The land not only remembers, it speaks a truth that our people have lived.

Preface

On April 23, 2021, in a landmark 7–2 ruling, the Supreme Court of Canada held that the Sńʕayckstx (Sinixt) are an Aboriginal People of Canada, a ruling with profound and lasting consequences for the Sinixt, all levels of government, and the non-Indigenous population of Canada. The court confirmed what three lower courts had also acknowledged: the Sinixt People enjoyed sovereignty in the Canadian portion of their territory for thousands of years. Wherever they might live today, they have rights protected by section 35 of the Canadian Constitution.

Prior occupation in the landscape was the legal foundation of the case, built by the uncontested evidence of the contemporary Sinixt who spoke about the enduring connection between their identity and the land. Being Sinixt means being in a direct, reciprocal relationship with the land and waters of the upper Columbia River region, the mountain territory of their ancestors.

This landmark decision has the legal effect of washing away Canada's 1956 extinction declaration and ushers in a new era. The decision also rewrites British Columbia's First Nations maps, so that they reflect the truth of Sinixt existence and identity. It forces the country's colonial governments to acknowledge what they have long avoided, and to face the consequences of the forced displacement of the Sinixt. The border between Canada and the US can no longer be an instrument of colonial injustice.

This story positions itself at the heart of shifting cultural attitudes toward land, people and culture. As the judgment confirms, the next chapter will be written by the Sinixt, as they choose how to organize themselves and reclaim all that was lost. Boundaries are dissolving on a global scale. The landscape is reasserting its power and authority. The people are coming home.

Slocan Lake pictograph. Photo courtesy of Shelly Boyd.

Introduction to the New Edition

In 1997–98, I first began to feel the presence of the Sinixt People in the landscape of the upper Columbia region, an experience that eventually led to the publication of the first edition of this book. At that time, there was little or no public understanding in Canada of the Sinixt – the Indigenous People of the mountains, rivers and lakes of the upper Columbia River. The story, in some ways like the tribe, had been declared "extinct." In addition, while the Sinixt were known and had rights and recognition south of the border, the bulk of their traditional territory in Canada was only a vague idea to many Americans. The impact of an 1846 colonial boundary on their identity, freedom and existence is central to the story.

It could be that as an American living in Canada, I was unconsciously drawn to this story. It's hard to know what about my personal and professional training made me wake me up and set out on an journey of understanding. With no real signs of a reserve, or a group of Indigenous People living in the region, my earliest research in the late 1990s was like walking blind in the written record. I gathered a scattering of dormant resources with the use of a land-line telephone and the inter-library mail-loan system. The day I finished reading a report about the Sinixt that had been filed with a library of government documents in Victoria, BC, is one I will always remember. In Randy Bouchard and Dorothy Kennedy's *Lakes Indian Ethnography and History* (1985), I learned about a Sinixt man named Charlie Quintasket, who journeyed from the Colville Indian Reservation in Washington State to the provincial capital in Victoria, BC, in the late 1970s, to try to draw attention to his existence. I stepped from my writing studio and knew the landscape would never look the same again. I am very grateful that Charlie Quintasket made that journey to speak his truth.

Writers joke about the best way to acquire knowledge on a subject: publish a book about it first. The book you hold in your hand reflects 20 more years of learning since the first edition. New content adds depth and significance to the story, and gives voice to some of the living Sinixt individuals who are most certainly *not* extinct. They continue to inspire and teach me, as I witness them carry their identity with pride, doing so in steady resistance to the colonial forces that have tried to reshape who they are. The narrative picks up a long-dropped stitch, a wishful connection between the people residing in the United States and their own history in Canada, thus creating continuity across time. I also acknowledge those Sinixt descendants not named in the book. All of their stories are important. I appreciate and love my Sinixt friends – for their laughter, their generosity, their dignity and their persistence. This book reflects *their* world – a place of story, meaning, humour and, most of all, a deep, unforgotten love for their territory. The Sinixt belong in the mountains. They are a great gift to the upper Columbia River landscape.

The book calls on two forms of knowledge to assist readers in achieving a deeper understanding. First and foremost, every word of the story of their culture as presented here has been confirmed and accepted as true by the contemporary Sinixt themselves. Second, because the story also exists within a colonial context, it refers to written materials, published history and textual memories, information that was often recorded by the hand of non-Indigenous People but nonetheless reflects the knowledge of Indigenous generations. For the Sinixt, these written records, reviewed critically and used selectively, can be an important validation of what they know to be true already. The result is a tapestry, combining threads of history, ethnography, science and personal essays on the natural world. I have used the terms "Sinixt" and "Lakes Indians" interchangeably in the text, respecting both the contemporary Indigenous and established colonial terms for these people. Many contemporary Sinixt individuals in the US in fact refer to themselves first as "Lakes," and also as "Indians." The use of this term is complex, but the ceasing of the use of "Indian" by those who have adapted to attach their identity to it is also problematic. In the words of Sinixt singer-songwriter Jim Boyd: "Seven generations high/built your nation with a lie/Indians got no more to lose/Except the name ya made us use."

The strictest attention has been paid to historical and ethnographic accuracy, with contemporary Sinixt leaders, local historians and academic experts reviewing the text prior to publication. To allow for free legibility, the text contains no footnotes. An extensive list of supporting documents can be found at the end of this volume in a bibliography and end notes. Many cited sources are now available online, thanks to efforts by private individuals, institutions and governments.

A brief editorial note is necessary regarding the spelling of the names of some of the rivers mentioned in the text: Kootenay is spelled "Kootenai" in the US, Okanagan is spelled "Okanogan" and Pend d'Oreille is spelled "Pend Oreille"; for simplicity, this book will use the Canadian spelling throughout.

It's important to acknowledge that visual record of Lakes Indian material culture and people at or just after the time of contact is extremely limited, with precisely labelled photographs of traditional cultural practice especially rare. This has led to the composition of drawings – with the help of an illustrator and architect – of what often existed only in verbal descriptions from Elders or simple sketches from anthropologists' field notebooks. Readers can use their imaginations to envision the beauty and harmony of Sinixt territory as reflected in their seasonal rounds, their village sites and their pictographs. The book's maps, created by Charles Syrett, have been based largely on the work of Randy Bouchard and Dorothy Kennedy, scholars who worked for years gathering information. In their year 2000 report, they produced a series of maps that assemble and rely on many different sources of information from Elders. Their important work spells and identifies place names with a "practical orthography," one that relies on standard fonts to express sounds unfamiliar to English or French speakers. The maps in this book follow their convention. The map notes, alternatively, spell the names using the international font system of the Salish language, which developed over thousands of years without a written form. I am grateful to the Salish School of Spokane for making this twinned record possible and invite readers to note the differences.

With respect and gratitude to the Sinixt People, and to all those who have assisted me, either in print or in person, I offer that any and all errors found in the text, maps or illustrations are mine alone.

As I learned about the land and the nearly forgotten Indigenous story, I quickly perceived that the settler culture's use and valuing of resources differs significantly from that of the First Peoples. In the first edition, it was not my intent to judge one way or the other as superior, but to recognize that respecting this difference might be an essential step toward cultural reconciliation. Twenty years ago, the path to tolerance for Indigenous presence in landscape was steep and narrow. I navigated an uncertain terrain in which most cultural institutions did not acknowledge the historic presence of the Sinixt. Twenty years ago, Canada had not yet articulated a national goal to embark on what they called their "reconciliation" with Indigenous People. At the time, racism, often unconscious, was a far more dominant force than the acceptance of responsibility for colonial oppression. Some non-Indigenous people criticized me for writing about Indigenous People at all, telling me that it was not "my story to tell." This was, I realize now, a subtle form of silencing. While racism toward Indigenous People still exists across this culture, a groundswell of recognition has begun. In working alongside the Sinixt all these years, I have come to understand that integrating Indigenous perspectives into contemporary culture is not exclusively the responsibility of the Indigenous People. As Shelly Boyd so aptly reminds all of us, we, the settlers, need to listen well and with respect. We need to pick up our pens or cameras or drawing pencils, and dig in to help.

Even as non-Indigenous People projected doubts onto me in the late 1990s when I was working on the first edition, I was lucky to be visited by spirits much stronger than theirs, or my own. At moments when self-doubt nearly overwhelmed me, Sinixt People came to me in night

"Rivers and lakes dominate the valleys in Sinixt traditional territory and are an important part of our spiritual lives. The word in our language for 'water' originates from the word for 'the place where you pray or ask for support.'"

—Shelly Boyd

dreams. Dressed in brightly coloured, fringed buckskin, they beat a drum, sang and danced to me from the shoreline. I floated past them on the Columbia River in a sturgeon-nosed canoe and woke inspired and reassured. One night, I dreamed of a group riding their horses down Nelson's Elephant Mountain and right onto Vernon Street. Strong, healthy and fit, they were trimmed from head to toe in blue jay feathers. Sometimes, a mysterious, disembodied voice sang to me. This happened when I visited the Colville Indian Reservation. I always came awake from each of these dreams humbled and enthralled. With the hair rising on my pale-skinned arms, I wondered what had just happened, and why. Only many years later did I learn from Sinixt/Arrow Lakes cultural facilitator Virgil Seymour what the dreams really mean. *You got tapped on the shoulder by the ancestors, Eileen.* Virgil assured me that I had always been on the right path, writing about his people, and that the ancestors knew it. *You can tell this story, Eileen. Anyone can. So long as it's the Truth.*

Virgil the human being left this world in 2016, but his strong spirit continues to reflect in his "Indian name" **sṅk̓lipqṅ** (Coyote head). His spirit shines bright across my writing desk. I will always thank Virgil for his clear words and perceptions. He taught me that I write as much about the land as I write about the First People. He demonstrated that we can all be part of the story of the land, if we stick to the truth. Then, as now, I hold fast to the historical record and to the reality of the contemporary Sinixt. They still know exactly who they are. The spirit of Coyote continues to light the way.

I can understand why many Indigenous People in Canada don't like the word "reconciliation." When a beginner-writer, I was taught decades ago that "–tion" words should be used sparsely. Grammarians call these –tion types of words *abstract* nouns. They reflect theory, not practice. They are not concrete, and instead represent things that can't be held in the hand. Things without a scent, a colour, a temperature or a taste. They remove us from what is real, and help us dwell in what is not true. I still use these words sometimes, but I am watchful of how they separate readers and even this writer from what I know to be true, from what is actually happening, and where it is happening, and why it has happened. This book attempts to reconcile the colonial past by remaining passionately local, grounded in *place* – because this is what I know. I have come to believe that only through each of our human spirits learning to love, respect and engage fully with the *local* places where we live, can we strip away the tyranny of a restless and wounded colonial spirit. The spirit still drifts and wanders across North America, separating us from the land, the water and each other.

Join me, as the healing road continues.

1.
Parting the Veil of Time

The upper Columbia mountains rise sharply east from the gentle buttes of the expansive Interior Plateau. They include the Monashees, the Selkirks and the Purcells, three stone spines rippling north-south in the shadow of the Continental Divide. Maps label this cordillera hosting a great western river the "Columbia Mountains," harkening to a time when geographical features echoed grand impulse with voyageurs bravely searching out a path to the Pacific Ocean. The early explorers from Europe who attempted to follow the Columbia River to the sea were often humbled by the serpentine upper Columbia valleys and peaks of the river's youthful beginning. As I grew to understand the critical role played by the Columbia River in the history of this place, I began to use the colonial term upper Columbia, as I do now. For the Sinixt, however, this region is not the upper Columbia, nor is it the West and East Kootenay. These mountains are a homeland they call the Place of the Bull Trout. It's a landscape of melting snow where the bull trout

The Incomappleux River, a name based on the Sinixt place name Ṅ kmaplqs.
Remnants of a thousand-year-old cedar forest survive
at the back end of this river valley. Author photo.

once thrived. A place of interconnected cold-water streams and rivers where the ranging fish could roam.

The Columbia Mountains possess a natural beauty appealing to the eye and spirit, but a geography that has long been challenging for colonial commerce and economic prosperity. As in the deeper past, the numerous streams, rivers and lakes of the region are fed but also confined by the steep, azure mountains rising around them, leaving little room on the valley floors for extensive cultivation, commanding vistas or sprawling cities. Some of the most arable farmland has also more recently been flooded permanently by water storage reservoir. True to the dense mountain systems that surround them, the present-day inhabitants of the upper Columbia are proud isolationists not unlike island dwellers, with a choppy granite sea separating people from the vast Interior Plateau to the west and south. It is often difficult to live here, but most seem determined to stay.

The rugged upper Columbia landscape forms a commanding backdrop for many human stories across time. These stories of determined people and tireless mountains reach further back than living memory can recall: Stories of fur trade exploration in a region filled to bursting with a wide variety of mammals, many of which are now extinct or threatened. Stories of missionaries establishing introduction to early Christian churches on sandy beaches or beside massive waterfalls that have since been silenced by dams. Stories of miners and farmers moving rocks out of the way to search for precious metals, or to plant orchards and raise livestock in valleys that have since been converted to reservoirs. Stories of railways being forged almost inconceivably from the steep sides of the mountains, railways whose tracks are now being lifted, one by one. And even before all of these events, even before European culture entered the area, stories of a prehistorical, pre-colonial Indigenous culture rest on the numerous spines of this landscape. The often unspoken memory of this region's First People helps to define the region's haunting but spiritually uplifting energy. In the long narrative that defines this place, a pre-contact culture has lived here with dignity, determination and perseverance. Their nearly forgotten story is being more and more remembered.

The mountains, for their part, have never forgotten.

I have learned about upper Columbia Indigenous history only through persistent effort. Not long after I arrived in the region in 1994,

Kokanee spawning in Caribou Creek. Author photo.

I began to ask questions. Did any prehistorical culture make a life here? Who were they? How did they live? What did they eat, make tools from, live in and wear? My questions were spurred by my developing belief at that time that landscape has a narrative of its own, that place speaks with a wordless certainty of its past. That geography actually has memory. If this is true, if a region can in fact hold and express the stories of human experience in relation to the natural world, then a full understanding of the upper Columbia landscape as home depends on knowing more about all the human history across time. It depends on parting the veil of time that has descended over this place and peering into the open face of the mountains. On listening as far back as my mind and heart would take me, listening for stories that could be felt, even if they could not be heard or read.

Slowly, I began to allow the stones littering beaches to press into the soft skin of my bare feet. I listened to ice-cold water tumble furiously into the lake during spring freshet. I made myself swim in the coldest, cleanest lakes I have ever experienced. I often noticed, as I stroked the dramatic watermarks etched in the stone cliffs at the shoreline, signs of how much water levels could change in a natural spring flood. I watched kokanee return to spawn in the quiet autumn waters. And I learned to smell snow on the wind. As I explored the region throughout the seasons, I came awake to the idea that certain places where I stood might have been campsites, winter villages or fishing grounds for a culture previous to my own. My eyes began to search for physical clues that would reinforce my gut feeling that Europeans were not the first ones here. The upper Columbia has no reserve lands set aside for First Nations, however, and no interpretive centre that details and explains prehistoric inhabitation. It has only fleeting, visible hints of Aboriginal heritage in Castlegar's Zuckerberg Park and small displays in several museums. Obvious clues of an Aboriginal culture thriving here in former times are rare. But I had a feeling, a feeling that could not be ignored. Responses to the questions I asked long-time residents offered little detail. Comprehensive information on prehistory was not readily available to the

Durrand Glacier and Durrand Peak.
Photo courtesy of Madeleine Martin-Preney.

general reading public. Most historians, museums and archives focus research and displays on the heady days of mining and city construction, not on a time when the landscape had a different purpose.

I heard many rumours about the region from long-time inhabitants or more recent arrivals: that the crease of mountain and water where Nelson sits was "the valley of the lost souls" and therefore too sacred to ever have been lived in; that "nomadic" Indigenous People only "passed through" the upper Columbia region to hunt, coming east from the Rocky Mountain trench, or up from the US; I even heard that the snow in Revelstoke was too deep in winter to support human inhabitation. As I walked in the woods, climbed peaks or floated on Kootenay or the Arrow Lakes in a battered aluminum boat, I felt increasingly that an important chapter in the upper Columbia landscape's narrative had gone missing. I could not shake an intuition that the mountains knew something I had not yet learned, something I needed to know. My attempts to define with words what initially began only as a feeling became a five-year-long journey of research and discovery. That journey has now stretched well beyond the book's initial publication, into a trek spanning nearly a quarter of a century. I am still walking, still learning. Learning how much I do not know.

MAPS AND MEANING

In traditional times, the Sinixt had to negotiate a vast, steeply mountainous and varied terrain without the use of a car, train or horse. While they travelled primarily by canoe on waterways, an extensive network of foot trails also connected one upper Columbia tributary valley to another, also allowing access to higher elevations for hunting, mining stone materials or making spiritual quests. Often called "grease trails," they functioned as intertribal trade routes to transport valued items such as bear grease, **sp'its'n** (Indian hemp or *Apocynum cannabinum*), cedar root or bitterroot. No doubt many minor trails also existed that took Lakes Indian women to favoured places for gathering roots, berries or plant fibres. Noticeable signs of all heavily used trails have disappeared, though modern roadways sometimes follow their path, as did the early wagon roads and horse paths of early settlers. Aboriginal knowledge and use of these trails at the time of contact provided invaluable support and assistance to the early explorers and settlers negotiating unfamiliar terrain.

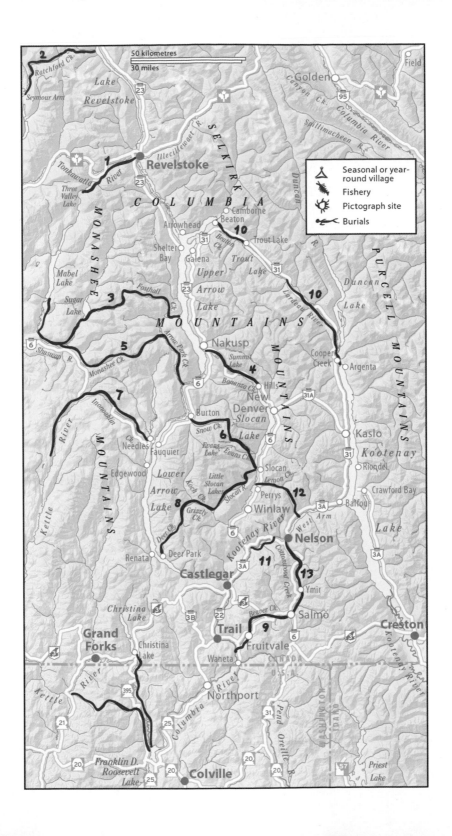

Map labels:

50 kilometres
30 miles

2 — Ratchford Ck.
Seymour Arm
Lake Revelstoke
23
1
Golden
95
Canyon Ck.
Columbia River
Spillimacheen R.
Field

SELKIRK
Illecillewaet R.
1 — Revelstoke
Tonkawatla River
23
Three Valley Lake

MONASHEE

COLUMBIA

Duncan R.

Camborne
Beaton
10
Arrowhead
Trout Lake
31
Beaton Ck.
Shelter Bay
Galena
Upper Arrow Lake
Trout Lake
31
10
Lardeau River

MOUNTAINS

PURCELL MOUNTAINS

Duncan Lake

Mabel Lake
Sugar Lake
3
Fosthall Ck.
6
Shuswap R.
Monashee Ck.
5

Arrow Park Ck.
Nakusp
Summit Lake
4
Bonanza Ck.
Hills
New Denver
Slocan
6
Burton
Snow Ck.
6
Evans Lake
Evans Ck.
Slocan Lake
Cooper Creek
Argenta
Kaslo
31A
Kootenay
31
Riondel
Crawford Bay

7
Inonoaklin River
MOUNTAINS
Needles
Fauquier
Edgewood
Lower Arrow Lake
Koch Ck.
Little Slocan Lakes
Slocan R.
Slocan
Lemon Ck.
Perrys
12
Winlaw
3A
Balfour
Lake
West Arm
3A

Kettle River
8
Grizzly Ck.
Deer Ck.
Renata
Deer Park
Kootenay River
Nelson
Cottonwood Creek
11
13
Castlegar
3A
Ymir
Christina Lake
3B
22
Beaver Ck.
9
Salmo
6
Creston
Kootenay River

Grand Forks
3
Christina Lake
Waneta
Trail
Fruitvale
CANADA
U.S.A.
Kettle River
395
Columbia River
Northport
31
Pend Orielle R.
IDAHO
Priest Lake
57
21
25
Franklin D. Roosevelt Lake
20
20
Colville
20

Today, the memory of these trails offers insight into the natural geography of the landscape. This and subsequent maps have been recreated based on references from historical records such as diaries and government reports. All references in square brackets indicate which explorer or settler first identified the trail and are extracted from *First Nations' Ethnography and Ethnohistory in British Columbia's Lower Kootenay/ Columbia HydroPower Region* by Randy Bouchard and Dorothy Kennedy. The trails identified here are likely to comprise only a portion of those used in former times.

1   West up the Tonkawatla River as far as Three Valley Lake. [Sandford Fleming, 1883]

2   North from the head of Seymour Arm on Shuswap Lake along the Seymour River to Ratchford Creek, crossing the Monashees through Pettipiece Pass. [Walter Moberly, 1865–66]

3   Along Fosthall Creek over the Monashees to Shuswap River/ Sugar Lake/Mabel Lake [Walter Moberly, 1865–66; James Bissett, 1868]

4   Up Nakusp Creek to Summit Lake and then alongside Bonanza Creek to the north end of Slocan Lake. [George Dawson, 1889]

5   From the north Okanagan across the Monashees to Arrow Park Creek by two routes, one more northerly, one more southerly. [Walter Moberly, 1865–66]

6   From Burton up Snow Creek and over the Valhalla Range to the south end of Slocan Lake. [William Mosely, 1965]

7   West from near Needles, following the Inonoaklin Creek Valley [W.G. Cox, 1860s; James Teit, 1930; William Mosely, 1965]

8   From the south end of Slocan Lake up through the valley of the Little Slocan River, west along Koch Creek, then southwest via Grizzly, Greasybill and Deer creeks to Deer Park. [George Dawson, 1889]

9   Along the Columbia near Waneta into the Beaver Creek Valley, then northeast to Salmo. [Rollie Mifflin, early 1900s]

10 From the northeast arm of Upper Arrow Lake following Beaton Creek and Wilkie Creek to Trout Lake, then from Trout Lake along the Lardeau River valley to Kootenay Lake. [James Turnbull, 1860s; James Bissett, 1868]

11 Portage around the two Bonnington Falls on the south side of the Kootenay River, along a low bench of land where the Kootenay Canal now sits. As many as 14 small and unidentified portages in addition to this one existed on the Kootenay River from its mouth east to the two waterfalls. These were used to varying degree depending on seasonal water levels.

12 From Lemon Creek to Six Mile Lakes and down Duhamel Creek to the West Arm of Kootenay Lake. [George Dawson, 1889]

13 From Nelson around upper and lower Cottonwood Falls, up the Cottonwood Creek drainage to Salmo. [Chief James Bernard referred to this area as "access to caribou hunting" when anthropologist Verne Ray interviewed him, circa 1920s–30s. Prior to colonization, large herds of caribou once roamed the mountain forests south of Nelson, drawn to valleys during annual, autumn breeding.]

The memory of these mountains stretches far back. Geology tells us that even human activity thousands of years old has only a momentary presence in the longer arc of time that bends around the landscape and its formation. Glaciers once covered much of the Columbia Mountains. These were massive sheets of ice thick with a strength capable of carving bedrock. Around 13,000 years ago, as the most recent ice age came to a close, the climate began to warm and the glaciers to melt. As the ice liquefied and broke up over the next 5,000 or more years, its massive, shifting force scoured U-shaped valleys and loosened rock to form glacial till, rock and sand of various sizes. Water and time then began to polish the pebbles, stones and sands that the shifting ice had deposited on various beaches. The movement of glaciers has helped form the varying undulations of the upper Columbia terrain we all love: alpine peaks, subalpine ridges and low shelves of land near to the water's edge. As the glaciers shifted and shrank, the terrain drained seasonal snowmelt into the valleys where, for eons, sizable bodies of ice remained. When this ice itself finally gave way, it left behind the deep, clear lakes we see today: the Arrows, Kootenay and Slocan. Increasingly, rivers flowed free from the ice and all the waters filled with a wide variety of aquatic life. Rushing tributary streams carried silt and sand down from the high peaks, gradually creating alluvial fans as they met the shore. These broad deltas of sand and soft soil transformed over time to host rich wetland ecosystems.

Even before all the ice was gone from the valleys, human culture moved into the region. Archaeological material uncovered at Kettle Falls, Washington, and Deer Park (north of Castlegar, BC), suggests that people came upstream from the Interior Plateau sometime after 10,000 years before the present (b.p.). Evidence gathered by a limited number of archaeological investigations in the upper Columbia valleys points to those using the landscape several thousand years ago being the distant ancestors of a culture anthropologists and archaeologists call Arrow Lakes Indians. The Lakes Indians are also known by their self-chosen name: in a linguistic spelling of their own language, **Sn̓ʕay̓ckstx**, broken down into meaning and pronunciation as: Place of the [sin] Bull Trout [EYE-ch-kiss] People [tahh]; in a contemporary anglicized form Sinixt (sin-EYE-ch-kiss-tahh). Prior to Europeans arriving in the early 19th century, the Lakes Indians lived a hunter-fisher-gatherer lifestyle on the fringes of the region's lakes and rivers. Archaeological evidence of permanent village sites dating from 6000 b.p. to the time of European contact exist all over the upper Columbia region: from Kettle Falls, Washington, north to Christina Lake / Castlegar ; from the Kettle River valley east to Bonnington Falls, Grohman Creek and the West Arm of Kootenay Lake; along the length of the Slocan and Arrow Lakes valleys, and at the north end of Kootenay Lake along the Lardeau River and Trout Lake. This is a Salishan tribe, sharing traits with other British Columbia Interior Salish people such as the Okanagan, the Nlaka'pamux (Thompson) and the Secwepemc (Shuswap). The language they speak is a dialect of **n̓səl̓xčin̓**, the language also spoken by the Okanagan people living to their west and the Spokane and Skoyelpi (Colville) people living to their south. Before European contact, the Sinixt lived

Artist's reconstruction of the Slocan Narrows site near Lemon Creek, British Columbia. By Eric S. Carlson, used with permission of Nathan Goodale.

in subterranean pit houses in permanent villages of 50–200 in winter. While the whole tribe was led by one head Chief, each village had a local Chief, whom they called a "thinker." These men or women thinkers from various villages formed a council for the entire tribe. The social organization of the Sinixt has been classified by one anthropologist as matrilocal, with next generations choosing to reside with the wife's family rather than the husband's, in order to capitalize on the knowledge of plant and medicine foods.

The Sinixt moved systematically about the region within a finite circle, especially in the warmer months, as they performed seasonal rounds from one food source to another before returning to permanent winter village sites for the long winter. Their carefully timed movements demonstrated intimate knowledge of the forests and waterways and an ability to maximize and tend food resources as they came available. Following a spring, summer and early autumn of intensive food gathering and hunting in various places, they settled down for a season spent by the fire: checking nearby traps, weaving or sewing and telling stories. Given the rhythms of the upper Columbia climate, food preservation and storage were important aspects of their culture. The religion of these people was and continues to be closely linked with the natural world. Like other Interior Salish, they express spirituality through the vision quest, winter dancing and the sweat lodge. The Sinixt consider dreams, visions and the acquisition of guardian spirits from the natural world to be essential qualities of their religious life. Prior to European contact, in fact, boys were sent out into the wild alone and girls were secluded in special retreat dwellings immediately before the onset of puberty. There, they fasted and prayed to receive adult wisdom, often in the form of a guardian spirit, who would be with them throughout their lives. These spiritual connections to nature were not generally revealed in a public way, although some tribal members with greater power would paint pictures of their guardian experience on rock. The pictographs then became destinations for later generations of questers. Some examples of these important spiritual signposts are still visible on rock cliffs in the region, though many have weathered away. Sweat lodges also hold religious value in contemporary life, with all parts of the sweating process having extensive ritual and spiritual significance.

The life led by the Sinixt appears, as with most Interior Salish tribes, to have been relatively peaceful, prosperous and balanced. They were not an aggressively warlike people, though they were known to avenge raids by neighbouring tribes or recover women who had been stolen as slaves. The Sinixt themselves did not own slaves. Despite long winters during which large portions of the Columbia and other rivers were iced over, the upper Columbia provided enough fish, game and plant foods to keep the villages fed through the dormant time, and the Sinixt fiercely defended these resources. The historical and ethnographic record details wars fought with Ktunaxa (Kutenai) neighbours to the east, and also disputes with Secwepemc (Shuswap) neighbours to the north and west, usually over fishing or hunting grounds, sometimes over women. Their relations with neighbours to the south, with whom the Sinixt shared the salmon resources at Kettle Falls, appear to have been peaceable. In particular, the Sinixt relationship with the Skoyelpi (Colville), who remained at and around the great fishery at Kettle Falls, was sisterly and mutually supportive, as it remains today. Intermarriages between these two sister tribes were very common. For early settlers, their distinct identities often blurred together under the label "Colvilles."

Accounts of the extent of territory and resources the Sinixt protected vary widely, from their own contemporary estimation (the Monashee subrange of the Columbia mountains east to the height of the Rockies, north to the Big Bend of the Columbia River and south to Kettle Falls) to lines drawn by limited information gathered from recent historical record (the Monashee subrange east to Bonnington Falls, north to Revelstoke and south to Kettle Falls, Washington). Some estimates include the Kettle River valley on both sides of the international boundary and extend east as far as the west shores of Kootenay Lake. Some estimates continue to the height of the Purcell mountains on the opposite shore. Wherever lines might be drawn, it is clear that the Columbia Mountain system that hosts the upper reaches of the Columbia River comprises the core of Sinixt territory. These are the people of the headwater mountains and rivers of the fourth largest watershed in North America.

They were here, but what happened to this upper Columbia Indigenous culture? Why does the contemporary landscape display so little sign of them? And why have many people outside of the region never heard of them? Relative to their long lineage in this place, the process of their disappearance was as swift as the rivers they had always travelled. As with so many Indigenous People, the erasure involved displacement, conquest and cultural change. Much of it stemmed from the rapid and widening influence of colonial exploration and settlement as two forces of acquisition met each other. United States gold rush activity moved north into the region as the Dominion of Canada spread west across the prairies and east across British Columbia. Precious minerals found embedded in upper Columbia rock spurred the rapid development of railways. And then a fresh wave of modern conquest came to seal the process, with the region's taming of its wild rivers flooding of much of the landscape's archaeological record of its deeper past.

The first official colonial contact between the Sinixt and Europeans in today's Canada is often marked as 1811, when David Thompson entered the upper Columbia region in his search for a navigable route to the Pacific, travelling up from the south. But the presence of Europeans had been felt earlier in Sinixt territory, when Thompson had travelled up Kootenay Lake in 1808, attempting to reach the Columbia from the east. Even earlier, first contact came in the form of disease, arriving in either the 1770s or 1780s as a smallpox epidemic, likely spread through intertribal trade. This epidemic was the first of many to affect the Sinixt over the next several decades. Measles and influenza followed in succession, then possibly smallpox again, to reduce the population even more. More measles and then diphtheria ravaged their numbers. In response, they regrouped closer to the core of their territory. It is important to note that by the time Thompson arrived, and then trade forts began to be established in the 1820s, the numbers of Sinixt living in their own mountain landscape would have already been drastically reduced by these diseases, from perhaps as many as several thousand to as few as several hundred. In addition to this dramatic decrease in population, the Sinixt would have experienced a weakening of their entire culture, as they buried many more dead than remained survivors and adjusted their inhabitation patterns to survive and rebuild.

In the wake of the first waves of disease, the Hudson's Bay Company (HBC) quickly established two trade forts along the upper Columbia: one (only briefly) at the former head of Upper Arrow Lake, at the site of the now flooded community of Arrowhead (Fort of the Lakes, or McKay's House), and one very successfully for a much longer time near Kettle Falls, about 25 miles south of the 49th parallel (Fort Colvile, later spelled Colville). In the 1850s, as a response to the newly established US–Canada boundary and the impact of American tax law on the British company,

---

(*facing*) David Thompson, explorer and cartographer for the fur trade, kept extensive journals in which he measured and noted geographic points. These helped him create a map for the fur trade. His observations during his travels through the upper Columbia River region between 1807 and 1812 were largely practical and usually specifically related to mapping. His journals, and those journals, diaries and letters of other early explorers, did not catch everything about the Indigenous experience, nor were they trying to. Unfortunately, settler historians depended on these sources for many years, with omissions or oversights in them often contributing to misunderstandings of Indigenous identity.

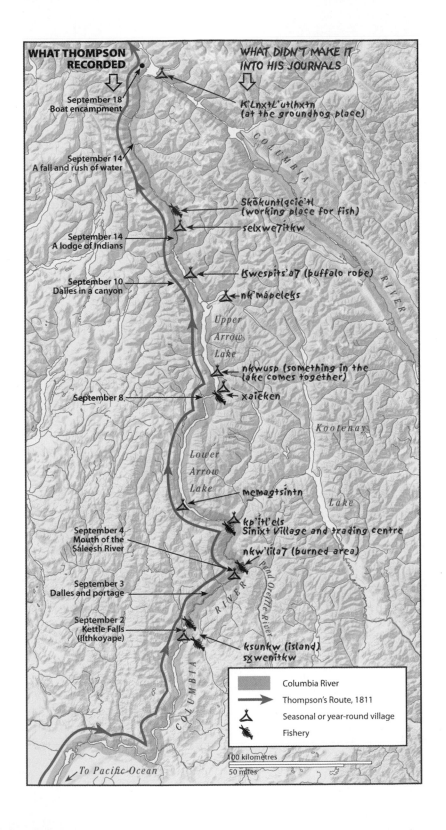

WHAT THOMPSON RECORDED ⇩

September 18
Boat encampment

September 14
A fall and rush of water

September 14
A lodge of Indians

September 10
Dalles in a canyon

September 8

September 4
Mouth of the Saleesh River

September 3
Dalles and portage

September 2
Kettle Falls
(łłthkoyape)

WHAT DIDN'T MAKE IT INTO HIS JOURNALS ⇩

Ḵ'LnxłŁ'utłhxłn
(at the groundhog place)

Skŏkuntłgcie'łl
(working place for fish)

selxwe7itkw

ḵswespits'a7 (buffalo robe)

nk'mápeleḵs

Upper Arrow Lake

nkwusp (something in the lake comes together)

xaīeken

Kootenay

Lower Arrow Lake

Lake

memagtsintn

kp'itl'els
Sinixt Village and trading centre

nkw'lila7 (burned area)

ḵsunḵw (island)
sxwenitkw

Pend Oreille River

COLUMBIA

RIVER

COLUMBIA

To Pacific Ocean

	Columbia River
→	Thompson's Route, 1811
⛺	Seasonal or year-round village
🐟	Fishery

100 kilometres
50 miles

a third fort was built at Fort Shepherd, just north of the international border beside the Columbia River. The presence of the latter two forts especially changed how the Sinixt used their homeland. They spent winters around the prosperous trade centres in rectangular mat lodges rather than live in traditional pit house villages upstream. Gradually in this way, the Sinixt moved southward to the lower portion of their territory for a longer portion of the year. They were attracted to the trade encouraged by fort managers and also grew increasingly dependent on missionaries, who offered smallpox vaccinations to accompany baptisms into the new faith. The HBC announced the closure of Fort Shepherd in 1870, though trading at the fort continued until the summer of 1871. Fort Colville ceased operations in 1871, decisively ending the era of fur trade and exploration. After its closure, the US government finally established an Indian Reservation in central Washington to house many of the tribes that had lived along the upper Columbia and traded at the fort, including the Lakes. This reservation had been in the works since 1853, when Washington Territory was created and a transcontinental railway was being planned across territory still relatively "unsettled" and dominated by the presence of First Nations. Between 1853 and 1872, US government officials drew maps, took account of Indian populations and met with leaders from the various tribes, among them the Lakes Chief, Gregoire. Their negotiations extinguished freedom in vast portions of their traditional territories but preserved tribal access to the salmon fishery. That access had been promised earlier, by an oral agreement between HBC Governor Simpson and the Salmon Chief at Kettle Falls.

But as Sinixt descendant, historian and professor Laurie Arnold points out in her essay later in this volume, the US government altered the original agreement within months. The fishery at Kettle Falls was initially preserved, but the root digging, berrying grounds and Skoyelpi villages of the Colville valley were not. For the Sinixt and their sister tribe, the days of peacefully co-existing with missionaries and trade fort managers along both sides of the Columbia while maintaining some form of the original hunter-gatherer lifestyle in their traditional territory appeared to be over. Compounding this loss was an apparent decline in salmon runs at the once prolific falls. US Army Colonel John C. Tidball commented in 1883 that the salmon numbers at this fishery were down, given extensive harvesting at the mouth of the Columbia to supply canneries.

Within a few decades, with mining and settlement interests rising in the region, the reservation boundary was redrawn again in the 1890s, this time to exclude the fishery at Kettle Falls and remove the Lakes traditional territory surrounding the Kettle and Columbia rivers that touched the international boundary. While the reservation shrank, its number of inhabitants rose, with census rolls from that time listing an additional few hundred Lakes and Colville Indians, many of whom moved south not to abandon their territory, but to be with family members. A large, geographical gap thus formed between the homeland of Lakes Indians on the US reservation and their traditional lands in Canada. The fur trade's clear understanding of the traditional territory and identity of the Lakes tribe did not persist with the next wave of arriving settlers. According to the research of Andrea Geiger, no reserve lands were set up in Canada for the Sinixt, in part due to a government Indian agent missing their presence when he passed through the region in the early 1880s. The Canadian government's misconception of the origins of the Lakes Indians, and an oppressive desire to define them as "American" Indians, was its own form of border patrol.

Canadian upper Columbia newcomers called for the Indians from "Uncle Sam's domain" to go back where they belonged and cease to hunt or fish the resources that they considered belonged to settlers. The Sinixt saw their movements as north and south within their existing territory, not across countries. The continuation of this seasonal migration demonstrated their draw to the cultural practices of their ancestors, something perhaps impossible for the new arrivals to understand. Though the Sinixt wintered farther south, historical record demonstrates that they continued despite pressure from conquest and the drawing of the international boundary to consider the upper Columbia a place of traditional importance. However, maintaining even a portion of the Sinixt traditional way of life in the upper Columbia region became increasingly difficult. Their seasonal appearance appeared to settlers to be nomadic, invasive or illogical. This confusion, fed by ignorance and racism, may have magnified tensions between settlers and those Sinixt attempting traditional rounds. In addition, settlers may not have wanted to encourage the use of land by Aboriginal people, since it might complicate their own ability to capitalize freely on the mineral and timber resources the mountains and rivers offered.

A few families held out with their seasonal returns in the hope that a reserve might be established in Canada, which it finally was, in 1902. But the Canadian government's choice of Oatscott (near present-day Needles, on the west shore of the Columbia) did not adequately address the Sinixt People's method for using the region's widely distributed resources in their traditional ways, with certain families frequenting certain areas in deeply embedded cultural practice. The Christian family, for instance, refused to live on the isolated reserve located on the west shore of Lower Arrow Lake because it would require abandoning important family gravesites and removing themselves from familiar fishing or hunting grounds near Brilliant, not to mention impinging on another family's use of land encompassed by the reserve. In addition, the reserve had no road access, no ferry, no school and no health care. To complicate matters further, records show that many of those living at Oatscott were of mixed ancestry, some of them Shuswap or Ktunaxa who had intermarried with Lakes. So, by the time anthropologists entered the more remote corner of the upper Columbia just after the turn of the century to gather cultural and historical information about the region's First Peoples, the presence of the Sinixt was already faint and growing fainter, making an accurate depiction of even the recent past in BC very challenging for those early scholars such as James Teit and Verne Ray. Of course, the loss of Indigenous culture before it could be recorded and understood was a story occurring across Canada, not just in the upper Columbia. However, the geographic tricks of this relatively isolated region, coupled with the transborder nature of Sinixt Territory, magnified the Lakes' separation from the much larger Canadian portion of their home landscape.

The ambiguous profile of the Sinixt at the time when Canadian anthropologists began collecting data about British Columbia's First Peoples after about 1900 sowed the seeds for future decades of academic and historical misunderstanding. Between 1902 and the 1930s, a small number of Sinixt lived on the Oatscott reserve, a family lived on at the mouth of the Kootenay River, and a few more pockets of Sinixt returned annually to hunt, fish and gather wild foods as far north as Revelstoke. But free crossing at the border became more and more difficult. Strict enforcement of BC game laws denying rights to any non-residents of BC discouraged hunting practices that dated back thousands of years, based on a border that dated back less than a century. Fewer and fewer Sinixt

Sinixt People, likely on the shores of lower Arrow Lake, early 20th century.
One of the canoes is canvas, the other traditional bark.
Photo taken circa 1900, courtesy of Vancouver Archives.

living in the United States made the journey north. In 1953, Annie Joseph, the last known Arrow Lakes Indian woman listed on the Oatscott reserve rolls, died. The following year, an investigation of allotments in the North Half was conducted by a British Columbia commission, attempting to determine if Canadian Indians had been issued Colville allotments. The timing may have been a coincidence, or it may have been a reflection of the colonial policy that an Indigenous person could not have rights, property or any other entitlement in two countries.

A few years later, the Canadian Government declared the Arrow Lakes Indian Band "extinct." At that time, 257 "Lakes Indians" were enrolled with the Colville Confederated Tribes of Washington State. Even more may have been living off-reserve and simply not been counted. For nearly a decade, the US and Canada had been quietly and seriously discussing a plan to create large water storage reservoirs in Canada, to enhance power production and buffer spring flood in the US. An engineering document that did not account for cultural use of land by

Aboriginal people, the Columbia River Treaty was the two governments' plan to eliminate the possibility of another great flood like that of 1948. The Canadian and BC governments, eager to receive financial compensation in return for US control of the upper Columbia's water, could not have been highly motivated to account for the Lakes Indians' historic use of the region's resources during contemporary times. To account for the Sinixt certainly would have complicated a water treaty process that involved the flooding of valleys used traditionally by them for a very long time. The government's apathy and/or avoidance, nestled within a widely held belief at the time that Aboriginal people were part of a "vanishing race," was typical of the era. Those who could not survive in a "modern" world were destined to disappear. The bureaucratic extinction of the Arrow Lakes Indians in Canada was consistent with this belief.

For nearly a century, despite efforts on the tribe's part, the story of the Sinixt was confined largely to references in the deeper layers of the historical record. Even though local and provincial governments received and had on file many archaeological and ethnographic reports confirming the Sinixt prehistorical and historical presence, government officials still have not widely or publicly acknowledged this fact, referred to the reports, or facilitated the telling of the landscape's true story to the general public. In their formal treaty negotiations with neighbouring tribes that do have rights in British Columbia, the government of BC has published maps that do not mention the Sinixt. They have encouraged the tribes north, east and west of Sinixt traditional territory to move forward with land claims negotiations, in a way that further complicates matters and certainly denies the truth.

Thus, the demise on paper of the Arrow Lakes Indians in 1956 has nearly caused the extinction of an important chapter of natural and cultural history in Canada's western mountain region. Silence about their story was for many years compounded by the lack of information about upper Columbia pre-colonial history in school curriculums, local history books or museum displays. Multiple generations grew up knowing next to nothing about the truth of the region's Indigenous history. A sole exception to mid-century government apathy was H.W. (Bert) Herridge, former member of parliament for Kootenay West, who began a personal quest for information on the Arrow Lakes Indians in the late 1940s. Inspired by his own boyhood recollection of seeing Sinixt summer villages just north of Nakusp at the mouth of Kuskanax Creek, and by the presence of pit house depressions on his Nakusp property, he decided to write a popular history. He indicated to Selkirk College Library in 1971 that he had been collecting papers and information to do so and intended to start writing soon. Unfortunately, Herridge died in 1973 before he could. Had Herridge been able to write his book, things might have been different in the later 20th century. Were it not for Charlie Quintasket's visit to the British Columbia government's capitol, contemporary upper Columbia residents might never have had full access to this story of a landscape and its First People. The more recent presence of Sinixt People who arrived from Washington State in 1989 to protect burial grounds (an ongoing peaceful occupation of the Vallican heritage site by the Sinixt); the legal pursuit under the Department of Immigration by a Sinixt man named Robert Watt; and, finally, the Colville Confederated Tribes' decision to pursue a hunting rights test case against the government of BC have all been continued efforts to call the government's attention to the issue. The government's response has been at best uncomfortable and avoidant, and at worst disrespectful.

Uncovering the region's buried or flooded prehistory has been and will continue to be an arduous task, akin to marking a trail up a mountain and across a minefield of potential error, misjudgment or mistruth. Knowing and honouring the Indigenous presence of the Columbia Mountains requires an extra amount of digging, a more than careful review of what one reads, and a listening ear tuned to the faint sound of a natural river, barely audible over the deafening roar of water passing through dams. A quick search online does not suffice. Paying attention to the deeper past of a landscape is an acquired skill, one that involves sifting through a mixture of fact, myth, intuition and fragmented dream. But the listener is always rewarded with a more enriched sense of the human stories that have formed this place and a more complete understanding of the rich and complex mountain ecosystem that once hosted the Columbia River. Nature does not dominate our lifestyle as it did in the days of **Sn̓ ʕayckstx**, even though the contemporary berry picker, hiker, hunter, fisher, herbalist, prospector, birder, biologist or logger can testify to its ongoing cultural significance. Wild landscape is an important story, a story happening many times. And in the book of where we live, our love of place connects this contemporary settler culture with that of the Indigenous People, building a bridge of mountains across time.

2.
Rivers as Highways and Byways

Indigenous plants take on enormous significance in all human Indigenous cultures. For the Sinixt, in traditional times, every living plant in the forests along the rivers and lakes of the upper Columbia region had a potential use. Plants thriving in this interior wet-belt ecosystem supported all aspects of their lifestyle, from transportation and housing to clothing, cooking and healing. Shrubs, flowers, ground covers and trees that regenerated year after year were the warehouse for their building and crafting needs. When I walk in these woods, I marvel at the variety of the region's evergreen trees in particular. Being wetter and more moderate than much of the BC interior, but still hot and dry in spells, the upper Columbia has a wide range of conifers. The site of one of North America's most northern boreal rainforests, it has a much wider variety of plants than most interior forests separated from the moderating maritime influence. The upper Columbia mountains capture some of the clouds scudding east from the coast mountains and hold them as they release the rain. Western red cedar, several types of fir, pine and spruce,

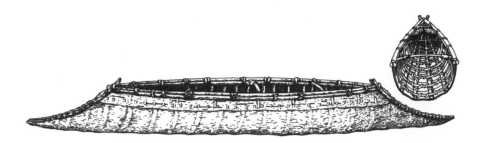

"The chief, with wife and daughter, accompanied us in their canoe, which they
paddled with great dexterity, from ten to fifteen miles. They make their canoes
of pine bark, being the only Indians who use this material for the purpose;
their form is also peculiar and very beautiful. These canoes run the rapids
with more safety for their size, than any other shape."

—Artist Paul Kane on the Arrow Lakes, 1847

and even, in a few rare patches, yellow cedar have found a home in the
rainforest mountains. Hemlock, a moisture-loving tree common in the
coastal temperate rainforest, thrives along creeks in the upper Columbia
region where soils never freeze hard. Yew, a tree prized by the Sinixt for
the strength of its wood in making bows, also grows in a few locations.
And the larch, or tamarack, a unique deciduous conifer, spreads bright
burnished needles across the steep blue mountain slopes each October.

Of all the region's variety of cone-bearing trees, one stands out above
the rest for its gifts to the Sinixt culture. One of five different pine species native to southeastern BC, it offered bark in large, thin sheets that
could be worked into canoes of dexterity and strength. While less
numerous today, the western white pine once thrived in the upper Columbia valleys. Ecologists theorize that before European settlers began
arriving in the region, white pine was the dominant conifer. Thriving
on low-intensity fires, once common to the south-facing slopes of the
valleys, that occurred naturally every few decades, it flourished in the
rhythms of this disturbance. The extensive fires set by settlers in the
1880s to make mineral finds broke this pattern and may have resulted in even more density of pine as the vegetation recovered. Through

the early part of the 20th century, a matchstick factory in Nelson took advantage of the increased supply of white pine, contributing to its declining population. Then, around 1930, a fungal disease called blister rust arrived from the coast, killing great numbers of the trees that remained. Today, all fires close to human interface are tightly controlled, limiting the low-intensity, natural disturbance that once encouraged the white pine to regenerate. Blister rust continues to affect the health and longevity of many of the area's pines, western white pine among them. The Latin and scientific term, *Pinus monticola* ("pine dwelling in the mountains") describes the tree's ecological preferences. The common name, white pine, refers to the pale colour of its wood when cut into matchsticks.

A relatively uncommon, mature white pine grows along Hume Creek in Nelson, within sight of my kitchen window. For today's upper Columbia residents dependent on automobiles, powerboats and fibreglass technology, it is hard to imagine the white pine having any more significance than simply being one of the many conifers that grace the slopes of the mountainous valley where we live, providing wood to be logged, or habitat for the region's wild animals. The Sinixt dialect word for this tree, **tl'i7'b7lekw**, hints at its significance, translating as "bark-canoe wood." Derived from the name for the canoe itself, **tl'iy 'a5i7**, the name points clearly to the cultural significance of the tree prior to European contact. The size of the white pine in my neighbourhood would have appealed to Sinixt canoe builders. It rises 50 feet or more, forming a distinguished spread of branches trimmed by a spiky lace of greenish-grey needles that sway elegantly in strong winds. Near the top, branches hang heavy with long cinnamon-brown cones that curve gracefully to a point. When I stand at its base, the tree is so large that my arms, trying to encircle it, reach only just beyond the diameter. The bark is rough and grey and scratches my cheek. The pitch oozes clear, golden and gooey. When I follow the trunk skyward with my eyes, I cannot imagine the strength and technique required of Sinixt men to strip the bark of such a tree without metal or machine tools.

So culturally significant was this tree to the lives of the Sinixt People that its name is not merely scientifically descriptive or poetically observant, but intensely practical and referring directly to the tree's specific use. This, the language tells us, is the tree that provides the bark for canoes. This, we can infer, was an important tree in the region before

European contact, both for its wide availability and for its role as a sort of spine for the culture. Many of the earliest European visitors to the region have left records of the Interior Salish canoe used by the Sinixt and other Interior Plateau tribes, in part because of its unique appearance and great utility. Fashioned so that the bow and stern curved not up to a point (as was common in so many birchbark canoes farther east, and in Pacific coastal dugout canoes) but sloped down to lie flat on the water, the canoe struck most explorers or settlers who saw it as remarkably adapted for the tumultuous waters of the rivers it travelled. It was described variously by those early visitors as being sturgeon-nosed, looking like a moose without horns in the water, or having a bow that warded off the rapids like the thrusting beak of a bird. David Thompson, no stranger to canoeing himself, particularly praised the design, noting that a canoe sturdy and large enough to hold six people could also be carried easily on the shoulder by one individual in a portage.

Compared to fibreglass canoes commonly used on upper Columbia waters today, such durable and light technology is remarkable to contemplate. Within the geographical context of the Sinixt, their ability to build such a strong and elegant vessel just makes sense. Water-borne people, they lived at all times close to lakes or rivers. They travelled primarily by watercourse, moving from salmon fishing spots to the entrance to hunting grounds always in their canoes, navigating around the region's towering mountain valleys by following the valley's rivers. They understood clearly the geographical challenges: that rivers could be treacherous by turn and sometimes impassable, too. So, unlike the great Haida vessels, their canoes needed to be supple and responsive, and easily portable on land in order to facilitate a portage. And they needed to be low to the water for stability as they moved through river rapids. The bark of a mature white pine, exceptionally thin at about two centimetres and yet very strong, was an excellent choice, making a canoe of great durability and flexibility of use. The last known traditional canoe to be made by a Sinixt man was that commissioned from Baptiste Christian by James Teit, during the time in which Teit interviewed the Christian family at the mouth of the Kootenay River in the spring of 1909. By the time Teit returned in July, the canoe was finished. The canoe was sold and shipped to the Berlin Museum, where it was stored until Second World War bombing destroyed it.

Nancy Wynecoop in
1936. Photo taken by
William Elmendorf.
Courtesy of the
Wynecoop family.

Here is the process of constructing a traditional canoe from start
to finish, paraphrased from Sinixt Elder Nancy Wynecoop (recorded
in notes taken by ethnographer William Elmendorf), with additions
from a narrative by the Arrow Lakes pioneer settler C.J.C. Slade, who
recalled a Sinixt man living around Burton named Louis Joseph making one in 1911. Nancy Wynecoop told Elmendorf that prior to building
a canoe, Sinixt men held a ceremony that included dancing, fasting
and sweat-bathing, to help make them more agreeable with each other
and focus their constructive energy. Such preparations reflect a reverence for the work and strongly suggest the cultural importance of

successfully constructing canoes. Living without a canoe in the upper Columbia prior to European contact would have been akin to living without a car in today's culture. Prior to the arrival of metal tools in the region, traditional Sinixt canoe builders would often strip the bark off a standing tree with the help of adzes made of sharpened stone. Sometimes, they felled a mature tree. After scraping off the outer bark, they split the inner bark on a vertical line and peeled off the heartwood in one sheet. Turning it inside out, they oiled it with deer tallow, to prevent cracking and maintain flexibility as it dried. They marked the outside shape of the canoe on the ground with stakes and fastened the gunwales to these stakes. Next, willow ribs were fastened to the gunwales, using willow bark twine. The bark was sewn onto the ribs, using cedar root. An additional layer of bark was fastened less securely onto the outside of the craft. All seams were glued with warm pine pitch. On the bow and stern of the canoe, the bark was folded over rings of willow. Extra layers were added for strength, shaped into a point, and sewn. A frame of woven poles was placed in the bottom of the canoe and covered with loose grass to sit on.

Traditional Sinixt Interior Salishan canoes no longer grace the waters of the upper Columbia River and the Arrow Lakes, though Spokane, Washington, resident and Sinixt descendant Shawn Brigman has spawned a renaissance of the original technique. He has also developed his own unique adaptations with the use of modern materials. The "bark-canoe wood" still grows here, and sometimes a white pine of full maturity can be seen rising resplendent toward the sky. When I gather its cones or clip its branches, I think about the effort required to peel bark in one unbroken sheet. I think about the light and sturdy canoes once gracing this water. These are vessels that grew, it seemed, out of the very landscape that made them possible.

RECOVERING SINIXT ART AND ARCHITECTURE

contributed by Shawn Brigman, PhD

My geographical movement back to ancestral Sinixt territory above the 49th parallel happened because of the late Virgil Seymour (Sinixt/ Arrow Lakes facilitator 2013–16). In June 2013, Virgil, with assistance from Jessica Morin, invited me to display my traditional conical tule mat lodge during a Selkirk College Aboriginal Youth Conference in Castlegar, BC. This opportunity gave me the confidence to continue exploring my Sinixt heritage in British Columbia. Another cherished memory that remains with me is being reunited with my late aunty Evelyn Arnold (Sinixt) at the conference. There, she was able to stand in my conical tule mat lodge on display at the Mir Centre for Peace with her long-time Sinixt cousin and friend Virginia Mason.

I. How I Implement the Sculpting Process

My cultural recovery practice centres on art and architecture specific to the northern Plateau Indigenous Peoples, including the Sinixt. My goal is to celebrate traditional Sinixt life patterns. I do not construct static relics of the past, but create continuity with the present and future in this living art and architecture. Objects include tule mat lodges, pit house/house pits, and bark sturgeon-nosed canoes. I also create smaller hand-held scale implements like basketry, tools and fish basket traps. All these are living implements linked to our geographical village and fishing sites. The smaller items could be packed into the bark sturgeon-nosed canoe for water travel to regional villages, and hunting, fishing and gathering sites. The cultural recovery practice usually begins with a review of relevant ethnographic reports, visitation to museum collections housing examples of an implement, and attending material workshops where cultural practices have endured. Next, I move into the field, harvesting and processing traditional materials. The process is not linear, but cyclical, with any given step occurring at any point during the process.

II. Bark Sturgeon-Nosed Canoe

Included in the Elmendorf (1935–36) notes was an outlined doodle sketch of a sturgeon-nosed canoe with a pointed bow, but with perhaps a vertical or square stern. The sketch has a recognizable rocker along the length of the bottom of the canoe. Recovering my first bark sturgeon-nosed canoe was an interdisciplinary process, making use of my educational background in architecture, my industrious nature in

Tule lodge at Mir Centre for Peace. Photo courtesy of Shawn Brigman.

harvesting and processing materials, and the triangular influence of historical ethnography, photography and Elder presence. I attended two workshops in June 2012, provided by communities still specialized in the continuity of bark sturgeon-nosed canoes as living embodiments: with the Kalispel Tribe, I learned about western white pine bark and its harvest from the forests of Priest River, Idaho; and with the Yaqan Nukiy Ktunaxa (Lower Kootenay Band) in Creston, BC, I learned about material identification and processing.

After attending these two workshops I set out to harvest materials from the Kettle Falls region to sculpt my first bark sturgeon-nosed canoe. When the diverse collection of materials is found in the forest, this does not guarantee that they will be of good enough quality to be used in bark sturgeon-nosed canoe making. One does not know the quality of all the diverse pieces of materials until they are harvested, processed and sculpted by hand. I learned with love, blood, sweat and tears that bark sturgeon-nosed canoe making is a large undertaking. It requires a big commitment, because the canoe requires specific material found only in the northern Plateau, upper Columbia River region. These materials are rare. They can't be purchased off the shelf at a material supply store. I scout the forests ahead of time, looking for trees of canoe-making quality, spending time, energy and gas. In the last nine years since I began this work, I've noticed that the forests in northeast Washington are drying up. They don't have the wet forest-feeling that they did when I attended the first western white pine bark harvest in the summer of 2012. Often the quality of the material is low, resulting in lost time and energy harvesting new material to replace non–canoe quality material. As a result, I average building only one bark sturgeon-nosed canoe per year. However, the dedication is worth the effort, for when a completed bark canoe rehydrates on ancestral waters it breathes the ancestral forests from which it was harvested. The whole experience of the forest is presented to the paddler just as it has been for my ancestors, since time immemorial. My goal is to visit my ancestral traditional territory in the Nakusp and Revelstoke area, where the white pine is more numerous, and where many forests have that wet feeling. I would like to create a bark canoe harvested from Sinixt territory north of the 49th parallel.

Shawn Brigman's *Salishan Sturgeon Nose Canoe*.
Photo courtesy of Shawn Brigman.

III. Salishan Sturgeon Nose Canoes, est. 2013

In 2013, I developed an original canoe interpretation, with a unique frame assemblage and fabric skin attachment method now widely known across the northern Plateau region. I call this a *Salishan Sturgeon Nose Canoe*. More than 30 of these canoes have been sculpted and are in circulation. In a gallery setting, the pigment used on the translucent ballistic nylon gives each canoe an original tint and celebrates the interior framework by making it visible. The *Salishan Sturgeon Nose Canoe* design has been implemented in art installations, and for youth and cultural programs across the northern Plateau culture region of British Columbia, Washington, Idaho and Montana. In 2015, Selkirk College secured grant funding for me to sculpt a *Salishan Sturgeon Nose Canoe* for the Aboriginal Youth Conference at the Nelson Campus. I demonstrated my technique at a "skinning the canoe" workshop. The canoe was blessed and launched several years later at Selkirk College

Dugout/sturgeon canoes at Kettle Falls. Photo courtesy of Shawn Brigman.

"Charlie Slade told me years ago that he remembers the Indians scuttling their pine bark canoes to preserve them underwater. When they wanted to use them again, they dove down, lifted out the rocks and brought them to the surface. Nothing hurt the canoe more than it getting too dried out."

—Jerry Louis, 2001

during the 2019 One River, Ethics Matter Conference organized and hosted by the Mir Centre for Peace in Castlegar.

My dedication to a northern Plateau recovery arts practice has also had a visible and positive impact on regional tribal communities. The recent awakening of spirit around water, river and salmon has included a return to canoe culture on the ancestral waters. During the 2016 canoe prayer journey, four *Salishan Sturgeon Nose Canoes* brushed the water of the Missouri River to Standing Rock, North Dakota, joining canoes from across the Pacific Northwest and Alaska.

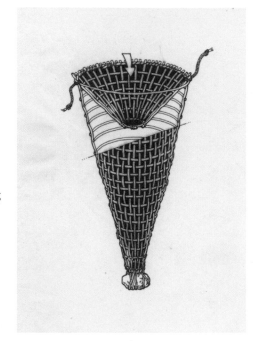

"All the small streams in Lakes country had one."

—Nancy Wynecoop, describing the conical basket traps used to catch fish

IV. Funnel Basket Trap

Back in 2011, the first time I reviewed the Elmendorf (1935–36) notes, a sketch of the Sinixt fish basket trap caught my attention. The handwritten notes listed the Salish language concept (**sc̓líwl̓**), a quick description of how the implement was employed in all small rivers, and the accompanying doodle sketch. With my educational training in School of Architecture, these field notes felt and read like my own personal sketchbooks exploring the recovery of such implements. The only thing missing was the naming of the material used for the implement. The Northwest Museum of American Arts and Culture in Spokane, Washington, had one of these baskets in its collection. In September 2016, I scheduled an appointment to hold and analyze the implement for materials, shape, function and dimensions. With available time in 2019, I set out to harvest red osier dogwood material and sculpt the conical-shaped fishing implement specific to the dimensions in my sketchbook. In June 2020, during the COVID-19 pandemic, I was delighted to return to a childhood stream where I fished as a youth with a pole, line and hook,

Fish trap sculpted by Shawn Brigman. Photo courtesy of Shawn Brigman.

upstream of the historic Kettle Falls fishery. I video-recorded a demonstration of placing the fish trap into the stream, doing so in honour of salmon recovery along the upper Columbia River, and posted it to the social media page of the Inchelium Language and Culture Association. As I worked with the funnel fish basket trap, I realized that its shape echoes the same technology and form as the pointed ends of the bark sturgeon-nosed canoe frame that I had sculpted in 2012! This particular bark sturgeon-nosed canoe then paddled across the river to the June 2020 Salmon Ceremony at Kettle Falls fishery, perhaps for the first time since before the construction of Grand Coulee Dam.

V. Paddle Carving

The Sinixt language term for paddling a canoe (noted by Elmendorf in 1935–36) is **ʔaẋʷmn̓ a'xwəmən** ("brush the water"). This imagery of "brushing the water" has deeply influenced my canoe making work. Historically, rivers connect all the ancestral villages on the Columbia Plateau. As a Plateau-specific cultural form, the bark sturgeon-nosed canoe represents the marriage and food-gathering patterns, Indigenous ways of knowing and being, and even a fish, the sturgeon, important to upper Columbia tribes as a traditional food. The bow and stern of the historical bark canoe relates to the shape of the nose of a sturgeon. Perhaps it was the fish that once inspired the shape and design.

In June 2018, I caught my first **c̓m̓tus** (sturgeon) near Kettle Falls, likely a hatchery fish released between 2009 and 2013. I did so for traditional food purposes, but also to examine the form, shape and relief textures of the fish, to manifest in relief carvings on paddles. A few weeks later, I attended the 2018 Kettle Falls Salmon Ceremony. At the canoe-landing site, one of the gathered nations sang their "sturgeon song" in addition to the "salmon song." One of my *Salishan Sturgeon Nose Canoes* had made the journey to the falls along with all the community dugout canoes representing the surrounding tribes who had once gathered to fish at the falls. The canoe I had sculpted was able to hear the "sturgeon song" for the first time. I now incorporate the sturgeon geometry – external plates on the back and sides of the sturgeon fish known as scutes – into the contemporary paddles I carve. The ancestral connectivity and continuity of village life on the rivers makes this cultural resonance possible.

Traditional art forms and natural materials are the essence of my art and architecture recovery practice. My practice embodies getting out on the land and remembering or relearning these materials. When I have finished making a tule mat lodge, fish basket trap or a bark canoe, it is empowering to reflect back and know that all the materials I have processed into beautiful sculptural and functional form were once alive in the forest.

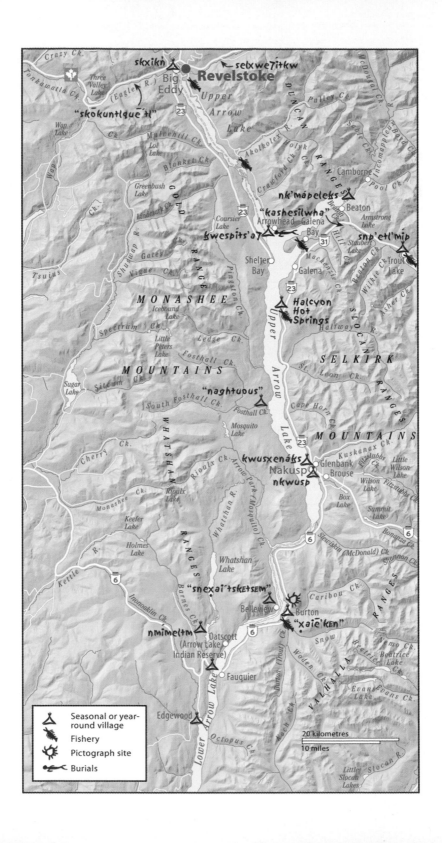

Crazy Ck.
Tonkawatla Ck.
Three Valley Lake
skxikṅ
selxweʔitkw
Big Eddy
Revelstoke
(Eagle R.)
Upper Arrow Lake
"skōkuntlguēʔl"
23
Wap Lake
Mulvehill Ck.
Lol Lake
Blanket Ck.
DUNCAN
Pulley Ck.
McDougal Ck.
Incomappleux
Boyd Ck.
Sable Ck.
Greenbush Lake
GOLD
Akolkolex R.
Holyk Ck.
Crawford Ck.
Camborne
Pool Ck.
Landmark Lake
Coursier Lake
RANGES
nk'mápeleks
Beaton
"kashesilwha"
Arrowhead
Galena Bay
Armstrong Lake
kwespits'aʔ
23
RANGE
Shuswap R.
Gatey
Tsuius
MONASHEE
Icebound Lake
Spectrum Ck.
Little Peters Lake
Fosthall Ck.
Vigue Ck.
Pingston Ck.
Shelter Bay
Galena
31
Mackenzie Ck.
Beaton Ck.
Halcyon Hot Springs
Staubert Lake
snp'etl'mip
Wilkie Ck.
Trout Lake
Asher Ck.
SELKIRK
Halfway
St. Leon Ck.
Sugar Lake
Siteum Ck.
MOUNTAINS
Ledge Ck.
South Fosthall Ck.
"naghtuous"
Fosthall Ck.
Mosquito Lake
Upper Arrow Lake
Cape Horn Ck.
23
MOUNTAINS
RANGES
Cherry Ck.
WHATSHAN
Rioulx Ck.
Arrow Park (Mosquito) Ck.
Whatshan R.
Kuskanax Ck.
Silverstubbs Ck.
Little Wilson Lake
kwusxenáks
Glenbank
Brouse
Nakusp
nkwusp
Wilson Lake
Fitzstubbs Ck.
Box Lake
Monashee Ck.
Rioulx Lake
Keefer Lake
Holmes Lake
Whatshan Lake
6
Slewiskin (McDonald) Ck
Summit Lake
Bonanza Ck.
Shannon Ck.
6
Kettle R.
Inonoaklin Ck.
Barnes Ck.
RANGES
6
"snexaiʔtsketsem"
Belleview
Caribou Ck.
Burton
"xaieʔken"
RANGES
nmimeltm
Oatscott (Arrow Lake Indian Reserve)
6
Burton (Trout) Ck.
Snow Ck.
Nemo Ck.
Beatrice Ck.
Beatrice Lake
Fauquier
Woden Ck.
Koch Ck.
VALHALLA
Evans Ck.
Evans Lake
Edgewood
Lower Arrow Lake
Octopus Ck.
Little Slocan Lakes
Slocan R.

Legend

🛖 Seasonal or year-round village

🐟 Fishery

☀ Pictograph site

Burials

20 kilometres

10 miles

Revelstoke to Fauquier

Skxikn̓: Large village opposite Revelstoke. Trading, trapping, hunting, berrying and salmon fishing.

Sĺx̌ʷʔitkʷ: "big water." Illecillewaet is likely derived from this place name.

N̓kmaplqs: "head of the lake." Now Comaplix. Both Comaplix and Incomappleux (from the French fur traders) are derived from this place name. The large village (largely under water) was important for huckleberries and root digging. Chinook salmon and bull trout spawned in the river.

Qʷspíc̓aʔ: "buffalo robe." Now under water. Important village for root digging (tiger lily bulbs) and salmon fishing. Fort of the Lakes was constructed in this area.

Halcyon Hot Springs: Early pioneer Edouard Picard described Indigenous People salmon fishing and using hot springs (late 19th c.).

Kwəsxnaqs: "long point." A village used well into the 20th century. Now Kuskanax.

N̓qʷusp: "cinched, gathered, clenched." Now Nakusp. Important for salmon and bull trout fishing. Burials and sweat houses at the mouth of Nakusp Creek.

xaieken: A sizable village near the mouth of Caribou Creek. Sinixt People told Clark Marshal that they burned for huckleberry growth up in the drainage.

N̓mimĺtm̓: "having whitefish." A seasonal caribou hunting village. Now Whatshan, which may be derived from another Indigenous word for the area.

MAP REGION 1: based on maps compiled by Randy Bouchard and Dorothy Kennedy in 2000 for the Columbia Power Corp. Map uses their practical orthography. Glossary uses linguistic symbols provided by the Salish School of Spokane.

3.
Revelstoke to Fauquier
Journey into the Heartland

SNOWSHOES AND SNOWSHOE HARES

The farther north into the Columbia mountains one travels, the deeper grow the winter snows. While formally classified as an interior temperate rainforest, this ecosystem has also been called a snow forest. The snow falls in deep drifts, though winters are still temperate enough to support many rainforest species. The accumulation of winter snow dominates the moisture cycle through the relatively hot, dry summers, as higher-elevation drifts melt to moisten the air, keep streams cool for fish and water the forest.

Prior to the 1960s and extensive hydroelectric development, the wintertime Columbia and its tributaries settled into an annual, icy silence. Left to its own devices, the upper river's natural flow pattern saw it surging in spring and early summer, then slowing to a shallow channel by early autumn. When winter temperatures arrived, many portions of the river froze over. In particularly cold winters, the surface of Upper and Lower Arrow Lakes and Slocan and Kootenay lakes also froze hard. The Sinixt/Lakes Indians evolved a complex system of winter and summer villages in response to the Columbia's natural rhythms. They capitalized on the ebb and flow of the river to make travel easier, riding the rapid current of spring snowmelt downstream to the major salmon fishery at Kettle Falls in the late spring. Months later, they pushed their sturgeon-nosed canoes laden with dried salmon against the slower currents of early autumn, paddling more easily upstream to hunting grounds and winter homes. As they went, they gathered the late-arriving coho salmon from back eddies and along the shoreline. Their traditional, subterranean, cozy dwellings formed the heart of their winter lifestyle.

From 1300 to about 1850, a global Little Ice Age resulted in plunging temperatures that would have exaggerated winter conditions in the region. Glaciers in the upper Columbia mountains likely expanded during this time. Snow must have been deeper than usual and winters may have endured longer. The impact of this change stressed various cultures differently worldwide. The most resilient suffered less. The impact of this Little Ice Age in the upper Columbia region can be traced through the journals of European explorers of the upper Columbia region, with cartographer David Thompson sledding bales of fur cheerfully across frozen rivers and British botanist David Douglas grumbling about the ice and snow that clung to the river and its banks well into April. Being stranded by winter ice was a theme that continued as more settlers arrived. In the winter of 1861–62, a miner caught by snow and the river icing over was forced to winter unprepared in the vicinity of Revelstoke, BC. Without the generosity of a Sinixt family living nearby – who shared their preserved food, perhaps bedding and certainly dry wood – he might not have survived until spring.

With a snow culture adapted across thousands of years, the Sinixt knew how to survive and even thrive in all weather. Inside the pit house dwellings, they tended their fires, listened to traditional stories, wove baskets, made tools and prepared soups enriched by dried salmon and caribou. As snow accumulated around and above the pit houses, it insulated them further from the cold. When they ventured outside

Photo courtesy of Mike Graeme.

"The banks on either side [of the Columbia River near Revelstoke] presented only high hills covered to the top with impenetrable forests.... The snow was very deep in the ravines or narrow gorges.... The most common trees are the Norway pine [*Pinus monticola*] and the cedar: the last is here, as on the borders of the sea, of a prodigious size."

—Explorer Gabriel Franchère, 1814

on sunny days, well-dressed hunters could follow the blue-shadowed tracks of the snowshoe hare (*Lepus americanus*) dipping and weaving through the snow-laden forest. This humble mammal rewarded the tribe with fresh meat and a fur unparalleled for its warmth.

Nancy Wynecoop translated the Sinixt word for the hare as "long ears," in her story about Mountain Goat and Huckleberry. The English common name, snowshoe hare, refers to the regional rabbit's long, broad feet, well-adapted to the snowy upper Columbia forests. In winter, long ears is white. In summer, the hare sports a greyish-brown coat that also gives it a low profile as it nibbles on horsetail, wild strawberry, raspberry and the young leaves of willow, alder and birch. When the days grow shorter, the falling light triggers the hare to moult its brown fur. Stiff hairs sprout on its feet, allowing it to float on top of the abundant snow, surviving on bark and branch tips and eluding capture from wolves, coyotes, lynx, foxes and golden eagles. Long ears prefers dense forests, wetland areas and river valley thickets, where there is lots of vegetation for food and shelter. North of the international boundary, as the mountains thicken and the valleys grow narrower, that sort of habitat is plentiful.

Hares are one of the most common mammals across the north. Scientists say they form an important ecosystem link between vegetable- and meat-eating mammals. E.H. Kreps, author of an outdoor survival manual from the early 20th century titled *Woodcraft*, observed their use by tribes as he travelled from the Great Lakes region into the northern boreal forest, from east to west. Kreps sings the praises of the rabbit hair blankets he saw being used by many of the Indigenous cultures in winter-bound regions as "the warmest bedding I know of." Sinixt Elder Bob Campbell and others have told me that it was likely women or young boys who did most of the winter hunting, with the help of snares. He once described how Sinixt women cut the snowshoe hare's pelt into one long strip, doing so immediately after skinning, and that they wove that strip into a blanket. Kreps adds specific techniques that may have been widespread. Indigenous women in other areas worked with the skin when it was fresh, or "green," pulling it off the body, scraping it quickly and placing it butt end down over a stick. After that, they cut the hide into one long strip, starting at the bottom and working up. As they cut, the strip of untreated hide rolled in on itself, transforming it into a sort of tube with all the fur facing out.

Women stockpiled these furry strips outside in the snow over days and weeks, until they had enough to bring the "green" hides back into the warm air, where they would thaw and quickly weave them.

The ethnographer James Teit mentions widespread use of rabbit hair blankets by the Sinixt. They wove the pelts, he said, on a simple loom of four sticks. Kreps describes a similar loom, with a length of twine wrapped around the four pegs. He details how Indigenous women began the blanket by looping the thawed strip of pelt over and over around one length of the twine, using their fingers to regulate the size of the loops. Once one looping row was finished, the weaver simply looped the next row back through the first, continuing until the entire blanket was a series of interlocking loops. As the untanned pelt dried, the loops stiffened and held their shape, forming a sort of rabbit fur chain mail. The long, silky hairs filled the spaces made by the loops, trapping air to maximize warmth.

Kreps claimed that a rabbit hare blanket had kept him warm down to −40° F. Teit recorded from Sinixt Elders that it was common for tribal members to possess one fur blanket for sleeping and another as a robe tied at the neck for winter expeditions in the snow. Strapped on a Sinixt traveller's feet would be another essential winter tool, one perhaps inspired by the fluffy rear paws of the furry hopper – a pair of snowshoes to stay aloft in the deep drifts. Made from the branches of red osier dogwood (*Cornus stolonifera*), the Sinixt snowshoe was distinct from those of neighbouring tribes and adapted for use in especially steep mountain terrain. Without much of a "tail," it was almost circular and slightly turned up at the toe. This shape facilitated climbing slopes, and assisted a hunter in setting a snowy snare for the low-profile hare, provider of much winter protection. For the young hunter, there might be a special meal of fresh rabbit, roasted or stewed over the fire, and a feeling of pride in having contributed to his family's warmth and nourishment.

Winters since traditional times have changed in more ways than just a warming climate. Frozen water, once a recurring factor in the river's natural and human history, has also become more a part of its collective cultural past, due to the operation of dams in the warming, anthropocene landscape in which we live. With trapped water being released bit by bit to make electricity to warm homes, the Columbia spreads wide, soft and gently lapping year-round. Warmer seasonal temperatures

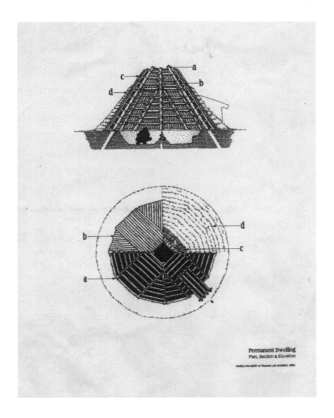

Permanent Dwelling
Plan, Section & Elevation

"On the part of myself and friends who wintered on [the] Columbia River
above the lakes [Upper and Lower Arrow] I have the pleasure to state
that the Indians treated us well and hospitably."

—William Cameron, May 18, 1862 (Referring to Sinixt People living
in pit houses/permanent dwellings in Revelstoke and area.)

due to climate change may have been influenced by what science calls
a "heat sink," the absorbing of large amounts of warmth into the still,
deep waters of reservoirs throughout the summer. This summer warmth
radiates out from the water through the colder months, keeping the water from freezing and raising ambient temperatures in the valley. The
memory of the resilient survival in deep snows among iced-over rivers
is still alive, however. It has migrated to the higher elevations of the
Columbia mountain system, where frozen flakes still fall with abundance and the abundant tracks of long ears dance among the trees.

HENRICUS AND THE PRIEST'S PEN

In about 1740, more than half a century before any colonial religious contact in the upper Columbia region, Circling Raven, a prophet from the Schitsu'umsh (Coeur d'Alene) tribe, dreamed of odd-looking men wearing long, black robes and carrying crossed sticks. These black-robed men would bring some sort of medicine, he understood from the dream. They would teach a new way of life. The first of many waves of epidemics ravaged the upper Columbia and Kootenay river region several decades later. Indigenous People struggled to develop immunity to European diseases even before fur traders arrived. Traditional medicine men were overwhelmed. Their long-practised healing techniques were no match for smallpox, diphtheria and measles, nor did plant medicines help. Around 1800, Iroquois hunters, who had converted to Christianity after their contact with the fur trade, came west over the Rockies. They demonstrated some Catholic worship practices to the vulnerable Salish tribes. That contact may have been a factor in three separate delegations of Schitsu'umsh travelling to a Jesuit centre in St. Louis, Missouri, between 1800 and 1840, asking for the black robes to come.

And, eventually, they did. Catholic missionaries arrived from French-speaking Canada in 1838, offering the first mass beside the upper Columbia River at the Big Bend, in October. As they travelled down the Columbia that first year, the Reverends Blanchet and Demers found the Lakes tribe living in villages along the upper river's main stem to be of a "mild, peaceable character." The first Oblate baptisms were at the Sinixt village "buffalo robe," where the Columbia empties into Upper Arrow Lake. The church also briefly operated a mission on Upper Arrow Lake at Fosthall Creek (St. Peter's Station). These Oblate missionaries stayed only a few years. Baptisms and religious conversions by Jesuits from the United States continued from 1845 and spanned the next several decades. As priests came to understand the importance of the annual salmon fishery and fur trade activities in the lives of the tribes, they established St. Paul's Mission church, in Kettle Falls. These missionary priests kept detailed records of baptisms, marriages and deaths. According to historian Andrea Laforet, the primary written sources of genealogical information concerning Sinixt families prior to the 1880s can be found in these records. Those holding the pens wrote in a mix of French and Latin. They also listed traditional Salish language names,

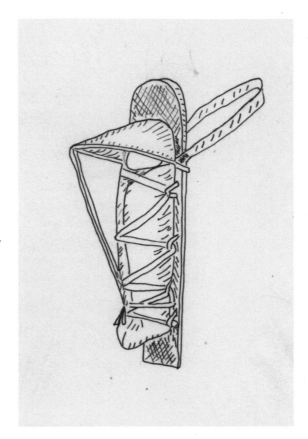

Tracing of a sketch by
James Teit, found in
*Salishan Tribes of the
Western Plateau.*

using phonetic spellings that provide few clues to translate the meaning
of these names. They recorded the age of the individual at the time, the
date of baptism, and a Christian name, chosen by the priest.

From that information, Laforet has been able to extrapolate approximate birthdates of those baptized. "Kessewilish," the Lakes Chief at
the time, was baptized as Gregoire in 1840 (b. circa 1800). According to
Laforet, the Jesuit father De Smet noted in 1846 that the missionaries
had the strong support of Gregoire (Kessewilish). In other sources, the
Jesuit father Joset referred to the Lakes as a whole as "Snaicksti" and
described them as "noble-minded." They naturally behave, he said, in
"more the Christian way." He and other priests said they found that the
Lakes living along the upper Columbia to be "well-disposed" to con-
version. This can be explained both by Kessewilish's leadership and by

strong spiritual practices that existed prior to colonial contact. Laforet writes that baptisms and marriages of Sinixt adults surged "between 1846 and 1852, with a smaller but still consistent number through the mid-1850s." The Catholic records present a stream of adults and children. Sgogemeïns as Josephus (married 1849/baptized 1800–1809) and his wife (with no Sinixt name noted) as Catherina (1849/1829). Skwegen as Franciscus (1852/1792). Tilgasket as Philippus (1849/1809). Ntsostiken (Insgonstokin) as Henricus (1849/1819). The list of Sinixt People within a web of relations continues for pages, providing a window into the well-populated past of the upper Columbia River region.

Given the continuing impact of European diseases, the new faith became almost immediately associated with survival. Priests were often the only non-tribal people who understood the apocalyptic scenes as illness overtook villages, wiping out up to 80 or even 90 per cent of inhabitants. Father Joset described a smallpox epidemic sweeping across the inland northwest in 1853–54, leaving a Jesuit priest at St. Paul's mission surrounded by many sick Sinixt and Skoyelpi people. Without a supply of vaccine, he improvised – by withdrawing "matter" from a sick man of strong constitution who had largely healed and then inoculating the man's family. They lived, as did many of the people he helped. Inoculations also appear to have served as a sort of leverage for some priests, who either promised the vaccine to those who would convert, or simply required people to attend mass in order to receive them.

Christian missionary impacts have left a complicated legacy to unravel, one that involves lost language and the interruption of traditional spiritual practices. Woven through all that has been lost are these enlightening records that the priests kept, now an important signpost of Sinixt presence in their traditional territory, upstream to Revelstoke. Tracing the sparse, pen-and-ink notations in the record books has allowed Laforet to sketch out a thick trunk of Sinixt People born before European contact, living in their territory on both sides of the boundary. The extent of the Lakes diaspora follows branches that radiate from that centre. Some descendants initially lived on the North Half of the original Colville Reservation. When that opened to settlers, many families went to the south half of the reservation, settling in Omak and Inchelium. Many of the Lakes families descending from those listed in the Catholic documents can be found there today, including Richard Desautel. Other Lakes descendants from those in these records hold contemporary identity within modern tribal organizations, including the Spokane, Kalispel, Flathead, Yakama and the Okanagan Nation Alliance.

Filed by legal counsel for the defendant in the recent Aboriginal rights case *R. v. Desautel* (2016), Laforet's report neatly undermines the British Columbia government's assertion that an extinction of the Sinixt was justified. While government lawyers argued that the Sinixt had largely begun to abandon the "Canadian" part of their territory prior to the establishment of the boundary, the birth records make it clear that a large number of Sinixt People were living above the boundary through much of the 19th century. Desautel's multiple-times great-grandfather surfaces in the report as a leader named Ingonstoken Ntsostiken, or, Henricus. Translated from the Latin as "home ruler," the baptismal name may have referred to Ntsostiken's role as a local leader of a Sinixt traditional village known as Ṅ k ʷlíla?, an area encompassing the mouth of the Pend d'Oreille River. His wife Henrica (Agagupitsa) is also in the records, as are at least two of their daughters, "Josephine Harry" and "Justina."

The 1846 border may have impacted the way the Sinixt interacted with church missionaries. The Catholic records from the 1860s record numerous baptisms and marriages north of the border, at the site of Ṅ k ʷlíla?, transcribed by the Jesuits as "kolilè." This area around the mouth of the Pend d'Oreille River had been in use by the Lakes people prior to contact. It became the location of the Hudson's Bay Company's Fort Shepherd, constructed by the British in the early 1850s to replace Fort Colville when US tax law made life difficult for the HBC. Laforet points to a notation in the St. Paul's mission diary from 1870. The Sinixt, the priest wrote, were at that time repeating "the old song" that it was too far to travel to St. Paul's for sacraments, particularly for the elderly and ill. The mission in Canada appears to have been a long-held desire. It may have been Henricus himself who advocated to the priests for the establishment of a mission above the boundary. The priest's sarcastic response is a difficult historical pill to swallow. Yet the fragment of historical information inked in the diary by his hand affirms the Lakes people's strong loyalty to the length of their traditional territory, as it existed for them without a boundary, and their loyalty to the protection and care of their Elders.

The church did not oblige the Sinixt request for a mission above the international boundary. That same year, the HBC fort just above the boundary closed, and in 1872 it burned to the ground. The loss of both Fort of the Lakes and then Fort Shepherd, the Catholic refusal to construct a mission for the Lakes people on the Canadian side and, finally, the establishment of a US reservation that stopped at the international boundary without one existing yet in Canada all contributed to the Lakes having been abandoned in the now "Canadian" part of their transboundary territory – abandoned by the same cultural forces that had dramatically reshaped their spiritual and economic lives since contact.

THE MURDER OF CULTUS JIM

The upper Columbia landscape is a place of geographic nooks and crannies, twisting roads and surprising views. Everywhere, the newly formed energy of its glaciated peaks expresses a strength and grandeur that moves people emotionally, makes them want to stay here even when they are only passing through and compels many journeys, both physical and metaphoric. It feels as if some of the region's stories are held tightly in these nooks and crannies. They lie buried beneath deep drifts of snow through the winter in the deeply clefted valleys, where the sky is a flat lid of grey cloud rather than a curving blue roof. But in spring, the melt begins. When the natural world awakens and the air warms, the earth is again exposed. This is when I feel the stories most strongly as they loosen from the land. They seem to seep down from the thawing alpine to float gently onto the morning stillness of the lake. On their quiet current rides the truth of the past. One grey April morning a few years ago, I drove 200 kilometres northwest from Nelson, pushing my way through the mist draped along the mountain flanks, to follow the path of a ghost. I will admit that I have not always believed in ghosts. But living here has changed me.

I drove north in the shadow of the Valhalla Range along the Slocan Valley's twisting floor until I reached the lake feeding the Slocan River. I climbed the highway rising around Slocan Lake, watching the water spread below in a way that seemed like paint washing across canvas. At New Denver, I veered west through the mountains to Nakusp to enter the heart of the Arrow Lakes valley. I turned north again onto the highway that fringes Upper Arrow Lake until I reached Galena Bay. The ghost I was tracking was not of the sort my sons once cut from paper and stuck to the window at Halloween. This was an unseen but somehow still noticeable presence, rising up from the terrain like a feeling rises in my own heart.

At Galena Bay, I hoped to understand the spectre of loss that seemed to hang on the curls of April's springtime mist.

In August 1894, a Sinixt man known by settlers as Cultus Jim arrived at the mouth of a creek that emptied into what we now call Galena Bay. His people had used this area around the north end of the lake for hundreds if not thousands of years. Jim came with his wife Adeline in a pine bark canoe, to set traps in the creek and hunt bear up the drainage. In addition, the **kəkn̓i?** (kokanee, or redfish) were returning and the berries were ripe. A few years earlier, he had been chased from a major village site of his people, a very old place called **N̓kmaplqs** (Comaplix), around the corner in Beaton Arm. A settler named Evan Johnson had set up there near the Incomappleux River and Indians weren't welcome. Jim and his wife may or may not have known right away that a settler had established at Galena Bay too. But they were soon to find out. The arrival of miners and settlers in the late 1880s and early 1890s made traditional seasonal rounds an uncertain and sometimes dangerous experience for the Sinixt. Often, miners began working staked claims in early spring, before any Sinixt had yet arrived from winter homes on the US side of their traditional territory. In spring, the land often appeared free for the taking to the settlers who were arriving. The well-documented story of Cultus Jim represents the inevitable clash of two cultures, two ways of life, two views of resource use. It tells of the universal ability colonial land ownership has to inspire misunderstanding. And it locates the final demise of an upper Columbia Aboriginal experience that depended on freedom of movement across its sovereign territory, defining resource use differently from an agricultural or industrial culture.

I turned off the highway just above the ferry terminal and followed Hill Creek Road for a while before I came to the head of Galena Bay. Here, summer cabins spread out close to the high water line, with "No Trespassing" or "Private" signs marking all the driveways. No smoke rose from any of the chimneys and all the cabins looked deserted. I drove a ways farther along the bay, until I found a friendly "For Sale" sign, with an inviting arrow pointing to a driveway that could offer me shoreline access. I rather liked the sound of the name Cultus Jim, until I found out what it meant. The network of trade forts in the northwest depended on a form of jargon known as Chinook, a mix of English,

A settler named Eli Edge displays ocean salmon, likely Chinook, from the Incomappleux River. Photo courtesy of the Arrow Lakes Historical Society.

French and a few Aboriginal languages, primarily that of the Chinookan people inhabiting the area around the mouth of the Columbia River. Given its function as a language bridge between the colonial world and the Indigenous one, Chinook jargon sometimes expresses derogatory and stereotypical views of the Aboriginal experience. *Cultus* is a Chinook jargon word. It means "worthless."

When valleys are flooded and transformed into reservoirs, their geography has to be deemed worthless enough to justify flooding. Inundation or "impoundment" of water in these valleys dramatically shifts a landscape's potential from active to passive use. Prior to flooding, the Arrow Lakes valley hosted many fertile and productive agricultural settlements: pastureland, orchards and gardens. And prior even to the agricultural period, hunter-gatherer villages of the Sinixt People dotted the shores of Upper and Lower Arrow lakes and the deltas of the Columbia River along its narrows between the two lakes, capitalizing on good fishing, trapping and wild plant food patches. By the 1950s, 32,000 of the 48,000 arable acres of land in the Arrow Lakes valley were deemed worthless enough as landscape to be converted into a silt-lined bathtub. And that is what happened in 1968, when the Keen-leyside Dam was finally completed and the water seeped across the soil to fill the valley. I climbed out of the car and measured the expanse of blackened silt, gravel and sand between the high-water mark and the edge of the water. Beginning in January and up until May, Keenleyside Dam slowly drains enough water from the reservoir to make room for spring freshet. During this "drawdown," the landscape uncovers the "worthless" secrets of its past. I stepped onto the exposed silt, my boots shifting on its fluid carpet. The deadened soil seemed to reinforce the prophecy of the Columbia River Treaty, that the sparsely populated valleys of the upper Columbia have very little value by comparison to urban communities downriver that need protection from flooding, or affordable hydroelectric power. My boots plodded through muck for several hundred yards. Normally, the outwash of the creek would be at the high-water mark. But at drawdown, the creek meets the reservoir much farther out. Finally, I could hear and see the quiet rumble of Hill Creek, cutting a twisted path across the moonscape of silt.

I walked along the barren creek bank until I reached a cluster of stumps, their roots still clinging to the soil where they had once flour-ished. The stumps hinted at what the shoreline would have looked like in August 1894: a riparian with cottonwoods, willow, berry-producing shrubs, and of course, mosquitoes. Sam Hill was like many early min-ers and settlers: taking a risk with hard work and isolation in hope of a strike, wary of claim jumpers, and possessing a gun with a hair-trigger. Sometime after the canoes slid into the shore, Hill encountered Jim on the trail. Jim asked Hill to leave so that his traps would not be disturbed. Hill, in the process of putting in a garden, refused to go. He told Jim to leave. Jim claimed prior use and defended his right to stay. According to testimony given by Jim's wife, Adeline, at the coroner's inquest, Hill threatened Jim with his gun. Jim turned to get his gun, but before he could cock it, Hill raised his rifle rapidly and shot Cultus Jim three times in succession. Hill, on the other hand, testified that he and Jim fired together, with Jim's bullet whizzing past Hill's head and Hill's bullets hitting Jim. Newspaper accounts of the incident are generally sympathetic to Hill. This is not surprising. Though there aren't many accounts of aggression between the Sinixt and settlers in the upper

Stump from logging visible during reservoir drawdown. Author photo.

Columbia, the articles about the trial in the *Kootenay Mail* suggest that many upper Columbia settlers had arrived in the region predisposed against "Indians." The poignant testimony of Adeline was overwhelmed by witnesses who say Hill fired only in self-defence, and by accounts of "trouble" Cultus Jim had caused in other places near Galena Bay as settlers arrived. Hill was acquitted of manslaughter on October 6, 1894.

I settled onto one of the stumps to watch Hill Creek tumble into the lake. Jim was killed in August, about when the kokanee begin their return home to spawn. That day, the creek must have been splattered with the first of the redfish, as well as the blood of a displaced man. Jim, "worthless" in the eyes of many new settlers, loved the landscape of his ancestors and had always called it home. In the clash between the First People and the new arrivals, his death may have been as predictable as the return of the spawning fish littering the creeks each autumn. But that does not justify the loss, or make the abruptness and violence of Jim's death any less disturbing. I stood and walked down to the very edge of the shore. Looking south across the grey stillness of the Upper Arrow

Reservoir silt. Author photo.

"Harry [Murphy] remembers a short ways up Mosquito Creek…he came across rock & bough steam baths. They used long cottonwood roots for binding. It was like rope when wet…. Many Indians came up from Burton to trap on Mosquito Creek."

—Arrow Lakes Historical Society H-82

Reservoir, I felt pangs that extended beyond the murder of Cultus Jim. How much of the rich and productive ecosystem that once surrounded the Sinixt has been overwhelmed by the rising water? I wondered then, as I do now, if the landscape that now shows itself as starved-out silt in Galena Bay was actually as worthless as BC Hydro once determined, in order to justify flooding it permanently behind a dam.

"When they [Cultus Jim and his wife Adeline] came back in the afternoon they saw the white man working on his garden. Jim said to him: 'I told you to get away from here,' The white man said he wouldn't get away from the place and that he didn't care for Indians and then went and got his gun. She was standing a little back when Jim came to her and asked her for his gun. She told him not to take the gun but he took the gun from her. The white man fired. Jim did not shoot. The white man fired three shots and [the] Indian [died]."

—Testimony of Adeline, reported by the *Kootenay Mail,* June 9, 1894

THE PRAYERS OF MY GREAT-GRAMMA ADELINE

contributed by LaRae Wiley

I have always felt a spiritual connection and yearning for the Arrow Lakes. As a child, my father told me that our family was from Canada and *that* was our traditional homeland. I even thought my great-uncle had a ranch near Northport; my great-grandmother, Adeline, had an allotment on Flat Creek nearby; and most of our family was buried at the Pia (**Piyʕáʔ**, "red-tailed hawk") Mission site on Kelly Hill. We knew we were Arrow Lakes people who had been forced out of our northern homeland. I didn't learn how I was directly linked to that forced exodus of our people until a few years ago when I discovered that "Cultus" Jim was my great-grand-mother's first husband. I can only imagine her pain and the loss that she experienced on that day. There was no justice for Jim and Adeline. No justice for my family and the loss of their homeland. My family, like most Sinixt/Lakes families, has experienced many layers of loss.

We were forced off our traditional lands in British Columbia, and we moved, for our own safety, to the southern region of our traditional territory. This was called the North Half of the Colville Reservation. Then in 1892 an act of the United States Congress removed the North Half of the reservation from tribal control and opened it to settlers. Some Lakes families forced from the North Half moved to the remaining reservation. Even farther from their traditional homeland. This new place, Inchelium, wasn't home… The landscape, the plants, the animals were not what the Lakes people knew and loved. They were refugees.

But no one would even grant them that title. By 1956, the Canadian government had declared the Arrow Lakes people extinct. Murdered, erased, homeless. That is the hand my family was dealt.

But there is perseverance and great strength in the Arrow Lakes people. I saw that strength first-hand in my great-grandmother. I knew her when she was at the end of her life. I have many good memories of Adeline. She wore her long grey hair in two braids, with a kerchief covering her head. I remember being in awe that a person could be so old. She had wrinkles in her wrinkles. As a child, I remember visiting her, holding her hand and lifting her crepe-like skin between my little 5-year-old fingers. One of my granddaughters does the same thing to me now and it makes me smile, remembering Great-Grandma. She would tell my dad, "you have lots of chicks, lots of chicks," in her Salish-accented English. There were five of us and we loved listening to stories my dad told us about Great-Grandma. One story I loved was about her winter dancing when my dad was young. Adeline was living in Chewelah with our grandma, Dad and his older sister, Gale. It was winter and Adeline was up for nights, singing and pounding her staff on the kitchen floor. My dad and Gale would yell, "Grandma, go to bed! We have school in the morning!" She kept singing and sang for a few nights. The kids didn't know it but she was "winter dancing." She was keeping her spiritual traditions alive by singing medicine songs and praying for her family, her ancestors, her homeland. I think of her strength and all she lived through and I know that same strength is found in me and my family. As I prepare each year for our family's winter dance, I am so grateful that Adeline was able to survive, so that I could be here laying fir boughs in my sweat, baking huckleberry pies, smudging our giveaway gifts and winter dancing with my five grandchildren. Every day they learn our language, sing our songs and live our culture at their Salish immersion school. The strength and perseverance of our ancestors is why this is possible. I don't know what will be made possible by and for the future generations of Arrow Lakes people. But I do know that no matter what a government decrees, we will always be Arrow Lakes people. **Kṅ sṅ ʕay̓ čkstx uɬ putíʔ kṅ aláʔ.** I am Sinixt and I am still here.

THE COLLECTORS

When Charlie Maxfield walks on the beaches of the Arrow Lakes, he carries an old car aerial in one hand. If he sees something large and promising on the surface of the silt and sand, he kicks at it with the toe of his boot for a closer look. If it is small, he turns it over with his homemade tool. Charlie Maxfield collects Aboriginal artifacts, vestiges of the Neolithic culture used by the ancestors of the Sinixt People. He has boxes full of hard, physical evidence that people lived here before contact. He has theories about their use of the upper Columbia valleys, their population, their favourite fishing spots. He has read many of the scattered archaeological reports, studies and surveys about the region's shadowy prehistory. He dismisses the majority of these studies as limited in their understanding. *How many of them were written by people who have lived here all their lives?* His question points to the value of place, and the importance of locality.

After I have spent a day with Charlie, I wish that he would share his perspective by writing his own study. Charlie's precisely numbered collection stretches around the floor of his living room, right underneath large windows that offer a commanding view of the section of the reservoir between Nakusp and Fauquier, his collecting range. This was, before the Keenleyside Dam, the fast-running portion of the Columbia River that linked Upper Arrow and Lower Arrow lakes, a portion of the river marked as "the Narrows" on older maps. When the reservoir water starts to fall sometime in January, Charlie heads out onto the newly exposed silt, car aerial in hand. He says he always thanks BC Hydro for the dams at the beginning of a new season. The endless cycling of the reservoir upturns fresh archaeological material year after year. This is a positive perspective on dams that I have never heard. Amateur collecting through digs is illegal. Even walking on the beach and searching for articles lying on the surface as Charlie does is frowned upon by professional anthropologists and archaeologists, as well as by contemporary First Nations cultures. Collecting artifacts connects to the controversial colonial practices of appropriation and display.

"The lack of thorough archaeological work conducted prior to the flooding of the Arrow Lakes valleys is nothing short of criminal."

—Grant Keddie, archaeological curator, Royal BC Museum

Charlie has been told by more than one academic that he should leave a spear point where he sees it; that he should not touch a grinding pestle when he finds it in a pile of cobbles. But Charlie collects, and he loves to do it. Over the course of a year, mostly in the winter when he is off work, he spends a lot of time roaming the sand and silt, crossing to the other side of the river in his small boat, searching. He walks for hours, leaning into the cold wind, accompanied by his dog and, occasionally, a six-pack. Each piece in his collection has an elaborate story connected to it, about the weather that day, the way the artifact revealed itself, its exact location, his theories about why it was there, or how it got there. Each piece is intimately tied to the place where it was found, the upper Columbia region, where Charlie has lived all his life. In that way, the collection maintains its connection to the place where a tool or implement was used.

Travelling with him across the sand in his muddied pickup, I learn as much about the pre-dam terrain as I do about collecting. He takes me to what looks like a sand dune in the middle of a drawdown desert near East Arrow Park and makes me bend down to see what only a sharp, trained eye could otherwise notice: a confetti of black stone chips from tool-making litters the sand. I listen to his description of the dune. *Before the dams, this was a rise above a creek, nice high ground safe from seasonal flooding, with a view of the river, but out of the wind. Perfect place to sit for hours, making arrowheads.* I stare at the drifts soon to be covered again by water, marvelling at his ability to recreate a forgotten landscape, a place where he has lived that has been transformed. Walking with Charlie is like exploring the surface of an unfinished jigsaw puzzle with a blindfold on. I listen to his narrative about how life might have been lived, how the landscape might have looked for the Sinixt before European contact. Sometimes, I stare hard out the window of his pickup, trying to see what he sees. His mind seems to roam between the shadows of prehistory, his own boyhood memories and the current, dramatically altered terrain that spreads around him. It is clear that Charlie is collecting more than artifacts. In the course of his search for bits of very old stone, he has learned about daily life, patterns of settlement, diet and the cultural practices of the Sinixt People. If I could be time warped, he says to me as we walk out onto Cottonwood Point at the former townsite of Burton to look at a mound of fire-broken rocks resting on the surface that he theorizes were once used in a sweat lodge,

Author photo.

"To me, the archeological record has survived! Perhaps not in its pristine scientific sense, but when I hold one of these pieces in my hand there is a connection that transcends space and time."

—Collector Janice Palmer.

I would ask for just one week before David Thompson arrived, so that I could see what life was really like for the people here.

After spending a day with him, I realize that Charlie also wordlessly examines and reflects on his own attachment to the upper Columbia whenever he strides along the beach. He seems to go out collecting in part because he loves the place where he lives. He explores directly beneath the glare of winter sun, walks across the sandy muck of a childhood friend's family farm flooded by the dams, or floats across the glittering, aquamarine river he has fished since childhood. In the end, his passion for discovering archaeological material seems to thinly mask a greater passion for the natural history of the Arrow Lakes valley,

Obsidian flakes at the Narrows. Author photo.

"Of a total of 152 sites recorded on the Arrow Lakes only 12 (8%) remained more or less intact and above the high water level; 140 (92%) had been destroyed beyond salvage."

—Archaeologist Gordon Mohs, 1977

for the landscape as a home as much as a commodity. I can't help wondering if his attachment to this heartland of Sinixt Territory bears any similarity to what must have been felt by the prehistorical people themselves, those whose artifacts so interest him. As strenuous as life must have been for them without modern conveniences, they loved it here, too. Though he never says so, Charlie seems to know that.

Charlie is not the only collector. He has friends who collect, too. And he knows of even more people throughout the region. From Balfour to Castlegar, and in all the valleys between, there are many collections held in private hands, assembled by individuals over the last 100 years. The local museums have some materials, but much of the physical evidence of a culture prior to our own is hidden in living rooms, boxes, drawers or jars. No one appears to have had to dig to find these things; they have been gathered off beaches and along scoured-away riverbanks, or upturned accidentally by plows. One of the most extensive collections, assembled by now deceased Keith and Ellen Edgell, numbers 3,500 pieces. They donated their collection to the Royal BC Museum. It now rests in the museum's archival tower, far away from the landscape where it was carefully assembled between 1958 and 1978. While the Edgells had hoped that donating it to the museum would allow it to be seen and studied by all, funding restrictions have led to the collection being left in the dark for years.

Collecting is controversial, and I can understand those who say it is the wrong thing to do. But after a day with Charlie Maxfield, I can understand why he does it. Our culture has had such a brief opportunity to develop a deep connection with these valleys, this water and the mountains that rise all around us. We want to hold in our hand an unyielding piece of Indigenous lineage in this landscape, to know that several thousand years of inhabitation is not an abstract possibility, but a real, hard truth with great power and presence. People can live in a place for a very long time. And here, in a region that hosts the confluence of two major rivers, they did live. For a very long time. Charlie Maxfield's admirable love and knowledge of the Arrow Lakes valley has been developed after only a handful of decades. Whether or not collecting was responsible for or merely fed an existing attachment to his home is anybody's guess. But the significance to the landscape of a drift-net weight, an argillite arrowhead, a granite pounder or a schist commonknife is not lost on Charlie. That's what keeps him searching.

MAP REGION 2: based on maps compiled by Randy Bouchard and Dorothy Kennedy in 2000 for the Columbia Power Corp. Map uses their practical orthography. Glossary uses linguistic symbols provided by the Salish School of Spokane.

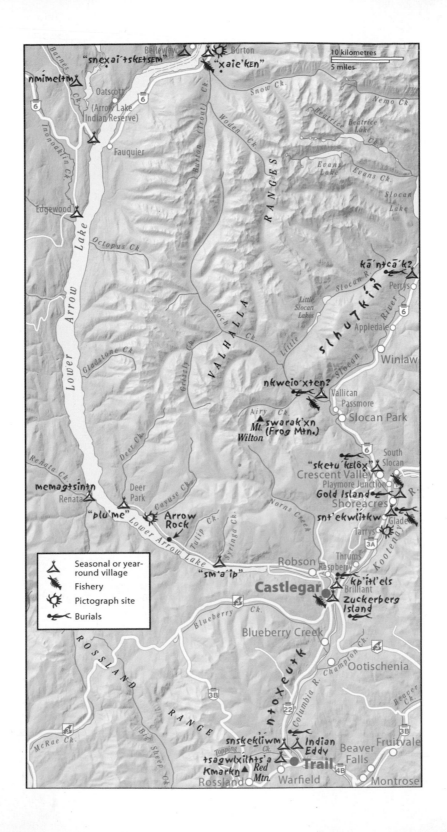

"snɛxaíˈtsкɛtsɛm"
Burton
"xaieˈкɛn"
Bellevew
nmimeltn̓

Oatscott
(Arrow Lake
Indian Reserve)

6

Snow Ck.
Nemo Ck.
Beatrice Lake
Beatrice Ck.

Fauquier

Woden Ck.
Burton (Trout) Ck.

Evans Lake
Evans Ck.
Slocan Lake

RANGES

Edgewood

Octopus Ck.

Taonooaklin Ck.

Koch Ck.

VALHALLA

Slocan R.
kā́ntcāˈk?
Perrys
6
Appledale

sɬuʔkiɲ

Little Slocan Lakes
Little Slocan R.

Winlaw

Lower Arrow Lake

Gladstone Ck.
Grizzly Ck.

nkweioˈxten?
Vallican
Passmore

Deer Ck.

Airy Ck.
swarak'xn
(Frog Mtn.)
Mt. Wilton

Slocan Park

Renata Ck.

memagtsintn̓
Renata

Deer Park

"pluˈme"
Arrow Rock

Cayuse Ck.

Tulip Ck.

Lower Arrow Lake

Syringa Ck.

Norns Creek

"sketuˈкɛlôx"
South Slocan
Crescent Valley
Playmore Junction
Gold Island
Shoreacres
snt'ekwlítkw
Glade
Tarrys

6

Kootenay R.

"sm'aˈip"
Robson
Raspberry
Thrums
3A

kp'itl'els
Brilliant
Zuckerberg Island

Castlegar

Blueberry Ck.

Blueberry Creek

Ootischenia
Champion Ck.
3

Columbia R.

ROSSLAND RANGE

McRae Ck.

3B

Big Sheep Ck.

ntoxeuʔk

22
Beaver Ck.
3B

snsкeкliwm
Indian Eddy
tsagwlxilhts'a
Kmarkn
Red Mtn.
Rossland
Warfield
Trail
4B

Fruitvale
Beaver Falls
Montrose

Topping Ck.

Legend

- ⌂ Seasonal or year-round village
- ⚘ Fishery
- ☼ Pictograph site
- ⋯ Burials

10 kilometres
5 miles

Məmʕaʔčiń tń: "log used for crossing," A centre for hunting mountain goat, this village was on the west shore of Lower Arrow Lake. Likely Renata.

Plu?ḿ: "smoke lingers." Related to **Ń pluʔčíń** (name for the Seyler Valley and the basin area at the northwest end of this valley south of Kettle Falls (having smoke at the mouth).

Arrow Rock: Arrows in rock crevices noted by several early explorers/travellers. Likely underwater, or destroyed by reservoir and road building.

Smʕaʔíp: "large log leaning against a tree." Prior to dams, Lower Arrow Lake started here.

Kṗ iƛ̓s: "people peel roots." Salmon fishing, trading, root digging (camas). The Christian family lived here well into the 20th century.

"It [a salmon weir at the mouth of the Kootenay River] is rendered still more remarkable by a dike of round stones, which runs up obliquely against the main stream, on the west side for more than one hundred yards in length, resembling the foundations of a wall; it is nearly as high as the surface of the water, and is clearly seen at low water. On the opposite or east side is a similar range, of less extent. These are evidently the work of man, and not destitute of ingenuity."

—Alexander Ross, spring 1825

4.
Fauquier to Castlegar
Long Shadows in a Broad Valley

"The test sample at DhQkj 1 [Brilliant] has yielded information that shows occupation of the area from at least 4500 years ago to the present…. The potential for qualitative and quantitative data spanning a long period of time is great at this site."

—James Baker, archaeologist, 1984

TWO GREAT RIVERS MEET

Most valleys in the upper Columbia region cleave just enough to accommodate a small river or a narrow lake. The land around the confluence of the Kootenay and Columbia rivers is an exception. Here, the terrain flattens and spreads enough to host two rivers, one joining the other. The sky feels immeasurably large. The contemporary Castlegar valley is and always has been a bustling upper Columbia crossroad. Today, the region's only commercial airport (Castlegar), one of its last major industrial employers (Celgar) and two of its dams (Brilliant and Keenleyside) are situated in and around the valley. Cars travel the roads, airplanes buzz overhead and the waters of the two great rivers crash through concrete gates. At the confluence, contemporary commerce, natural resources and transportation meet. As they did in former times.

The open, relatively arid valley, with two mighty fish-bearing rivers coming together, was also strategic to the river culture of the Sinixt. With canoes their only form of long-distance transportation and salmon a dietary mainstay, the Sinixt had many reasons to live here. As salmon ascended both the Columbia and the Kootenay for spawning from July to October, fishing would have been good, especially at the mouth of the Kootenay. There, sockeye, Chinook and coho turned north through what is now known as Tincup Rapids to continue up the Columbia, or turned east into the Kootenay, destined for the Slocan River. The arid forest around these rivers would have also hosted accessible wild foods. The present-day ponderosa pine ecosystem dominating the fringes of the Columbia River south and north of the valley suggests that long ago the area around the confluence might also have been more arid forest filled with balsamroot sunflower in spring and Oregon grapes ripening in summer.

Sinixt Elder Charlie Quintasket has suggested that the place name for the village at the Kootenay river mouth, **Kṗiƛ̓ls**, may be derived from the word **sṗiƛ̓m̓**, or bitterroot (*Lewisia rediviva*). Bitterroot was an important feature in the Sinixt diet, and although it is not known to have grown here, it has been found in the mountains along the Seven Summits Trail south and west of Castlegar and may have been acquired through trade for salmon. Heavy use of the canoe positioned the confluence as a natural meeting grounds and strategic location for those Sinixt headed north toward Revelstoke, or east toward the Slocan Valley. It was also accessible to the Ktunaxa coming west from their territory to access salmon through trade. Early historical and ethnographic records supports this. In 1861, responding to conflicts between miners attempting to go up the Columbia and Indigenous People wishing to maintain their hold in the area, Gold Commissioner W.G. Cox acknowledged the domain at the confluence by posting the north side of the Kootenay River mouth as "Indian Reserve," although his actions ultimately had no lasting impact. Almost five decades later, anthropologist James Teit visited the valley in 1909. After several days of listening and asking questions of the Sinixt People living there, Teit concluded that the valley was the important old headquarters of the Lakes (Sinixt) people. As recently as 1983, archaeologist James Baker stated that the Sinixt village site of **Kṗiⱦls** (at present-day Brilliant) was by far the largest in the area, with carbon-dated remains indicating that it had been in use for thousands of years.

Colonial travellers and officers did not easily understand the significance of this valley to the Sinixt in the exploration and settlement period. Fur trade explorer David Thompson stopped overnight here on September 5, 1811. After an unsuccessful effort to find fish for a meal, Thompson "went off & directly met 5 men & 7 or 8 Women bringing me a small present of a Salmon & Berries, which made us camp for the night." As was typical for many of his journal entries, the explorer was more focused on compass measurements for a map than he was on tribal identities. Narrow focus and limited understanding continued when a Canadian Indian agent travelling through in the early 1880s missed their presence, and continued even when the Canadian government began working around 1900 to establish a reserve. Government officials were often confused about the specific identity of the Sinixt versus those of the neighbouring tribes to the south, east and west who sometimes fished here. With one government Indian agent in Kamloops, and not another one again until Fort Steele, officials travelled sporadically to the upper Columbia hinterlands between these two centres. Their knowledge of geography and Aboriginal settlement patterns was spotty at the best of times. Communication linking one decade to another was not good either, with one official often unaware of actions by a previous official concerning the land around the confluence. For example, although Commissioner Cox had posted the area on the north side of the confluence as reserve in 1861, Edgar Dewdney then claimed it as a townsite in 1865. And in the 1880s, that same promised land was Crown-granted by government officials and sold to J.C. Haynes, who planned to build a town called "Haynesville" on the bluff overlooking the river, but died before he could.

So, although the Castlegar valley had every historical and prehistorical reason to be considered significant and central to the Sinixt living in the upper Columbia at the turn of the 20th century, a reserve was instead set up at Oatscott in 1902, on the east shore of Lower Arrow

Lake, nearly 100 kilometres upstream. This decision was made despite detailed correspondence received from a man named Baptiste Christian, head of a large Sinixt family living at **K̓p iƛ̓ls**. Christian claimed that the area surrounding present-day Brilliant had been inhabited by his family "since time immemorial," and contained many gravesites the family wished to preserve. Unfortunately for his family, **K̓p iƛ̓ls** was a key location for settler economic prosperity. The government's decision to establish a reserve at Oatscott instead reflected the attitude at the time that First Nations were part of a vanishing race without a relevant role to play in Canada's future. In the government's eyes, such a vanishing race should not be taking up valuable, central land. The decision also demonstrated the great challenge faced by British Columbia, and all of Canada for that matter. To make room for the pre-existing Indigenous culture as well as colonial interests was impossible in many settlers' minds. Neither was accounting for Indigenous sovereignty through treaty any longer a policy of either the BC or federal governments. How could economic development and agricultural expansion co-exist with a hunter-gatherer lifestyle, two approaches possessing such distinct attitudes toward nature and its offerings? History suggests over and over that the vast Canadian wilderness was not large enough to house both perspectives. Certainly, the valley surrounding the confluence of the Kootenay and Columbia rivers wasn't either. The government's discounting of Baptiste Christian's requests indicate that he and his family had, in the government's eyes, lost sovereignty in the landscape. The next actions of the Christians demonstrate, however, that cultural ties to this corner of the upper Columbia were not to be so easily broken. The Christians became a strange brand of deeply rooted outcasts: they were sent away to the Oatscott Reserve but refused to leave the confluence valley. Though their names were on the roles at the Oatscott Reserve, they do not appear to have spent much time there. Their tenacity demonstrates that people can love and be extremely attached to places, that land, sky and water can be felt stubbornly down into one's bones, and that Indigenous sovereignty cannot be easily colonized. The Christian family's story is a reminder that calling a place "home" is a political act, but also one motivated by the urging of a soul.

Despite this unbending attachment to the landscape, circumstances had shifted to challenge them even more. Townsites were under construction, farm parcels were marked out. The village on a bluff overlooking the river was no longer widely known as **Kp̓ iƛ̓ls**. It was now 198 acres of Crown land marked out as "District Lot 9, Group 1." Despite its burial grounds and pit house depressions, despite its long association with the Sinixt People, the land registry said that **Kp̓ iƛ̓ls** was owned by the heirs to the estate of J.C. Haynes. The region's Indian agent, R.L.T. Galbraith, positioned at Fort Steele, visited Castlegar not long after the Oatscott Reserve was set up. He seemed unable to grasp the Christian family's deep connection with **Kp̓ iƛ̓ls** and requested more than once that they join the others living at Oatscott. The Christians refused. It was in 1909 that they enlisted the support of noted anthropologist James Teit. Teit interviewed them and recorded their family's use of the land over many centuries. Their efforts were furthered in 1910 when a Reverend John McDougall wrote to Indian Affairs in Ottawa, requesting that the Christian family be granted a small reserve to preserve their burial sites and the dwellings they had built on the north side of the river mouth.

In 1910, Indian Affairs finally indicated a willingness to set aside a small amount of land for them. Unfortunately, Indian Affairs then learned that because the land at **Kp̓ iƛ̓ls** had already been Crown-granted, it would have to be purchased rather than simply "set aside." To that end, Indian Agent Galbraith was asked by officials in Ottawa to begin making inquiries into purchasing the parcel from the heirs of J.C. Haynes. For reasons the historical record does not make clear, the land was instead sold in the spring of 1912 to Peter Verigin. When the Christians found out, they were distraught. They wrote again to James Teit, who in turn wrote to Ottawa. Back in the west, Galbraith was instructed by Ottawa to ask the new owners to sell a small portion of the 198-acre lot back to the government, for use as a reserve for the Christian family. But Verigin was not willing to sell even a small portion of the land. He and his community of Doukhobors were also outcasts, oppressed people who had recently found freedom on Canadian land. They clung fiercely to that freedom, even if it negatively impacted another oppressed culture, one that greatly predated their own arrival, one with rooted bonding and cultural responsibilities lasting several thousand years.

Verigin offered that the Christian family could remain as guests. This arrangement, which appeared to satisfy Indian Affairs, did not satisfy the Christians. To be guests on land they had used in their family for many, many generations confused and perplexed them, as did Verigin's requests to build fences around their gravesites if they wished them to be protected from plows. Over the next few years, tensions between the new owners and the Christians mounted as gravesites were plowed open. Letters continued to be written by the Christian family and Teit. Finally their difficult situation was brought before the 1914 Royal Commission on Indian Affairs. In 1915, Inspector of Indian Agencies A. Megraw was asked to review the situation in the upper Columbia. He put in another request to Verigin that a small portion of the land he had purchased be sold to the Sinixt. This request was also denied. As the settlers made it increasingly difficult for the Sinixt family to remain at **Kṗix̌ls**, Baptiste Christian, the leader of the group, finally left with his wife to establish a farm in Marcus, Washington, close to many other Lakes Indians who had taken up homesteading there. Historical record makes clear that he did not leave willingly. Alex Christian stayed on alone, shifting his residence up to Syringa Creek, where he became known locally in Castlegar and Trail as "Indian Alex." He fished, hunted and trapped in the traditional ways throughout the broad valley he had always known, moving by canoe from one location to the other where he had small cabins and smokehouses: across from present-day Celgar; at the confluence of the Kootenay and Columbia; in Castlegar at the north end of town; and at Waterloo Eddy six kilometres south of town. He also had a trapping camp at Blueberry Creek eight kilometres downriver. He was described as generous and kind, a skilled hunter and well liked by many who knew him in the area.

Ancestral land can be partitioned, entitled, sold, built upon. Gravesites can be plowed, pit house depressions filled in, villages buried. But something remains, stuck like a rock in the current, noticeable even beneath all the smoothing of time and memory. When I enter the broad, beautiful valley surrounding the city of Castlegar, a feeling from the past reaches forward, reminding me of what the landscape lost when Baptiste Christian finally felt pushed out enough to move south to Marcus, Washington, when "Indian Alex" finally grew too old and sick to hunt and fish in the traditional ways. The history of **Kṗix̌ls** still shimmers across the current of the Kootenay River as the water frees itself from the gates of Brilliant Dam to meet its cousin, the Columbia. I see a tragically displaced family and a nearly forgotten culture in the hard, dancing shards of light reflecting off the free-moving river, especially on clear winter days when the sun reflects strongly against the snow and the shadows across the landscape are long. On those days, driving across the bridge over the Kootenay River beside the dam, I can almost see Alex Christian's azure shadow, stepping out to check a trap set into the deep drifts beside Blueberry Creek.

"The Lake Indians were regular callers at the Westley store [in Castlegar]. One family in particular, that made their summer home at Brilliant, near the confluence of the Kootenay and the Columbia Rivers, used to bring bear meat, birds and fish to Mr. Wheeler. He remembers them being most friendly."

—Historian Harold Webber, 1973

RESPECT FOR WHITE GRIZZLY BEAR

In October 2009, John J. Verigin, the executive director of the Union of Spiritual Communities of Christ, apologized on behalf of the broader Doukhobor community for the culture's role in displacing the Christian family. In attendance was another Sinixt descendant, Lawney Reyes, and his family. Reyes, Alex Christian's grandson, is a successful US author who has written extensively about his Indigenous and Sinixt heritage. The title of his book, *White Grizzly Bear's Legacy: Learning to Be Indian,* refers to his grandfather, Alex Christian, whom he calls "Pic Ah Kelowna," or White Grizzly Bear.

The apology took place near the end of a two-day visit in which Reyes spoke to students at Selkirk College and to the public at an evening lecture at the Mir Centre for Peace. A small group of us stood in long grass at the edge of the Kootenay River, assembled around a recently erected granite cairn memorializing the Christian family. I watched as Verigin explained how he finally understood the truth of what had happened between the Doukhobors and the Sinixt early in the 20th century. After that, Verigin approached Reyes and his family in a traditional Doukhobor gesture of recognition and apology. Bowing completely to the ground before the feet of Reyes, he placed his forehead on the earth. When he rose up again, he presented Reyes and his family with traditional gifts symbolizing his twin gestures, cloaked in the humility of a low bow to the ground. The story of the Sinixt, long denied access to the land that forms their identity, rests at the heart of the challenge faced by

Alex Christian in about 1914. Photo courtesy of the Canadian Museum of History, 26616.

"I want to stay in the home where I have always been and want that I have a piece of land made secure for me.... I also ask that the graveyards of my people be fenced and preserved from desecration."

—Alex Christian, 1914

Canada. How can any relationship between Indigenous Peoples and the colonial government find new and trusted ground without involving the land itself? In the golden autumn light beside the Kootenay River, I witnessed a powerful act that demonstrated the essence of the task before all colonial institutions and settlers.

Apologies by governments and institutions for harms done to the Indigenous Peoples have been in short supply. Humble, spiritual actions such as Verigin's have been even more meagre. Just a few years after his bow to the ground, I sat in a Castlegar courtroom, witnessing the start of a long legal battle, *R. v. Desautel,* the direct result of Canada's inability to apologize to the Indigenous People of the upper Columbia River region, for denying their existence. Almost a century after Baptiste and Alex Christian's forced relocation, Richard Desautel, a "Washington State" resident and Sinixt descendant, had come north to hunt in his

Harry Wong, White Grizzly Bear's grandson, paddling on the Columbia River near the confluence with the Kootenay, in a kayak maker's interpretation of the traditional canoe that Harry commissioned around 2010. Harry planted important seeds of education and awareness about the Sinixt canoe as he travelled and paddled throughout the region. Author photo.

traditional territory ("British Columbia") without a licence. An intractable provincial government had long refused to acknowledge even the Sinixt Aboriginal right to hunt, because to do so would inevitably also acknowledge that the Sinixt had been forced to leave and had rights in the region. Claiming that they had voluntarily left their territory, the government position denied the truth of history and the powerful connection between land and identity. When the judge asked him to give his plea that day, Desautel replied quietly "not guilty." One voice, one man's courage, echoing through time to join with the courage and eventually profound disappointment of White Grizzly Bear and his brother Baptiste.

"THE MEDICINE OF OUR HOME"

the perspective of Ladonna Boyd-Bluff

Ladonna Boyd-Bluff is an Arrow Lakes/Sinixt descendant, the great-granddaughter of Baptiste Christian. Baptiste was the oldest among his brother Alex and sister Marie (Mary) Christian, a family who lived along the Columbia and Kootenay rivers up to the early 20th century. Sadly, Mary was murdered in 1911 and both Baptiste and Alex were forced to move south below the 49th parallel in the years that followed. Ladonna, like so many **Sn̓ʕayckstx** (Sinixt) tribal members, has lived all her life below the international boundary, carrying with her a limited understanding of "Canada" and the upper Columbia landscape where her own people, her father's family and her tribe, originates.

As a small child, the youngest of six, Ladonna had a powerful dream, one in which she saw a small, old Indian woman, standing on the porch of an equally old shack. This elder lady bent down to speak with her. Ladonna felt a true love for this woman and a powerful connection. All her life, Ladonna has carried the memory of this dream with her, knowing in her heart that the woman in her childhood dream was her "Gramma Agnes," a relative she had never met. Agnes had been born to Baptiste and Adeline Agusta Christian, during the time when Baptiste, Alex and their sister Mary fought against the pressure of colonial settlement and were eventually forced to relocate.

Gramma Agnes knew the language. Dad could understand but never spoke it.

After Baptiste and Adeline and their family resettled on the Colville Indian Reservation, Agnes grew up, married Harry Boyd and had seven sons and one daughter. One of those was Louis, Ladonna's father. Like many of the Boyd sons, he enlisted in the US military. Much of the social activity

Agnes Christian Boyd, the daughter of Baptiste Christian. Photo courtesy of the Boyd family.

Ladonna with her brother Jim in 2011. Photo courtesy of Shelly Boyd.

in the military revolved around alcohol. When Louis returned home, he struggled with addiction. During her childhood, Ladonna did not hear stories of her people and their forced removal from their homeland.

I think it was too painful to talk about back then. Today, I hear about the stories of my family and understand the generational pain that comes with it. The strength of my ancestors and what they experienced to survive gives me the privilege and honour of living today. Our ancestors were forced from a homeland that they loved very much. Today we still feel that pain of removal, partially because we have not been able to live on the traditional territory of our people.

After many years of work in addiction services, Ladonna began to feel the tug of her Gramma Agnes again. In 2015, she decided to drive north across the boundary, to visit the homeland. She asked her brother, Jim Boyd, where she should go. Jim, who was the Arrow Lakes facilitator (2009–2012) and then chairman of the Colville Tribe (2012–2016), was familiar with the territory.

He told me: Just head up that way and tell me what you feel.

She knew exactly what he was saying and questioned no further. And so, along with her husband, J.R. Bluff, she headed north. They drove up Highway 395 along the Kettle River, crossed the boundary to Christina Lake, and continued east over the Monashee Mountains. After dropping down into the Columbia River valley at Castlegar, not knowing exactly where she was, and never having been told the story of the Christian family, she began to feel powerful waves of emotion.

It just took over me. It was strong. I broke down crying, even weeping. Upon return, I told Jim about it and he just smiled. I understood what he meant with his smile. WE both understood the power of the connection to our ancestors and the land. I've always had this sort of intuitive understanding and connection. My brother understood this about me.

Ladonna and her husband drove east and then north, through the mountain passes, all the way to Nakusp. There, they visited the museum and saw artifacts related to her tribal heritage.

What does it mean to be so grounded in place that one knows that one's own ancestors touched the stone arrow points, mauls or adzes on display in a museum? The Christian family's forced migration downstream along the Columbia to the Colville Confederated Tribe's reservation was an abrupt reversal of thousands of years of bonding and attachment. From a colonial cultural perspective, losing contact with homeland is woven so deeply into the fibres of contemporary ways of being in North America that it has become accepted as a norm. The restlessness and seeking across landscapes continues, generation to generation, as people move from one city to another, one country to another, one coast to another – following employment, personal preference or a dream of a better life. The story of a painful original detachment from ancestral homeland is one that was shared originally by all the settlers who arrived in North America. For settlers, it has resulted in living only on the surface of a place, in cities that have no obvious connection to their own relatives, or with a limited awareness of the natural rhythms of indigenous animals, plants and waterways.

The trauma of Indigenous dislocation, Ladonna explains, shows up in many, many ways. In her current work to develop Indigenous curriculum that both heals and instructs, she has come to perceive delicate layers of meaning in Indigenous languages. Words in the language of the land are imbued with a world view and spiritual understanding. She describes her

Camas. Photo courtesy of Valerie Huff.

visit north of the boundary and its powerful message in simple English words, words that hold a profound meaning for her and her tribe.

It felt so good. I want to go back as soon as possible. I know that the land is where you heal. I can still feel the medicine of our home.

"INDIAN CHOCOLATE"

The same year Ladonna Boyd drove north across the border for the first time in her life, I was crouched in the high grass beside the Columbia River, at the fringes of the soccer fields in Castlegar's Millennium Park. Blue abundance flowed around me, but this abundance wasn't a river current. Between the tightly mowed playing fields and the roiling path of Columbia River snowmelt, I had discovered a profuse tide of wild camas flowers (*Camassia quamash*). Camas rises annually with grace and wild beauty throughout the Pacific Northwest, blooming where moist conditions exist. High spring water conditions in the upper Columbia and Kootenay main stem valleys once provided riparian conditions especially favourable to the flower. As valleys broaden out, so too do flood plains expand. Those of the Castlegar valley once formed modest, seasonal prairies where the camas could thrive. Similar flood plains included those downstream around Marcus and Kettle Falls, Washington; along the Pend d'Oreille River between Cusick and Usk, Washington; around the meandering path of the Spokane River; and in western Montana and the Idaho panhandle.

In the first week of June 1866, Caroline Leighton travelled across the upper Columbia region with her American husband, through a landscape not yet influenced by settler agriculture. Revelling in its beauty, she came across expanses of camas along the lower Pend d'Oreille River that "at a little distance, we took…for a lake." Closer up, Leighton found Indigenous women from the Kalispel tribe, tending ovens dug into the ground, filled with thousands of bulbs. The camas, Leighton wrote, "looks like a little hyacinth-bulb, and when roasted is as nice as a chestnut."

Prior to being controlled by hydroelectric systems, a silted flood plain spread around the confluence of the Columbia and Kootenay rivers. The riverside land, formed originally by ancient deposits of glacial material, had for millennia received the settling silt and nutrients from the river, transforming it into a nutrient-rich flood plain. The Sinixt had lived in year-round villages for thousands of years on the riverside bluffs just above the water's high spring mark. When the spring floods receded, men made ready to fish for ocean salmon, fresh-water sturgeon, trout and whitefish, while women dug and harvested a much-beloved plant relation, ʔiʔtxʷaʔ (*Camassia quamash*). By early June, the blue blooms had faded, the ground was soft and the bulb was ready for digging. In her memoir of traditional Lakes culture, Nancy Wynecoop records the memories of her grandmother, Able One, describing how the Sinixt women moved into the moist, nourishing grounds to harvest the roots. *The high water had receded from the banks, and the rich sediment provided a place where camas grew large and shallow along the slough and back water.* Contemporary Sinixt People refer to ʔiʔtxʷaʔ as an important ancestor of the tribe, a being deserving of great respect and honour. For Able One, camas was "the king root," supreme and important. Helen Toulou, Shelly Boyd's Sinixt grandmother, once described camas as "Indian chocolate," a reference both to the dark hue when cooked, and to the sweetness. Cooking the camas converts its inulin fibre into a sweet, digestible carbohydrate. This dark, cooked hue informs the contemporary Sinixt translation of **ʔíʔtxʷaʔ** – "black camas." In traditional times dried cakes of the cooked bulb stored well for winter, sustaining the people as they waited for the salmon to return.

British botanist David Douglas travelled in the upper Columbia region in 1826–27, recording and categorizing plants, as well as collecting samples of native plants for use in British gardens. In May 1826, just before the salmon runs started, Douglas ranged around the Spokane River, collecting and observing. On the 11th, he spent the night at Spokane House with the legendary fur trader Jaco Finlay. The Hudson's Bay Company had recently abandoned the trading station, in favour of Kettle Falls upstream. Douglas does not mention Finlay's wife, but the fact that the botanist was offered a preserved camas cake and cup of tea for lunch suggests a woman's presence. Travelling up the Columbia River from Kettle Falls in April the following year, Douglas describes the great abundance of two other bulbs blooming around him – western spring beauty (*Claytonia lanceolata*) and yellow glacier (or avalanche) lily (*Erythronium grandiflorum*). His visit was likely too early for him to note any camas blooms, and though his journals do not muse about why these two flowers would be so profuse, it seems obvious to me that women gatherers played a role in nurturing their numbers.

In her own travel diary, as Leighton reflects on the root diggers she observed, she understands how camas and other plant foods could wield a powerful feminine influence. If a man takes an Indigenous woman away from the places where she has been accustomed to gathering roots and berries, Leighton writes, "she may not succeed, in a new place, in discovering them." The placement and tending of plant foods supported many Interior Salish tribes to form a matrilocal shape, with a tendency of the new husband to reside with the wife's family. Recent work of anthropologist John Ross, historian Lillian Ackerman and ethnobotanist Nancy J. Turner discusses with academic precision the way in which the knowledge of plant foods and medicines long held sway in how and where Indigenous People lived.

The once expansive camas fields at the confluence, as well as those farther upstream along the Columbia and Kootenay, and south across the international boundary, have all been greatly reduced or eliminated by settler agriculture and hydroelectric operations. Farmers and ranchers arriving in the late 19th century brought with them plows and grazing animals. They tilled the rich soil to plant orchards, and mowed around the trees. The practices tested or destroyed much of the indigenous plant's habitat. The ignorance of newly arriving settlers could also twist the meaning and significance of the time-honoured gathering process. Jimmy Quigg, who established a ranch in the 1880s in the confluence valley, told the *Nelson Daily Miner* (November 18, 1899): "The Indians had a big encampment near Robson, where the Kootenay empties into the Columbia. Here they had a few potato patches which they thought would give them a clear title to the country." Mistaking the camas for potatoes, Quigg goes on to describe how the Sinixt effort to protect the camas fields as "a favorite plan of theirs to show they were settlers."

Part of the process of setting the cultural record straight is to take in and accept the irony of Quigg's ill-informed judgments. These were not potatoes, but camas, and they demonstrated that the Sinixt, too, tilled the soil gently for their own purposes. But the impact of settlers had just begun. Only six decades after Quigg was interviewed, megaproject

Uncooked, salvaged camas bulbs. Photo courtesy of Valerie Huff.

dams on the rivers controlled spring floods, converting fertile riparian soil into reservoir shorelines. These changes dealt a nearly fatal blow to camas, creating a contemporary landscape devoid of nourishment. Yet, somehow, vestiges of camas have hung on, offering a whisper of continuity through time that reflects the flower's quiet strength and ongoing impact. Dr. Brenda Beckwith, an upper Columbia researcher and adjunct professor in the School of Environmental Studies at the University of Victoria, calls camas "a survivor." Highly adaptable, the plant persists at the fringes – in roadside ditches, woodland, small, remaining patches of flood plain and even cobbled soils that hug the river's edge. Surveys by the Kootenay Camas Project (KCP) have resulted in the cataloguing of 65 surviving camas sites. In her work with KCP, Valerie Huff has seen over 30 native pollinators at some of these sites. Most of them contain a mere sprinkling of flowers, compared with the tended ancestral patches of old, which must have hummed loudly with bees.

Knowing about the great losses can sharpen appreciation for both the persistence of this plant and the need to preserve what is left. That's where Beckwith, together with Huff and KCP co-founder Eva Johansson, have put values into action. When Castlegar's city planners began to clear an area of Millennium Park for the future development of riverside swimming pools in 2014–15, the city's plans inadvertently threatened a surviving, healthy patch of camas. With the city's permission, the KCP mobilized a salvage effort. Hundreds of bulbs were dug, transported to another part of the park and replanted. Most of them survived. Today, they thrive within a 1.1-acre camas preserve, the only protected area in Canada set aside specifically for camas.

In her research and work with the camas on the BC coast and interior over many years, Beckwith has salvaged thousands of bulbs. She never ceases to be impressed by the plant's ability to adapt. It can even thrive as a direct result of being dug up. Through their collective work with the plant, Beckwith, Huff and Johansson have formed a deep appreciation for the ways of Indigenous women. In the process of harvesting with pointed, fire-hardened sticks made of yew and ironwood (or today's metal rods and narrow shovels), women have learned to disturb and aerate the soil. Digging with gentle care can break apart the clumps of smaller root that can form off a "mother" bulb. Women replant them, taking only those bulbs that are mid-sized. Beckwith, like many contemporary ethno-ecologists, believes that Interior Salish

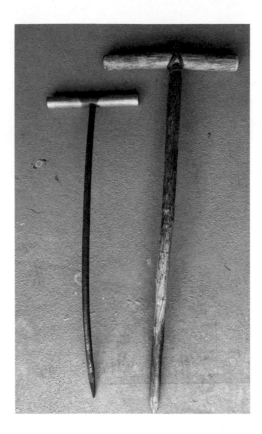

Contemporary digging sticks
in wood and metal, made by
Sinixt tribal member Brian
Phillips. Photo courtesy
of Shelly Boyd.

feminine cultures have long engaged in this form of specifically adapted plant tending. They cultivate, manage and support the abundance of plants that were once deemed essential for physical survival. "Once you start treating camas like a root vegetable," she says, "it reproduces vigorously. It behaves like the root vegetable and doesn't take long to remember how."

As well as encouraging increase through harvest practices, it's probable that Indigenous women took camas bulbs from one place of abundance and planted the overflow where they thought they might succeed. I have found camas growing in some pretty unlikely locations away from more obvious flood plains, most recently in a tight, rock-bound patch of soil watered by snow seepage from adjacent cliffs. Another pocket of camas spreads on a small plateau several hundred feet above Castlegar, at the edges of Verigin's tomb. Beckwith theorizes that the camas growing there could signal a much higher maximum level of rivers and flood plains three to five thousand years ago, as the glaciers in the region gradually melted away. It's entirely possible that the habitat and harvesting of camas is many millennia old. Today's seemingly isolated locations share a significant trait: they are also located close to traditional Sinixt village sites. In the past several years, Beckwith and Huff have often struggled to convince conservation agencies and governments that camas are as important as fish, ducks or boat ramps. A strike against the plant is its obvious visibility for only 3–4 weeks each year. After that, it is difficult – if not impossible – for the uninitiated digger to spot. Municipal governments and land owners can easily overlook the ephemeral flower, as the first settlers once did.

Over 150 years after Leighton first saw the camas fields, a few survivors waver in the wind around me, telling stories of bushel baskets, digging sticks and earthen ovens. The landscape has its own memories, and sensitive awareness can make the potential for harmony more visible, more audible and within our grasp. Camas is a true river flower – a signature plant of the snow-charged ecosystem, a potent reminder of survival and sustainability.

TIE YOUR HORSE TO A SUNFLOWER

In May, the rocky, sunny hillsides dampened by spring rain, from Kettle Falls north to the Castlegar valley, host a happy flower. Among the feathered clusters of ponderosa pine, the vivid, arrow-leaved balsamroot sunflower rises to sing a boisterous song. *Spring is here,* the blooms trill. *Spring is here! Balsamorhiza sagittata* is a faithful companion of the ponderosa pine open forest, where it finds the sun, scrappy soil and arid conditions that it loves. It is a true transboundary flower, opening its cheerful face in the hills and mountains around the upper Columbia from Kettle Falls north. I have found scattered flashes of yellow on rocky hillsides near Trail, BC, and as far upstream as Syringa and Deer Park. From that point, the upper Columbia's mountains gather in tightly. The shadows grow deeper and the forest becomes too damp for this flower.

Arrow-leaved balsamroot is – according to botanists – a member of the commodious "sunflower" family, one that includes such diverse members as asters, goldenrods, butterweed, pussy toes and mountain arnica. Several hundred species of sunflower are found in southern

Balsam root sunflower. Author photo.

British Columbia and northern Washington, including two that are Eurasian-born and extremely invasive – spotted knapweed and oxeye daisy. Given the sprawling and diverse numbers of this flower family, I am likely going out on a limb to say that the balsamroot is by far my favourite of them all. I do love the plant for its large, furry, grey-green leaves, the sturdy stems and lush flowers that rise up out of thin, dry soil, all the time smiling widely in the process.

In *A Salishan Autobiography,* the Sinixt/Skoyelpi Elder and writer Mourning Dove describes the importance of balsamroot in the Indigenous world that radiated out from Kettle Falls, where the great salmon fishery formed a seasonal locus. The women set out to pick the new shoots in March, a month Mourning Dove calls the Buttercup Moon, named for another, much earlier yellow flower. Indigenous women gathered balsamroot shoots "as soon as the ground thawed enough for her to use her digging stick on the tender white sprouts." According to Mourning Dove, the white sprouts were the first fresh source of nourishment after months and months of dried salmon, meat and roots. From these earliest shoots forward across the warming season, the happy plant offered a wide array of gifts to the gatherers. Sinixt/Skoyelpi Elder Martin Louie once described to researchers how young boys wrapped the long, arrow-shaped leaves around their feet and attached them with bunch grass stems. They would walk as far as they could before the leaf split, thus teaching themselves to step softly in the forest. Especially gifted stalkers would even be able to jog without tearing the leaves. The Salish word for the plant, **smúkʷaʔxn̓**, translates as "lump on the foot," a term that Louie said originated from this practice. Sinixt, Skoyelpi, Okanagan and possibly other tribes ate the flower buds after peeling off the outer layers. Women from many tribes gathered the seed from May to August. Tribes of the north Okanagan refer to the month of May as "sunflower seed month." Some tribes ate the small seeds fresh or roasted on a hot rock. Others dried and pounded them into a powder, to store them as flour or to boil into a winter soup. Women dug up tubers to make tea to ease rheumatism, cooked them into a poultice for medicinal purposes and dried and pounded them into a powder. The inner portions of the tuber were shredded, mixed with water and applied to hair as a tonic. Dried leaves were sometimes stuffed in winter moccasins for extra warmth, or smoked as a substitute for tobacco.

There were other uses, still. Many years ago, I met a Sinixt woman who wore a small ceramic vial of balsamroot sunflower pollen around her neck. Collecting it had been a painstaking process. By far the most unusual was offered by Skoyelpi/Sinixt Elder Louis Pichette, who told researchers in the 1970s that he liked to dig around the base of the plant and tie his horse to it. By the 1850s and 1860s, as the gold seekers and settlers arrived, more and more Sinixt and Skoyelpi adapted to and embraced the horse as an important method of transport. Born in 1897 into a landscape confined by the boundaries of the reservation's south half, Pichette grew up with horses and used them to get around. For the Lakes people today, horses remain an important tie to cultural traditions that have evolved to reflect their environment.

Anyone who has tried to transplant a wild sunflower as I did several years ago understands how this flower might double as a hitching post. Reflecting its willingness to attach deeply to the land, "lump on the foot" must never be taken for granted – for its sunny disposition or for its strength in planting itself. The tuber goes deep and attaches firmly in order to draw what it needs from the soil, and any attempt to transfer the plant's cheerful beauty into a cultivated garden risks failure. As a living totem of light, the flower blooms into a soft, springtime world, signalling a time when daily, traditional Indigenous life could be lived mostly outside again, under an ever-warming sun drawing the plant foods up from the soil and fresh salmon back to the river.

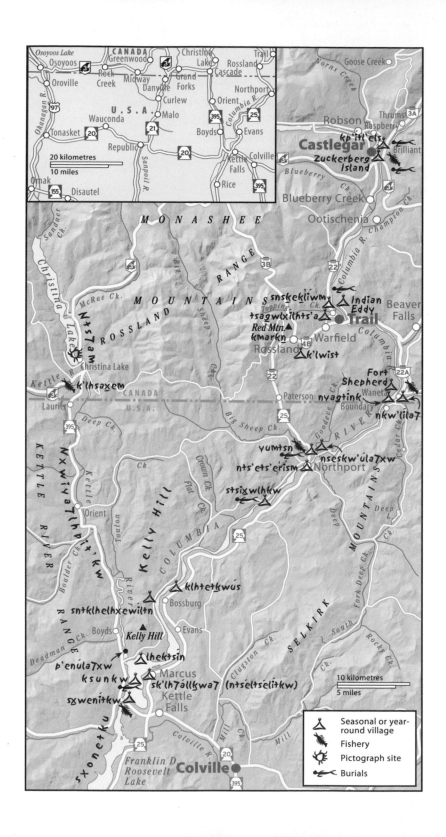

Inset map (top left):

Osoyoos Lake
CANADA
Greenwood
Christina
Lake
Trail
Goose Creek
Osoyoos
[3]
Rossland
Rock
Creek
Grand
Forks
Cascade
Northport
Midway
Danville
Okanagan R.
97
Curlew
Orient
Columbia R.
U.S.A.
Malo
395
25
Wauconda
21
Tonasket
20
Boyds
Evans
Republic
Colville
Kettle
Falls
Sanpoil R.
20
395
Omak
155
Disautel
Rice

20 kilometres
10 miles

Main map:

Norns Creek
Goose Creek
3A
Thrums
Robson
Raspberry
kp'itl'els
Castlegar
Brilliant
Zuckerberg
Island
Blueberry
Ck.
3A
Blueberry Creek
Ootischenia
Columbia R.
Champion Ck.
MONASHEE
3
Big Sheep
Ck.
3B
22
RANGE
McRae Ck.
MOUNTAINS
snsk̓ek̓liwm
Indian
Eddy
Beaver
Falls
ROSSLAND
Topping Ck.
tsagwlxiһts'a
Trail
Columbia
Red Mtn.
Nłsłám
kmarkn
Warfield
4B
Christina Lake
Rossland
k'lwist
Kettle
R.
22
Fort
Shepherd
22A
k'lhsaxem
CANADA
U.S.A.
Paterson
nyagtink
Wanet̓a
Laurier
Deep Ck.
22
Goodeve Ck.
Boundary
nkw'ila7
395
Big Sheep Ck.
25
RIVER
Cedar Ck.
NATIVE
Deep L.
Ck.
Kettle
yumtsn
nseskw'úla7xw
Crown Ck.
Plat. Ck.
nts'ets'erism
Northport
RIVER
Orient
stsixwlhkw
MOUNTAINS
Toulou
Ck.
COLUMBIA
25
Deep
Fork Deep Ck.
Kelly Hill
klhtetkwús
SELKIRK
River
Bossburg
South
Rocky Ck.
sntklhelhxewiltn
Boyds
Evans
Clugston Ck.
Deadman Ck.
Kelly Hill
lhektsin
p'enúla7xw
Marcus
ksunkw
sk'lh7állkwa7 (ntseltseli̓tkw)
Kettle
Falls
Mill Ck.
10 kilometres
5 miles
sxwenitkw
sxonetku
25
Colville R.
Mill Ck.
20
Franklin D
Roosevelt
Lake
Colville
395

Legend:

Seasonal or year-round village

Fishery

Pictograph site

Burials

Rossland to Omak, WA

Čƛawi̧xíc̓aʔ: "wash body." Seasonal village for deer hunting.

Sn̓sq̓ʷəq̓ʷliw̓m̓: "picking place up high." A centre for gathering Saskatoon berries and likely fishing kokanee.

K̓i̧ wist: "highlands."

Kmarqn̓: "smooth top." Now Red Mountain, important for huckleberry picking well into the 20th century.

N̓k̓ʷlílaʔ: "rolling water." A large village important for salmon fishing. Richard Fry and Justine Su-steel ran a trade station here from 1860 to 1864. Now Waneta Dam.

Ksun̓kʷ: "island." The main village for the Sinixt during the annual Kettle Falls fishery. Now under water.

"The [Lower Arrow] lake appears to be teaming with salmon from the sea."

—James Bissett, August 1868

"We used to go to Rossland to go huckleberrying.... There was a lot of Indians that used to go there, Rossland. Rossland there was some high mountains there. You could get a lot of Indians there, lots of Indians go there, pick huckleberries."

—William Barr

MAP REGION 3: based on maps compiled by Randy Bouchard and Dorothy Kennedy in 2000 for the Columbia Power Corp. Map uses their practical orthography. Glossary uses linguistic symbols provided by the Salish School of Spokane.

5.
Rossland to Omak, WA

Following the Salmon

SWIMMING UPSTREAM

When I wanted to connect personally with many living Sinixt Elders while researching the first edition of this book, I had to leave their traditional homeland and drive for the good part of an afternoon. I headed not north into the moist heart of the mountains, but west and south, descending onto the broad, dry Interior Plateau. I followed the drainage of the Kootenay River for a while, then crossed the Blueberry-Paulson summit to Christina Lake and Grand Forks before crossing the US–Canada border at Danville, Washington. There, I took up with the Okanagan River as it flows south toward the Columbia. Once I passed Christina Lake, the arid, early spring landscape bore little resemblance to the cleaved, still snow-covered peaks of traditional Sinixt territory. Ponderosa and jack pine scattered across rocky scrubland. The air felt dry, and the late February light had a fierceness that made me reach for my sunglasses. I was astonished by the height and breadth of the blue dome above me, a sky of endless emptiness no one sees much during an upper Columbia mountain winter. Three hours west and south from Nelson, I arrived in Omak, Washington, a small town perched on the northwestern corner of the Colville Indian Reservation. The pines and larch had headed for the hills, clustering thick only at higher points. The land was dry as a bleached bone, sparse with sage, bunch grass and rabbit bush.

At Elder Alvina Lum's house, I measured scrub alder, willow and cottonwood gathered along the quiet, late-winter river. These bare-branched fringes host swallows and kingfishers whose sharp-tipped wings laced the softening air. I was not entirely sure why I had come, though immediately upon arrival, I perceived a sizable irony, one of those cruel juxtapositions authored by colonization. Some of the Indigenous People of our region's interior rainforest – a place of steep mountains, gushing rivers and thick trees – now live in and call home a flat, dry, desert landscape that could not be more different from that of their ancestors if it tried. Later that day, I sat down with another Elder, Eva Orr, in her tidy kitchen. Another irony surfaced. I asked her to identify her most preferred traditional food. Her answer came without a moment's hesitation. Salmon, she said, her eyes lighting up. By road, the Pacific Ocean is a day's drive away, or longer, to the west. In 2001, my contemporary mind could not match either of the two landscapes with ocean fish – that of Eva's ancestors, where she herself has never lived, or that of her contemporary home, this desert. I had not yet learned of the upper Columbia River system's epic salmon runs during traditional Aboriginal times. When I asked Eva to clarify, she shot me a proud look and repeated her answer. Eva Orr did not mean canned salmon. And she did not mean kokanee, the freshwater salmon making a comeback in upper Columbia waters. She meant salmon. Salmon from the sea.

In the autumn of 1933, when Eva Orr was a young adult living in northern Washington, construction of Grand Coulee Dam began. The upper Columbia's flow was diverted around the site of the dam, thanks to the construction of a temporary coffer dam. Then the concrete walls went up. The dam was designed and implemented in large part to help control floods at the mouth of the Columbia that threatened urban safety and development. There was no documented intention to alter ecosystems or fundamentally damage a traditional rhythm of life for the Indigenous People of the upper Basin. But that is what happened. By the time the dam was completed in 1942, its concrete walls had completely shut out one of the Interior Plateau people's richest wild food sources. Salmon could no longer follow the scent to their home along the rushing Columbia deep into Sinixt territory, as far even as Columbia Lake: a 1,200-mile, 2,650-foot odyssey against gravity that fed many Aboriginal groups living along the river. The fishery once located at present-day Kettle Falls just west of Colville was one of the largest in the Interior Northwest, drawing Indigenous People from as far away as Montana to participate in the miracle of abundance. Eva Orr's answer refers to a rich heritage, a time she was just old enough to have experienced first-hand, before the dams severed permanently the Interior Plateau's connection with a distant ocean.

When fur trader Alexander Ross arrived in the upper Columbia in 1825, he commented that "the waters are, apparently at least, more productive than the land, for the salmon and other species of fish peculiar to the country sported about in every direction." Other early reports by traders and explorers identify significant sites for salmon harvest throughout the region: at the mouth of the Pend d'Oreille and Slocan rivers; on the Columbia River at Kettle Falls; on the Columbia River near present-day Castlegar; in the Slocan and Arrow lakes. The Chinook arrived first, a mighty species swimming up the Columbia in late spring that announced the start of a summer-long harvest. The sockeye

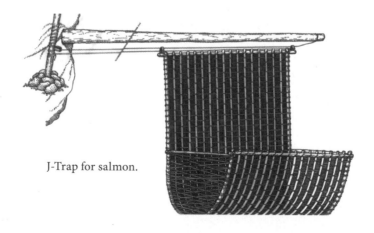

J-Trap for salmon.

and steelhead arrived in July. Another late-summer run of Chinook came after that, and then the coho finished the season in October.

Artist Paul Kane observed in his journals of 1847 that the Salmon Chief's basket trap would contain an average of 400 fish daily. He was told by the Salmon Chief of the time that the basket could gather as many as 1,700 fish when the run was at its peak. Back some distance from the falls, women laboured to preserve hundreds of thousands of pounds of salmon as winter food by splitting them into four vertical filets and laying them to dry in mat-covered lodges on shelving constructed with poles, or by smoking them in specially designed huts. The Sinixt and Skoyelpi used various methods for capturing the salmon. Basket traps were common at Kettle Falls. Chief James Bernard told anthropologist Verne Ray that the Sinixt tended to gather at a particular site during the peak of the run, between Hayes Island (now flooded) and the east banks of the Columbia, just above the upper falls. Nancy Wynecoop also identified this island, which she called **Ksuǹkʷ** (island) as a place for fishing that also had extensive women's bathing pools and men's sweathouses. Trading posts and ethnographers suggested in their reports that the boundary between Lakes traditional territory and that of the Skoyelpi (Colville) tribe was not strongly marked. According to Sinixt facilitator Shelly Boyd, the two groups have always been like sister tribes, with tight interrelationship through intermarriage. For those observing the tribes at Kettle Falls, the distinction between who was Lakes and who was Skoyelpi was not clear, leading to the label "Colville" that has often been used for both of them. To this day, the close bond between the groups remains strong.

In 1852, a Hudson's Bay Company employee named Angus McDonald was transferred to Fort Colvile at Kettle Falls, assuming the post of chief trader near the end of the fort's duration. After a dozen years living with his Nez Perce wife and her relations farther east, McDonald was fluent in several tribal languages. The sights and sounds of the fishery at Kettle Falls pierced his memory so deeply that he was able to describe it in great detail in a memoir many years later. His ear tuned to Salish languages, McDonald heard the Indigenous word for this place, **sxwenitkw** (**Sx̌ʷnitkʷ**), which he transcribed as "Shonet koo." The lively roar of stair-stepped waterfalls filled the air. Salmon moving upstream paused to gather strength for the leap. Fishermen and basket traps were ready.

Kettle Falls at high water. Photo courtesy of Colville Confederated Tribes.

McDonald remembered the salmon crowded so thickly "in the billows at the foot of the falls" that he mused that they might have as easily been shot with a rifle as speared. He painted a vivid picture of the human physical feat involved in bringing the fish ashore. The fishermen had to be both strong and graceful in order to pierce salmon that might weigh up to 100 pounds. Lifting a quivering fish from the current while standing on rocks slippery with mist and spray required balance, presence of mind and certainty of purpose. Those who wavered or wobbled could easily be swept away.

All of the returning fish guaranteed a reliable, renewing source of food for the Sinixt People. This was an annual, water-borne breath of life, a silver or scarlet flash of nourishment finding its way upstream. The impact of Grand Coulee Dam on the Indigenous way of life in the upper watershed was immeasurable. A long-held, reciprocal relationship between river, fish and people had been brought to an end. And yet, amid the impact of this massive loss, tribal Elders spoke of Coyote's Prophecy, the belief that the trickster figure who had originally brought salmon to the river would eventually return them.

The last upper Columbia salmon may have been one caught in the Slocan Pools in 1934. Until then, the arrival of salmon in the region was a miraculous feat of nature, one that connected the sharply creased peaks and steep rainforest valleys with a faraway expanse of salt water. Botanists call the Columbia River's upper, mountainous region a "coastal refugeum," their term for a sheltered area of more temperate climate in which some coastal plants can survive. Before the construction of dams, the upper Columbia was also a refuge for coastal fish wishing to spawn in freshwater creeks: Chinook, sockeye and coho, ocean dwellers, were linked to fingers of spawning creeks by the mighty, liquid-blue pathway to home, the Columbia River. These fish brought with them micronutrients that fed the streams, attracted numerous predators as they spawned, and enriched the waters and riparian areas of the upper Columbia enormously as they died and decayed. Plenty of evidence from early explorers records the biological and cultural miracle of the salmon's prolific presence in the region.

Visiting Eva Orr on the turn of the new millennium, I could not have foreseen how the spirit of Salmon would indeed rise over the next 20 years. Some Canadian biologists working in the upper Columbia River region at that time were not even aware that salmon had once populated the region. Most old-timers who remembered the fish in the river's presence had long passed away. When I asked one biologist working for BC Hydro if he thought salmon could return to the region he shook his head. *I can't imagine that ever happening,* he said.

Little did I know and understand then that for 80 years – since Grand Coulee's completion blocked the salmon – the tribes have never stopped hoping and working for the salmon to return. It is, they say, their responsibility to do so. At the heart of this long, challenging struggle are several Sinixt men, often working in the background and on the US side of the border, largely out of the view or understanding of most Canadians. Their dedication has helped the possibility of salmon reintroduction rise in public consciousness. It looks more and more likely that the Sinixt may return to their Canadian territory on the backs of the fish they have loved and celebrated for millennia.

THE WOVEN LANDSCAPE

Patti Bailey's home on the Colville Reservation perches on a rise above the Columbia River's reservoir shoreline. She explains that though she and her people have been pushed south from their territory in Canada,

Cedar roots being peeled and split. Detail of coiled cedar root basket from the Wynecoop family.

"The Lake [Sinixt] say that an old woman residing in 1909 near Burton City [on the Arrow Lakes] is the only [one] they know of still living who has made coiled baskets; but all the other old women have seen their mothers and grandmothers making baskets."

—James Teit

they always stayed close to the river. For many years, Patti has been learning and practising the art of basketry. She experiments with all sorts of techniques and materials, including cedar. Both yellow cedar and the more common red cedar grow on the reservation in the area around Twin Lakes, near where the Sinixt have their pow-wow grounds at Round Lake. That small part of the vast and arid reservation is like a patch of upper Columbia forest - cool, watery and wet.

"Each time I work with cedar (čápaʔx̌) there is a lesson or learning experience," she explains. "Cedar is a gift that requires gratitude, humility, and patience. Cedar's beauty holds light, and like human skin, it has many vital layers within. Cedar efficiently absorbs moisture, and as with all things, water is its life. I love the process, the seasonality, the smell, and the depth of generations of knowledge passed forward. I'm so fortunate to have learned from our Elders. I hope I can continue to pass that knowledge on."

The Sinixt were weavers and shapers of many forms of basket, used for many purposes. Baskets were their primary containers, their way of carrying, preparing, cooking and storing food. They used baskets to carry and store food, to haul water, to hold medicines and to transport household goods from one village to another. An essential part of everyday life, they were constructed in an artful, ingenious way with the most widely available, practical materials. Everywhere around them in the upper Columbia landscape, Sinixt basket weavers found lengths of workable plant fibre: branches, bark, roots and grasses. Making a basket was a complex and highly evolved skill. It involved forming three-dimensional space from linear material and in that sense was an exercise in geometry. It also involved an understanding of the chemistry of the material being worked with. Some plant fibres required heat for shaping, for example, and others moisture. Some materials needed to be worked right away, others could be stored for later use without damaging their workability. To weave and stitch also required a mixture of foresight and patience, as women conceptualized a framework and completed the long, tedious rows. Patience for this was provided by the human heart. So, between the hand, the heart and the landscape, a shape was born, an accomplishment that elegantly balanced the mental and spiritual process with the physical work of production. The containers held an integrity of place and space that was its own direct expression of valuing landscape.

The wide variety of plant species in the diverse upper Columbia mountain ecosystem allowed an equally wide variety of baskets to be produced. The presence of cedar and spruce meant that strong baskets made by wrapping split cedar or spruce root around a central coil, the type common to all Salishan cultures, could be made here. Cedar root was extremely durable, especially plentiful and workable. In the spring, women dug the pliable roots, working the ground with a fire-hardened stick, about 15 feet away from the trunk of a tree. Roots growing in a sandy riverbank were easier to obtain and the quality of roots was believed to be superior for their length and straightness. The roots were then washed, heated, peeled of their outer covering and split into thinner strips. Working with these prepared strips, a woman stitched tightly over a weft coil made of more bundled cedar root. The result was a basket so flexible and closely woven that it could contain water.

Birchbark baskets were also common in the region. They were made by stripping square or rectangular sheets of the outermost layers of bark from a paper birch tree. The sappy bark that was not used immediately could be heat-shaped or soaked later for use. Women made four diagonal cuts from the corners of the piece of bark and then the cut edges were brought together, overlapped and stitched, with the outside of the bark forming the inside of the basket. They sealed seams with pitch to make a basket watertight. Finally, they added a rim for strength, by stitching the raw upper edge of the bark to a hoop of willow or red osier dogwood, usually using wrapped cedar root. These sturdy baskets could be used for cooking. Fire-heated rocks were dropped into liquid held by the basket, for creating soups or stews. Green sticks of saskatoon berry bush or red osier dogwood were often placed in the base of the basket, to keep the rocks from coming in contact with and burning through or weakening the bark.

Birchbark baskets were constructed in many sizes and shapes, to be used as carriers for berries or fish, or as water cups or serving dishes. The Sinixt women also formed loose baskets made from weaving flat strips of inner cedar bark in a simple lattice pattern, to hold fish and other wild foods, or carry household items. They wove food storage bags made from tule blades, twined with willow bark or **sp'itsin** (Indian hemp, *Apocynum cannabinum*). They lined food storage pits with sheets of cottonwood bark formed into underground baskets, to protect the

James Teit purchased these baskets made by women in the Christian family for the anthropologist Franz Boas. Photos courtesy of the Field Museum.

below-ground earthen bins from rodents. They even made temporary berry containers, by bringing the top three points of the thimble-berry leaf together and holding them in place with a small stick. Lakes/Sinixt baskets were not intricately decorated, though some women used dyed strips of bear grass or bits of mahogany-red chokecherry bark in a process of overstitching called imbrication. Teit's notes from when he interviewed Sinixt women from the Christian family in the early 20th century suggest that the extremely wet environment of the upper Columbia River mountains may have limited the life span of many natural dyes, discouraging their use as decorative elements.

I have worked just enough with raw, natural materials to have a great respect for the challenge that Indigenous women once faced in creating and containing space with plant fibres. The spring before my visit to Omak, I was invited on a rainy day to harvest the inner bark of cedar from trees that had been felled on some private land near Kaslo. The day was an exercise in endurance and strength. First, in a steady, cool spring rain, I straddled a hefty cedar lying on the ground and used a cumbersome draw knife to scrape away the outermost, shaggy bark. Then I used another, sharper knife to cut and peel away the vanilla-coloured layer of exposed inner bark into the longest sheets possible, almost as I would strip a tubular orange of its peel. This exposed the heartwood beneath the inner bark, a remarkably cool and slippery expanse of tree flesh. After several hours, my hands were sore and blistered from the draw knife. My jeans were stained with cedar sap and soaking wet. Cold to the bone, I had developed a small insight into the relationship Indigenous women must have had with their landscape. Harvesting natural materials, especially in quantity, was no small task.

In former times, women would have taken bark very carefully off a live, standing tree: using an adze made of stone, cutting in to the depth of the inner bark near the base of the tree and then pulling up and away on the strip. They were adept enough at this to be able to separate the bark without damaging the tree's ability to transport its nutrients. After a few years, new bark would begin to grow in again over the heartwood, with the scar of harvesting shrinking over time. Once the women had taken off a sheet about 6–12 inches wide, they used a bone knife to separate the rough, shaggy outer bark, then folded the smooth strip into a bundle. Before carrying it home, they always expressed gratitude to the tree. After I had harvested my own sheets of inner bark, I drove home from Kaslo to dry off. Then, before the bark could stiffen, I completed the first step in processing. I stripped each wide piece of inner bark into several narrower ones and then separated each one of these long strips in half crossways to make it thinner and more workable. As I worked in my front yard, the sun emerged from the clouds to warm my hands, and I learned the finer points of how fibres can suggest or defy evenness of separation. I quickly grew absorbed as I worked with the cool, flexible material. It still felt alive as it passed between my fingers.

The strips of bark I harvested eventually aged to a pale cinnamon-brown and waited for years to be soaked and woven around a captured space. In this culture of plastic and metal, there seemed to be no urgency, as there would have been long ago, for me to create a container from this workable fibre. I kept the bark as a reminder that the crafting and weaving of appropriate materials is a fundamental quality of human experience, an extension of the feminine impulse to shape, contain and hold. The form and shape of baskets mimic patterns found in nature: the bowl of a bird's nest perched in a tree, the symmetry and integrity in rows of fish scales or feathers. Baskets hold value not only as objects but as symbols of a woman-culture's quiet ingenuity in experimenting with the landscape's fibres. Their shape is a metaphor for nature's unique symmetry and function. One day many years after that first visit to the Colville Reservation, I was asked to join a group of Sinixt basket weavers on the Colville Reservation. I sat in a circle with Sinixt women – Nancy Michel, Patti Bailey and Joyce Kohler – watching them laugh and talk as they formed bark and roots and grass into beautiful containers, much as their ancestors might have done.

On that first drive home from the Colville Reservation, I made a circle tour, heading east first, and then north. I traversed the middle of the Colville Confederated Tribes (CCT) Reservation and joined up with the Columbia River again at Kettle Falls, where I intersected the path of the salmon as they had once headed north into the upper Columbia Mountains. Salmon were caught in great numbers under the supervision of a "Salmon Chief" who presided over the communal basket trap set out in the most productive part of the falls. The fish were then distributed equally among all who came for them. Since I travelled at the time of low water and the end of an unusually dry winter, I was able as I crossed the Columbia to see portions of the rock beds that once formed the lower falls. Visible upstream were the rocky shadows of the upper falls, where the Sinixt once fished. I stopped to take a long look, trying to imagine salmon jumping over the natural barrier that has been dissolved by changes to the river. The tangled, white flow of a wild river strangled silent by 20th-century engineering prowess can still be recreated by the accounts of the missionaries, explorers and trade fort managers who recorded the large volumes of salmon the tribes harvested from the river.

Coming home along the ancient path of the salmon brought me across the border at Waneta, BC, where the Pend d'Oreille River drains into the Columbia on its east bank and the ghost of Fort Shepherd spreads out on a bluff along its west bank. No physical sign remains of the Hudson's Bay Company fort that ceased operations in 1871 and burned to the ground in 1910. It had only been established in 1856, so its relevance may have been shortened by the inevitable decline of the fur trade. Even for that brief time, it was important to hundreds of Lakes people who formed a village beside the fort that was a stone's throw from an old village site and burial ground for the Sinixt on the opposite shore. At **N̓ k̓ʷlila?**, beside the mouth of the Pend d'Oreille River, Richard Fry and his Sinixt wife Justine "Su-steel" established a trade station to replace Fort Shepherd when it was closed temporarily between 1860 and 1864. Mary Marchand and other Sinixt Elders identified this area as a significant settlement when asked in the 1970s.

As I drove slowly across the old steel bridge just north of the boundary, I looked out my window, trying to imagine the Sinixt village. To visualize mat lodges, fish-smoking huts and pine-bark canoes pushed into the shore, I must look beyond a massive concrete gateway, the Waneta Dam. Construction of the dam, initiated by Cominco (a mining company today known as Teck) in 1951, dramatically altered the terrain around the river mouth. Prior to the dam walls being constructed, the banks were levelled to make way for a concrete mixing plant. The post-colonial scrub, gravel and concrete, lit by the harsh February light, give no hint of the significant Indigenous settlement of this place. A pride and grandeur in the 250-foot-high Waneta Dam eclipses the

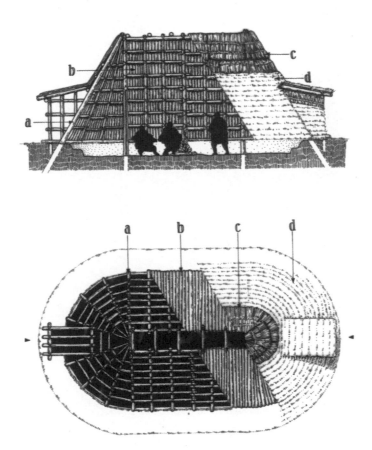

This type of shelter was used year-round in the fur trade era, in place
of pit houses. It's not entirely clear why the pit house ceased to be used.

depth of human history the dam's complex has buried. Seeing things
as they once were along the transborder path of the salmon will have
to be an exercise of imagination, accompanied by a trickle of shame
for the shortsighted conduct of the colonial culture that is my heritage.

The salmon, once so valued and now extirpated from these upper
Columbia waters, are an appropriate metaphor for the Sinixt, who must
struggle against the currents of myth to return to their rightful point
of origin in the region's cultural history. Dams are not only made of
concrete. And sometimes they keep out more than just fish.

Fort Shepherd. Courtesy of Library and Archives Canada, C36196/99.

"To me, that flat above the river's bank 3/4 mile north of the boundary is again picketed, and within the rough stakes I see the storehouse, two warehouses, men's quarters, and officer's lodgings, all of hewn and squared logs. I see more; the Indian village with its 200–300 men and women and children camped in the vicinity of the fort."

—Jason Allard, recalling Fort Shepherd in 1866

"Merchant Hendershott was aroused about 3 o'clock Wednesday by knocking at the back door of his store [in Waneta]…. and…found…a half frozen Indian, whose canoe had upset opposite the Waneta depot and left [him] to the mercies of the swells of the [Pend d'Oreille] falls. He swam to the shore near the Ft. Sheppard [*sic*] hotel and made his way to Hendershott's store. The hospitable merchant soon had a roaring fire going and pot of coffee steaming, which together soon thawed out the Indian so he could tell of his narrow escape and of the loss of his gun, clothing and canoe."

—*Northport News*, December 16, 1897

SWEET FRUIT

A dozen different species of blueberry and huckleberry populate the vast mountain interior of British Columbia, Washington and Idaho. All are members of the sprawling heather family, and most seek out forested habitats at middle to high elevations. While some Interior Salish tribes crown the saskatoon (service) berry as their most royal and prized of all the wild fruits, for the Sinixt, that honour goes to the black huckleberry, *Vaccinium membranaceum* – **st̓xaɬq** (sweet fruit). The densest populations of this fruiting shrub seem to settle in and follow the outline of Sinixt traditional territory. While picking the fruit is possible as far south as Mount Spokane and in high passes in the southern Selkirk Mountains, these areas hold no measure to the profusion of the upper Columbia region. One of the recorded areas of abundance is around the once large and spreading village of **N̓kmaplqs**, at and around the mouth of the Incomappleux River. Here, the Sinixt burned and maintained open areas to encourage profusion. Another place is **Kmarqn̓** (smooth top), today known as Red Mountain, important for Lakes people as a picking site well into the 20th century.

Though the Sinixt can no longer tend huckleberry fields north of the border as they did in traditional times, the fruiting shrub remains resilient and prosperous, largely due to wildfires and the large-scale clearing practices of industrial logging. Just after I relocated to the region, a friend took me to her favourite spot. On a hot August day, I stood in the tangle of alder and huckleberry bushes, close to the edge of a logging road, plucking one after another, following the ripe fruit deeper into the vegetation growing back from a clear-cut until I was surrounded only by the green web of leaves and the hum of insects. When I stepped across fresh bear scat alive with flies and laced with purple skin, I realized I had separated myself from others in my single-minded pursuit of the fruit. A picker must never forget that huckleberries also belong to the bears.

Nancy Wynecoop described efficient methods of many types of berry harvest that included the use of a comb fashioned from wood, woven tule mats under bushes to catch the fruit as it fell, and the shape of traditional picking containers, fashioned from birchbark, with a long string to hang flat against the lower body. Contemporary Lakes women have told me that they maintain careful spiritual practices to encourage a good harvest, just as their ancestors did. When Lola Campbell grieved the loss of her grandmother Eva Orr, she respected the practice of refraining from picking for a full year. It was important to do so in order to ensure good future harvest. "I am hoping for berries as big as my eyeball next year when I go out," she told me at a gathering for Eva's memorial. Women trained in the tradition keep their thoughts positive while they are picking. They show gratitude for the years when huckleberries are abundant, and acceptance when pickings are slim. They make offerings, usually tobacco, as a way of expressing reverence and gratitude.

"MOUNTAIN IN A JAR": A LIFELONG PASSION FOR HUCKLEBERRIES

contributed by Judge Wynecoop

Both of my grandmothers were Sinixt and enrolled in the Spokane Tribe, as am I. The tribe adopted them when Arrow Lakes traditional territory ceased to be theirs, as reservations were established to corral them. They told their many children that the upper Columbia River and nearby Christina Lake was their home ground, as was Low Pass near Bossburg, and Marcus. Their children's children (my generation) had only a vague sense of what being Sinixt meant. For me, that all changed when I attended a 2004 presentation given in Spokane by the author of *The Geography of Memory* at Auntie's Bookstore. I purchased the book before she began the program, and as I leafed through it and looked in the index there was my grandma, Nancy Perkins Wynecoop referenced nine times! – including the wonderful transcription of the Sinixt (Lakes) story, "Mountain Goat and the Origin of Huckleberry" (printed in purple ink, no less) told to my grandmother by her own grandmother, Seepetza (Able One).

I was born in 1934. My grandma Nancy delivered me. My Aunt Nettie told me Grandma's days, and often her nights, were given to service to others. Almost every new baby in the family was ushered into the world with her loving help. Nancy passed on in 1939 so I hardly knew her, but from my childhood on, I have picked huckleberries – with my other grandmother, May Etue Galbraith, my uncles and aunties, my parents, my brothers, and now, my wife Tina, children, grandchildren and good friends.

Back in the fall of '51, when I was a senior in Wellpinit High School, my Uncle Glenn, my brother Chick and I went on a camping and huckleberry picking trip to North Baldy. Glenn had heard from our neighbouring tribe of Kalispel Indians that there was a great crop of huckleberries that year. It was absolutely out of this world. The bushes were loaded with large, black huckleberries, and we could grab handfuls from the bushes. We never used pickers [combs made from wood]. Some did. You worked harder cleaning them later because of leaves and little sticks. Besides, that's not "picking." These berries were about the size of nickels and so juicy and sweet. That day the three of us picked 22 gallons! We filled four or five empty five-gallon ice cream containers, plus our extra picking buckets that we hung from our belts. When we got home my mom, Phoebe, saw them and she was completely overwhelmed. I wished that she could have got to pick with us in that patch. She loved picking huckleberries so much.

I prefer to pick from the huckleberry patches in the Selkirk mountain range close to the international boundary; we can't cross the border marked by that wide, clear-cut swath that changed our peoples' lives when it crossed us – but it is a clear, visible reminder. Salmo Mountain, Monumental Ridge, North Baldy, the mountains surrounding Priest Lake, all are known for their fine huckleberries. They are rich in flavour, abundant, and often so big "you have to roll them to the car!"

I long for huckleberry season. I think about it all year: Is there too much snow, or too little snow cover, hard frosts when the snow has melted and bloom time has begun, is there a drought? When the New Year is celebrated, I am quietly celebrating for a different reason: it is only six and a half months until I will start picking huckleberries again! I average 22–32 gallons each year. I begin at the lower elevations and work my way up as the season progresses. By the time the frosts set in I am at the top of the mountains. In 2020, I picked my last bucketful on September 29th, the latest harvest ever. I go two, mostly three times a week. It's about a two-hour drive one way and the travel up to the patches is on many miles of single-lane dirt roads where it is not unusual to meet a logging truck barrelling down with its load of logs. We squeeze past each other.

Judge Wynecoop in one of his favourite picking patches.
Photo courtesy of Tina Wynecoop.

Huckleberry patches vary from year to year. It's not always a sure thing where the most prolific patches will be, without a lot of scouting. I enjoy the search almost as much as the picking. There is one road I've named the "Never again road." It is a shortcut. The boulders run the whole length of the road and are remnant reminders of the last ice age. They are so big and so tall that my four-wheel-drive rig has to creep and bounce along. It is quite a balancing act to stay on the road and usually my passengers get out and walk behind out of respect for their well-being. The vistas from this road – to the south and west toward the Huckleberry Mountains with the Columbia River beyond – are glorious. The waiting berries are tantalizing. My son Jake, my huckleberry partner, calls this "shortcut" the "Every-damn-time road."

Our Colville/Sinixt friends, the tribal women who appreciate getting to join in and pick in my favourite patches, have noticed that each year I "wake the berries up" and "put the berries to bed." They call me the huckleberry whisperer, or the (unofficial) huckleberry chief, because they recognize my passion for being in the mountains. My wife refers to my picking as an "obsession" – but I know that purple is the colour of the blood that courses through me, pumped by my heart and spirit. In fact, when my blood is drawn for medical reasons, the vials take on a purple hue instead of red.

I can still point out the traditional places tribal people camped in the mountains, and I drive the same trails and roads they took. One trail is named "The Flowery Trail." It begins in Chewelah in the Colville valley and passes over the mountain to Kalispel territory at Usk. I'm sure my ancestors also had names for many such trails in the north country, above the boundary.

We freeze a lot of huckleberries. My wife makes pies, and preserves the berries in a way that leaves a little bit of room in our freezer for other things. I've suggested we buy another freezer. We give gallons to the cooks for tribal gatherings. We share berries with non-profit groups to support their fundraising auctions, and so on. Our two sons used to pick gallons and gallons to earn money for their college funds. Church ladies like to purchase from them. The irony was that the chips and pop and fuel it took each trip cost us more than what they earned. We could have just stayed home and wrote them a check. But what they truly "earned" was knowledge and respect for their family traditions – for the ways of the huckleberry. They have "the geography of memory" in them

Huckleberry.

now. In 2004, following her presentation, Eileen Pearkes autographed my new book. She inscribed it with a flourish: "Enjoy this journey."

And I have! I have so valued learning about my ancestral home, the wider horizon's grander view and the great depth of my Sinixt heritage.

The recipe for huckleberry jam the way my wife Tina makes it:

Place a gallon of fresh-picked, clean but unwashed huckleberries in a heavy-bottomed stainless steel pot. Slowly heat the berries to release the juices. If the berries are harvested early season then add a small amount – no more than a quarter of a cup – of sugar. (Unlike with common jam recipes, Tina avoids the recommended pectin and lemon and the large amounts of sugar.) Bring the berries to a rolling boil in their own juice, stirring constantly for four minutes. Ladle into hot, sterile pint jars and put a canning lid/ring on each one, then process to seal. When it is time to open a jar to put on toast, pancakes, ice cream, or just a spoon-load to eat all by itself, you will have the pure glorious fragrant mountain huckle-berry taste, the taste from "the time when they made things."

—Arnold "Judge" Wynecoop

WHAT A RIVER BODY SAYS WHEN IT SPEAKS

In the last, frantic year before Grand Coulee Dam was operational in 1942, federal scientists scanned maps and rapidly devised a salvage plan for the salmon and steelhead that would be stopped at the base of the new dam. Scientists planned to capture the fish, load them into unrefrigerated tank trucks and transport them by road, to release them into the Okanagan River or deliver to hatcheries where eggs could be salvaged. Their plan spoke with rational confidence that the salmon would quickly redirect into the Okanagan River. However, the plan morphed quickly to disaster, with many fish dead or dying by the time they arrived where they were being hauled. It was both an ethical and a scientific failure, one that decisively snipped in two a sustainable cycle built over millions of years. These hasty mitigation efforts in the early 1940s had also planned for the construction of four hatcheries. Only three were ultimately built, and then the federal government constructed another dam downstream of Grand Coulee, Chief Joseph. It was not until the early 2000s that the CCT successfully negotiated for that fourth, forgotten hatchery to become a reality.

In 2008, after years of the tribes taking the hydropower producers to court over their failure to properly support salmon mitigation efforts, the CCT signed a Fish Accord with the Bonneville Power Administration (BPA). *Everyone was trying to stay out of court,* Joe Peone, Colville Tribal fish and wildlife program director, has explained. A Sinixt descendant, Peone helped build the Fish Accord, which provided firm financial commitments to habitat and hatchery management, to at least support the struggling salmon populations below Grand Coulee and Chief Joseph dams. The federal agencies and tribes began to work together as partners "on the ground" at that point, to support tangible survival benefits for salmon. They would upgrade passage over federal dams, restore river and estuary habitat, and improve hatcheries. There was a catch, however. Some officials quietly told D.R. Michel – another Sinixt descendant and new executive director of the Upper Columbia United Tribes – that the words "salmon passage" (above Grand Coulee and Chief Joseph) were too politically sensitive in hydropower management circles at the time to be associated with the hatchery's construction. Another Sinixt descendant and historian, Mike Finley, was an elected CCT leader during the planning and construction of the hatchery. In our conversation, he described the attitude of government officials when they released funding for its construction. *It was like they were saying "Now take this hatchery and go into the corner and be quiet."*

Together, the men watched over the next decade as scientists and government officials continued to resist what the tribes had always known – that the fish had never forgotten how to swim upstream and into the Canadian mountains. Meanwhile, the hatchery's goals were specific, and applied only to restoring *downstream* fish: recover spring Chinook and summer steelhead, both listed as imperiled under the Endangered Species Act; sustain and prevent listing for summer/fall Chinook and sockeye; provide ceremonial and subsistence salmon from "hatchery extras," for the CCT tribe; and finally, increase recreational fishing for all people, in the middle and lower Columbia, estuary and ocean.

Unable to formally consider getting the salmon around Chief Joseph and Grand Coulee, the tribe and its leaders turned to restoring fish populations in the upper watershed where fish passage was not an issue. The fact that the Okanagan flows into the Columbia downstream of Chief Joseph (236 feet high) and Grand Coulee (550 feet high) dams meant that the river had never lost its salmon completely, though numbers had dwindled severely. After the hatchery was completed in 2013, the CCT in the US (funded by the BPA) and the Okanagan Nation Alliance in Canada (funded by the US-based mid-Columbia Power group via the Colville Tribe) launched an ambitious sockeye restoration project on the Okanagan River. Joe Peone was at the heart of the work. The BPA would not allow any federally mandated mitigation funds in the US to be used in Canada, he explained to me, so the CCT reached an agreement with the operators of the mid-Columbia dams (Wells, Rocky Reach, Rock Island, Wanapum and Priest Rapids), whose mitigation dollars from ratepayers *could* cross the boundary. And did. Fish biologists hired by the CCT acquired 28 riverside properties and some water rights with BPA money on the US side, transforming the channellized, straightened lower Okanagan River where they could – into something that twisted and turned again. Mid-Columbia power mitigation funds worked to improve passage into the Canadian lakes that had once formed about 40 per cent of juvenile rearing habitat, including Okanagan and Skaha. Joe Peone chuckled when he demonstrated that the solutions were not necessarily expensive. *We opened up Skaha Lake habitat with $2500 worth of lumber.* Chief Joe hatchery released hundreds of thousands of fry into the river. Tribal people gathered for salmon festivals, where they stood by the water, singing songs and beating drums, calling the spirit of Salmon home.

This combination of the rational and the intuitive worked magic, and the spawning sockeye multiplied: 108,000 returned in 2008; 200,000 in 2010 and 2011; and then, in 2012 on Tuesday, the 26th of June, 41,573 sockeye passed through the fish ladders around Bonneville Dam *in a single day*, headed upstream to the Okanagan River. Fish blogs and newspapers crowed with jubilation. By the time the spawning season was over, nearly half a million had returned that year. It began to sink in across the mainstream culture that ecological restoration could translate into recreational user success. Under D.R. Michel's leadership, the Upper Columbia United Tribes next hired Earth Economics, a consulting company, to study the positive impact of restoring "natural capital" to the upper Columbia economy. *We knew that if we continued to manage the system by focusing only on hydropower values and flood control – we would all lose. Our economic report proved that ecosystem values can create prosperity, too. Things don't have to be "either or." With a grass roots, cross-border approach, we can all win.* Indeed, Joe Peone told me that he sees the results downstream of Chief Joseph Dam. *Up to 300 fishing boats are floatin' around in Wells pool now, fishing the Columbia from early July until October.*

Among scientists, governments and policy experts, the whispered possibility of the returning of salmon above Grand Coulee into the tributary rivers and lakes of the upper Columbia began to turn on the ground-breaking, international, cooperative tribal effort for sockeye. In 2012, the Universities Consortium on Columbia River Governance hosted a conference in Polson, Montana, on the Flathead Indian Reservation. There, academics and tribal leaders discussed the coming possibility of renegotiating the 1961 US–Canada Columbia River Treaty, and tribal representatives began to connect the treaty with salmon passage – openly and directly. Over the next few years, broader discussions among governments and institutions led to a concept known as "ecosystem function" to be added to hydroelectric efficiency and flood control in the possible goals of a new treaty after 2024. Emboldened by the success of the Okanagan River runs, the tribes pushed further. Ecosystem health should not be one of the pillars governing Columbia River operations under a new Columbia River Treaty between Canada

Three-pronged spear.

and the United States, they asserted. It should be *the* foundational value in a restored river system. Persistently, patiently, and yet also radically, these leaders have reminded all who live in the upper region of the fourth largest watershed by volume in North America to think about the river differently, to see its potential and to believe that salmon could return. In them, as in my much earlier visit to Eva Orr, I have seen and heard the graceful focus of Sinixt People on the wisdom of the ancestors, those fishermen who stood poised on slippery rocks, spears in hand, with grateful hearts.

As they continue to work on salmon restoration into the third decade of the 20th century, the Sinixt do so in the context of an intellectual climate of grave concern over rising global temperatures. Scientists and governments have been measuring the effects of increasing drought in the mid-Columbia basin, and decreased snowpack on the east slope of the Cascades. Spring and summer outflows from the Columbia River remain persistently constrained by irrigation and hydropower production, nested within a broader value system that still is not ready to soften the economic model currently in place and take account for the needs of the fish. With industrial farming, a rapidly decreasing Odessa aquifer and financially stressed hydropower producers, water has become something scarce, something to parse out. Some especially pessimistic scientists are even ringing the eventual death knell for Columbia River fish that once numbered 16 million annually, swimming upstream for many millions of years as far as the Rocky Mountains to spawn. Columbia River Basin Indigenous tribes have observed ever-dwindling stocks of Chinook, steelhead and sockeye travel upstream through many fish ladders on the lower and mid-river, only to be stopped by the

Salvaged and moved above the reservoir prior to the unnatural flooding behind Grand Coulee dam, "the sharpening stone" has been marked by countless stone tools at Kettle Falls across thousands of years. Indigenous fishermen and women sharpened their spears and knives here.
Photo courtesy of Mike Graeme.

twin behemoths of Chief Joseph and Grand Coulee, dams that provide no passage to the hundreds of miles of cold-water habitat sheltered and fed by the Canadian mountains in Sinixt traditional territory. Oddly, I don't hear tribal biologists and policy leaders being pessimistic. Is it because they don't understand the science behind climate change? Or is it because, as Mike Finley says, *science needs to confirm what we've always known*, and science has not yet caught up. While hydroelectric development in the upper Columbia has been intensive, extensive and deeply harmful to ecosystems, there is, the tribes say, a supply of cooler water upstream that can give the fish summer and autumn flows to keep them viable. All at once, the storage dams in the uppermost watershed may have a new purpose.

Another feature of climate change is surprises. In 2012, a year of extremely high spring rainfall led to a great deal of water from the upper Columbia being discharged downstream through the system. A fisheries manager from the CCT got a call from some tribal employees working at a soon-to-be-operational hatchery just downstream of Chief Joseph Dam. Due to the high flows, a maintenance staircase at the base of the dam was being flooded by the spring runoff. There, employees found Chinook salmon using the staircase like a fish ladder, *trying to get around Chief Joe.* In years past, fish had made it through the fish ladders on the mid-Columbia and pooled annually on the downstream side. Enough salmon had congregated there every year, in fact, that Lakes tribal members had developed a fishery in the tailrace water. They adapted their fishing practices to use a special three-way hook they designed, one that could handle the turbulent tailrace water. For the tribes, Chinook finding that staircase was a sign that the fish still wanted to come home. I hear joy in D.R. Michel's voice to this day as it speeds up when he describes the event. *They looked at that staircase as a way around the dam. They had a desire to find that home. That desire was still there.*

About the time the salmon found the staircase, informal discussions over the Columbia River Treaty began to pick up speed. From 2012 to 2016, US tribes stepped forward as sovereigns to assert the needs of fish that had once flourished in the upper system, primarily salmon but also sturgeon, lamprey and others. *We weren't asking permission to be involved,* Michel has explained. *We demanded that governments make effort on behalf of the fish. Nobody had asked our opinion. We spoke up as sovereign nations who had lived for thousands of years beside the river.* In a series of meetings that eventually formed the US regional treaty recommendation, and at conferences on the ethics of the Columbia River Treaty, Michel and others detailed the great cultural losses the tribes had experienced, pointing to ongoing physical and mental health issues related to no longer having salmon as a primary part of their diets. The concept of *ethical* restoration of the river system gradually entered mainstream treaty discussions and eventually showed up in US and Canadian regional recommendations for treaty negotiators in a vague term defined as "ecosystem function."

In 2016, the CCT invited the public to a ceremony to call the salmon home, at the inundated Kettle Falls. The tribes who had traditionally gathered at Kettle Falls each built dugout canoes and paddled them to the falls from their respective territories. The people had never stopped going to the falls each spring to pray for the return of the fish, as was

Each year, the Sinixt travel to the Salmon Ceremony at Kettle Falls in this cedar dugout canoe that tribal hands created in 2016. Author photo.

their deeply ingrained tradition. But now, the effort would be public. Between 2016 and 2019, they held open ceremonies, feasted and sang beside the water. In the global community, tribes and governments began speaking of rivers as "persons." My email inbox started to fill with questions from readers. *What about the Columbia? Can it be a person, too?* Discussions around how to manage the Columbia for the 21st century broadened. Appointed Columbia River Treaty negotiators in the US spoke carefully and more matter-of-factly of "ecosystem function" as a confirmed value, if still a vague one, in how to apportion water. But the US and Canadian tribes were still shut out of the negotiating table. Then, in 2019, Canada announced that Indigenous People would be invited to sit with Canadian negotiators during treaty negotiations. Speaking at a conference in the autumn of that year, Canadian lead negotiator Sylvain Fabi described the decision as "long overdue." While Canadian Global Affairs staff members warned him about setting a precedent, he replied that *not* inviting tribal leaders would be to "miss the boat again," and added: "We want to be on the right side of history." Except that the still-extinct Sinixt had not been invited to join the table on the Canadian side. There was more work to be done.

In a short decade, the possibility of salmon restoration above the dam had swelled into a cloud, like spawn being released in a streambed. Momentum was building. That same year, 2019, the CCT decided to do some cultural releases of salmon into the waters above Chief Joseph and Grand Coulee dams. They called these releases of 30–60 fish in various upstream locations a spiritual "re-joining." The thousands of Chinook who had returned to spawn on the upper Columbia River in 1942 and met the wall of concrete had, in the tribal mind, never been able to make it home. This would close the loop on a broken cycle. As plans got underway, a hatchery juvenile salmon, released by the Spokane Tribe as part of their own spiritual and ecological healing, unexpectedly found its way home. Equipped with a rice grain–sized transmitter, it had miraculously survived a journey down the upper Columbia to the ocean – through two Spokane River dams, through Chief Joseph and Grand Coulee, through all the mid-Columbia dams and out to the ocean, before returning a few years later to swim up into the access channel at the Chief Joseph hatchery late in the season. The hatchery staff had already started closing the weir, Michel explained, but a rise in river levels immediately downstream after hydropower releases gave the fish a second chance to swim into the holding tank. When tribal employees "pinged" the late arrival, they realized that it had come originally from the Spokane hatchery, not the Chief Joe facility. Jubilation spread through the tribal world as more and more people realized that a salmon *could* return of its own volition if released in tributaries deeper in the watershed.

Given half a chance, the spirit of Salmon *would* return to the region.

As a recurring, ever-renewing food source, salmon demonstrate potential for natural systems to be abundant, expand and remain sustainable. As a spiritual being, Salmon evokes persistence and grace – survival through strife, mixed with courage and resilience. Born in fresh water, the fish transforms its entire endocrine system to be able to inhabit the sea. Near life's end, it reverts back to freshwater habitat, pushing persistently upstream to natal habitat, where it spawns for the future, then dies. The capacity to swim these long distances demonstrates awesome physical strength, as well as the focused desires of the fish. This global keystone species, even as it is threatened worldwide with habitat loss and climate change, does not want to disappear. It is at once mysterious and inspiring, and represents a perfect template for the healthy bonds that form not with *logos* (science) in charge, but with *eros* (love) ruling the day.

To that end, on one hot, breezy, summer morning in 2019, the tribes gathered at the shores of Grand Coulee Dam's 125-mile-long-reservoir, to release 30 Chinook into water that had not felt the belly of salmon in nearly 80 years. They gathered with passion in their hearts for a fish that had never been forgotten.

When I arrived at the boat access ramp at the mouth of the San Poil River arm of Grand Coulee's massive reservoir, many tribal members had assembled. Some women wore the colourful traditional dresses, scarves and beaded bags of ceremony and celebration. Tribal regalia is often handed down, generation to generation. Akin to "dressing up for church," donning these traditional skirts, head scarves, beaded necklaces and ribbon shirts is a sign of respect for the fish. Several tribal drummers had already formed a circle around "the big drum" under a cloth canopy, to shade them from the sun. These appointed drummers would pray and sing for the fish throughout the cultural release. Elders sat nearby in rows of chairs. With the reservoir lapping at his heels, Colville Confederated Tribes Chairman Rodney Cawston spoke of the hard work that had preceded the day, pointing in particular to D.R. Michel. That there was little to no room for change within the tightly managed Columbia River system had not stopped Michel from persisting, just like a salmon.

Beside Chief Joseph Dam's reservoir, sunlight glittered happily off the water, as if it knew that today, for just a few minutes, this would be a salmon river again. Michel's words echoed in my head as I watched more people trickle down the long boat ramp and join the group. *There are opportunities to change the system, to rebalance culturally, spiritually, economically and ecologically,* he had told me and others willing to listen, several times. *What keeps us going is our tie to the land, that responsibility. It's who we are.*

I was one of few with pale skin, hidden from the fierce summer sun under a broad-brimmed hat. Mostly those gathered were Sanpoil, Nez Perce, Lakes, Skoyelpi, Okanagan and other tribal members. Everyone waited. Waited for the salmon to arrive. Before settler contact, it was the same. Waiting. The homing was a miracle, a divine and mysterious gift. A runner would carry the exciting news upstream, arriving at the next village well ahead of the first spring Chinook. The people antici- pated. They loved. They waited. The mighty Chinook pushed their way against the spring snowmelt current that surged through the Colum- bia's streambed.

It seemed like many hours (but in the end was only one) before the piercing beep-beep of a truck backing down the ramp created a ripple of excitement. Drumming and singing began. The state-of-the-art fish transport truck owned by the CCT inched down the long road as people formed two parallel lines to the water. Over the past half-century, the Yakima, Nez Perce and Colville tribes have had more and more influ- ence in the Columbia River salmon hatcheries, exerting an ethics and sensitive awareness about how things are done. To that end, everyone had been assembled well ahead of the scheduled arrival, so that the fish would not be kept waiting. Water temperature in the truck's tank had been closely monitored. The needs of the fish, in a tribal management system, are paramount.

The drum reverberated through me, pounding against my ribcage from the outside in, awakening my well-protected heart. I was unable to recognize the words in the traditional Salish song that filled the air – words of welcome, praise and gratitude, I was told later. I watched as the truck stopped at the upper end of the long line of people. Several men from the CCT fisheries department hopped out. The suspense and ex- citement were palpable. Many people in the lines began to knock small stones together, imitating the sound of shifting riverbed gravel. The first net dipped into the truck's tank, bringing up the silvery flash of a fish. The air thickened with hope. The drum quickened. That first fish went head first into a rubber bag filled with water, and then the writhing bag moved through the river of bodies. I watched as many brown hands grazed against it, even though only a few strong arms held it firmly to pass from one to the next. When it reached the shore, the writhing bag was lowered beneath the water's surface. The first salmon pulsed out and darted away.

The air filled with 300 whoops of joy. My heart lifted and skin shivered. I was witnessing an ardour typically reserved in my culture for a pair of reuniting lovers, for family members, a new grandchild, or even for a favourite rock band when it takes the stage. I had never in my life heard such a pulsing unity of verbal joy for a wild fish. I stood, emotionally overwhelmed, up to my knees in the water, a little away from the line of people passing the fish as the drum beat them home, one at a time. Each one pulsed from the rubber bag and darted quickly off into the deep.

At some point, one of the fish brushed against my calf as it swam away. Excitement ran through me like an electric current. I had felt on my skin a desire for freedom. For a wild home. The emotional haze thickened around me as I watched the very last fish enter the water. What does it mean to be a salmon in this tightly rationalized world, to dart off into unknown possibilities, to risk survival in an unfriendly reservoir? The drum faded, then stopped. The truck pulled away, empty. The crowd's energy diffused, but within me, a strange feeling of astonishment only grew. What is this force of raw, physical and earthly desire, compared with the behemoth economic engine of hydroelectric development? What does it mean to love something or someone so much that you never give up wanting it to return? Women set out breakfast on a few portable tables. I was not hungry, but I crouched on a piece of reservoir driftwood and forced myself to eat. Sharing food is, I've been taught, a way to seal the prayers for the fish. All around me, the quiet but joyful chatter of tribal people continued, as if they were standing outside socializing after a church service.

Many contemporary Columbia River salmon have been embedded with a non-invasive, rice grain–sized telemetry tag to help fish managers make counts of returning fish. A few are equipped with larger radio transmitters for more technically precise and expansive research. The size of an AA battery, the transmitters sit in the stomach of the fish. The antenna wire comes out of the mouth and drags behind the salmon as it swims. Transmitters have helped science create maps proving the remarkable journey Columbia River salmon make – often ranging as far as the coast of Siberia in their fluid migration –but they are hard on the fish. These fish carried no such burden, Randy Friedlander from the CCT department of natural resources told me after lunch. In their spiritual and biological reach, Salmon's spirit would have as much freedom as possible. Successful survival would be a mystery for now – until and if spawn was actually discovered in places along the reservoir.

Some scientists call the uncanny ability of the salmon to home themselves a sensory knowledge akin to smell, one imprinted on the *otolith*, or the "ear stones" of the fish, located behind the brain. I think of it instead as an *extrasensory* perception, one far beyond the capacity of our own human minds to understand. The relentless logic of hydroelectric development has, for too many years, impressed itself on the body of the river. As I drove north into Canada again later in the afternoon, I realized that the cultural release by the tribes was not about overruling the otolith, as the logic of science had tried to do in 1942. The 30 fish swimming in the reservoir upstream of the dam represented tribal faith and belief in freedom and desire. The salmon had been first and foremost *Salmon*, a spiritual reconciliation for a broken promise. How many of those salmon might find their way across the boundary's invisible line? The Latin root of the word sacred (*sacrum*) refers to the bone that surrounds and protects the procreative organs. The tribes describe restoring salmon to the Columbia as their *sacred* responsibility. In surveys of the body of the river early the following year, tribal researchers found that the upper San Poil River, Nespelem Creek area and the lower Spokane River had all received the spawn of culturally released fish. The released salmon had found places to reproduce.

Walking upright into a world of great change, all of us can carry a protective reverence toward natural systems. We can expand a sense of love and gratitude. By calling up an ancient and mysterious form of *eros*, we may be able to avoid stumbling, falling or descending permanently into hopelessness. By fostering love for the river and its fish, we restore our human and sacred connection with the natural world.

MAP REGION 4: based on maps compiled by Randy Bouchard and Dorothy Kennedy in 2000 for the Columbia Power Corp. Map uses their practical orthography. Glossary uses linguistic symbols provided by the Salish School of Spokane.

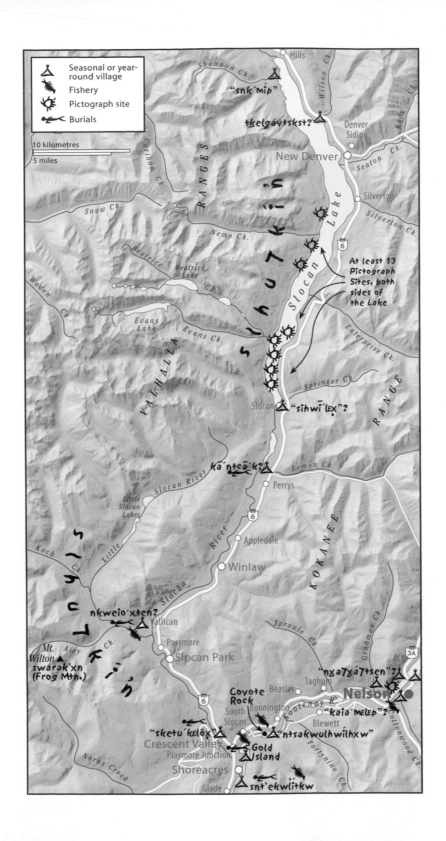

Hills

Shannon Ck.

Wilson Ck.

Kaslo Ck.

"snk´míp"

ɬkelgáytskst?

Denver Siding

New Denver

RANGES

Caribou Ck.

Snow Ck.

Nemo Ck.

Slocan Lake

Silverton

Silverton Ck.

6

At least 13 Pictograph Sites, both sides of the Lake

Beatrice Ck.

Beatrice Lake

Wolven Ck.

Enterprise Ck.

VALHALLA

Evans Lake

Evans Ck.

Springer Ck.

RANGE

Slocan

"sihwi´lex̣"?

KOKANEE

ḱáˊntcáˊḱ?

Lemon Ck.

Slocan River

Perrys

Little Slocan Lakes

6

Koch Ck.

Little

Appledale

Slocan

River

Winlaw

nkweio´xten?

Vallican

Sproule Ck.

Grohman Ck.

Mt. Wilton
swarak'xn
(Frog Mtn.)

Airy Ck.

Passmore

Slocan Park

"nɣaʔɣáʔɬsen"?

3A

Taghum

Beasley

Nelson

Coyote Rock

6

Bonnington

South Slocan

Kootenay R.

"kaia´MELEṗ"?

Blewett

Cottonwood Ck.

"sketu´kelóx̣"

Crescent Valley

Playmore Junction

"ntsakwulhwilhxw"

Gold Island

Fortynine Ck.

Shoreacres

Norbs Creek

Glade

snt'ekwli̓tkw

Slocan Lake to Slocan Pool

Sləẁqin̓: "pierce, strike on the head." Likely a reference to gaffing salmon. Anglicized as Slocan, the Indigenous term refers to the entire region.

Sn̓tk̓litkʷ: "much river food." This large village and fishery caught salmon and steelhead spawners that could not ascend the falls to Kootenay Lake.

T̓qlʕay̓čkst: possibly means "trout ascend," for a bull trout fishery. Today, Wilson Creek/Falls.

Sn̓k̓mip: meaning end of the lake or a pass, like mountain pass.

"The higher frequency of pictograph sites than campsites...makes it tempting to hypothesize that [Slocan Lake] was more important to prehistoric inhabitants from a religious perspective than it was from an economic one."

—Archaeologist Morley Eldridge, 1984

6.
Slocan Lake to Slocan Pool
Land of the Living

FROGS INTO FOOD

"The Lakes [Indians] were very careful about getting, preparing and processing food; if a woman stepped over or on a piece of food it invited a famine; carelessness was a great vice."

—Nancy Wynecoop to William Elmendorf, 1935–36

One contemporary account of Sinixt oral history has a story about a time long ago when the upper Columbia gave little food. Rather than abandon the drought-stricken land, Sinixt people retreated to riverbank caves. After much hunger and suffering, they discovered frogs that were coming into the cave offering themselves as nourishment. The people

Frog Mountain seen rising above the Slocan River.
Photo courtesy of Mike Graeme.

ate the frogs and survived. When the drought ended, a frog came into the cave, to tell the people they would again find food in the forests and rivers when they emerged. The story reminds any listener of how slim the margin is between abundance and scarcity when people depend on a wild landscape for sustenance. And even though Sinixt oral history warns against times of privation, a study of the records of early European contact indicates that in the upper Columbia region, the land, water and air provided all that a culture needed to keep its diet balanced and its people healthy. The Sinixt ate many types of fish and meat, starchy roots, nuts and berries, all harvested from these valleys. Cultures that subsist on wild foods with minimal agricultural effort must be highly nature-related. They pay attention to wild rhythms and the habits of animals and plants because they know that only by understanding and respecting these things will they survive. Indigenous cultures consume animals and plants with equal relish, but also with equal reverence. Unlike in a strictly agricultural society, their approach emphasizes receiving the offerings of natural systems rather than impressing their will on the landscape. Such cultures are rare now, but the relationship they have always had toward the places where they live still holds important meaning. It is a subtle yet important distinction that in the story the frogs "offered" themselves to be eaten. This spirit of an animal or a plant offering itself permeates the approach of any nature-related people to their food. Interactions with landscape and its abundance were reciprocal and receptive.

The first shoots of the chocolate tips peaking up through the slushy March snow. Fresh greens after months of only dried food. The avalanche lily in flower again on a mossy outcropping, a signal that it was time to collect the fist-sized roots beneath the soil. The arrival of deer to lower elevations as heavy snowfall increased higher up. The recurrent cycles of nature in these valleys would have had a deep, appreciative quality about them; not only for the beauty of the seasons but also for the nourishment and life energy being offered by the earth. The Sinixt traditionally held several ceremonies through the year that reflected their spiritual reverence for the process of seasonal renewal in the landscape. In late winter, they held a dance to bring good weather and good fortune. During this ceremonial time, the men danced single file through the village while women stayed in houses, standing and singing whenever men danced past. In the spring, after everyone cleansed their bodies to receive fresh foods by drinking teas of Oregon grape or sarsaparilla, men feasted the women while the women danced through an entire day in a "fruitful season" ceremony, celebrating the return of fresh plant foods that women would gather throughout the warmer months. In the summer, there was a "first salmon" ceremony, a joyous honouring of the fish that provided months of high-fat, calcium-rich and easily preserved food as they swam upstream.

Contemporary Sinixt People still respect and value at a deep level what nature offers. They collect wild foods as their people always have: with an eye to future harvests, with a natural conservationist impulse. This impulse to take care of everything that is alive has its own deep roots in their culture. It was a care their ancestors took not so much for ethics or for economy but directly for survival the following year. This attitude continues to bind the contemporary Sinixt to the rhythmic gifts of the natural world. Though there is evidence that the Sinixt control-burned to encourage the regrowth of huckleberries and tiger lily bulbs, that they supported the abundance of camas in how they dug the roots, and that they practised cyclical harvest to allow populations of plants and animals to restore, their approach to nature was neither agricultural nor industrialist. Until the arrival of European culture, they did not till the soil deeply, nor did they extract animal resources in a systematic way for monetary profit. Entirely dependent on the natural world as it presented itself, they worked cooperatively with the seasonal rhythms of the earth to harvest what was offered.

Early European explorers appreciated and capitalized on the nature-related lifestyles of the Interior Salishan people they encountered along the Arrow Lakes in the early part of the 19th century. Sometimes half-starved after the trip over the Rockies, these men often gratefully accepted dried salmon and caribou meat, or cakes of preserved berries moistened with bear grease, that they were offered by those wintering in villages along the Columbia River. Explorer diaries are peppered with accounts of weary travellers gorging gratefully on salmon, bear meat, caribou or goat – usually shared but sometimes traded by the Sinixt. The trading company officers establishing forts in the region after 1820 acknowledged and respected the hunting skills of the Sinixt men. Their skill helped them provide countless furs to the forts, which appeared to have a voracious appetite for the pelts. But, ironically, this success catapulted the Sinixt into a vastly different economic system, encouraging them to embrace the extractive methods of European and colonial cultures. After 1820, hunting became more than a subsistence activity to provide food, bone tools and warm clothing. It became a commercial pursuit. Half a century later, the arrival of permanent settlers from other parts of Canada, the US and Europe to the upper Columbia altered the subsistence lifestyle further. Creeks were no longer for kokanee or bull trout harvest, but sites for placer mines capable of producing mineral wealth. Summer and winter villages became townsites, ranches or market gardens. Berry patches became orchards. Spawning kokanee were just as likely to be thrown into the soil and used as fertilizer for flower gardens as they were to be smoked and eaten. The landscape had become a place of natural resources waiting to be extracted and transformed into material wealth – an enormous shift. Amazed by the abundance of fish in the rivers and lakes, settlers harvested as many as they could with no thought to the future, thus straining populations. Settlement activity left less and less room for the receptive, rhythmic way of life that had dominated the valleys for thousands of years. In addition to the displacement of the Sinixt People, the impact of logging, mining and townsite development disrupted or removed habitat for the animals, fish and plant foods, further altering the ancient patterns worn into the soil and water of the upper Columbia.

To those arriving with a different value system informed by the energy, excitement and conquest of colonial settlement, the upper Columbia lifestyle must have seemed primitive and limiting. Those who had come to believe that only agriculture and commerce bring prosperity saw the region as unfulfilled and primed for proper use. Yet human survival in wild nature is not an inferior way of life. It is just different. Subsistence requires ingenuity, careful planning, attunement to instincts and respect for natural rhythms. It requires an amalgam of mental and spiritual acuity, as well as physical strength, and breeds a form of humility and grace in the face of uncontrollable natural systems. The Sinixt's management of upper Columbia wild resources was both social and technological, much as it is today. Their lack of motorized technology and metal tools then had limited the size of impact they could have on the physical rhythms of the ecosystems, but it did not limit their spiritual understanding. Their culture responded to this constraint with gentle intelligence. They had no choice but to wait for flood waters to recede before establishing summer villages. In doing so, they witnessed the fecund life force that floods carry. The people searched the current for the fresh flash of a fish, never sure if the fish would return in great or small numbers. They prayed. They loved. They hoped. The story of the frog in the cave ends with the frog becoming a permanent symbol in the landscape, hopping and growing until it becomes Frog Mountain, a high peak in the Valhalla Range, visible driving south from Winlaw through the valley of the Slocan River. Frogs, in the end, are not just food. They remind us of faith, the enormous value of small creatures, and the delicate balance that makes wild survival, and even profusion, possible.

"When the fires were burning in the evening the house was lighted up like electricity. There was lots to eat."

—Nancy Wynecoop describing winter in a pit house
to William Elmendorf, 1935–36

THE SEARCH FOR A RIVER PEARL

A few years ago, I was walking along the edge of the Slocan Pool on the Kootenay River just west of Nelson when I noticed what looked like a scrap of the ocean nestled between two rocks. I reached to pick up an oval, dark shell that resembled half a mussel. I turned it over. Inside was a polished, concave surface of pearly white. At a place the Sinixt call "much river food," I had recovered the memory of *Margaritifera falcata*, the western pearlshell. In traditional times, the Sinixt gathered the freshwater mussels from the riverbed, relishing them. They and other Indigenous People throughout the inland Columbia River basin turned to these shellfish when stores of other foods dwindled, or for variety. Once abundant in streambeds from southern British Columbia to central California, the western pearlshell lived historically in the Klamath River system, the rivers of the Coastal Range, and in the main stem and tributaries of the Columbia River, including the Snake, Willamette, Kootenay and Walla Walla rivers. The creature has even travelled as far as the headwaters of the Missouri River, likely cresting the Rockies through glacial activity.

In the old days before dams, the free-running Kootenay River shot through Stonebyre Canyon just upstream of the Slocan Pool. After passing through that funnel of granite, the water carved an expansive arc beside a large Sinixt village. In spring and summer, the river pool was a cauldron, burbling with oxygen as it dispersed the water's energy from the falls. The current scrubbed riverbed gravels and enriched the suspended nutrients, priming the habitat for spawning Chinook and steelhead trout, those who knew they could go no farther upstream. It was a rich habitat for spawning fish, just the right habitat to support "much river food" – including the freshwater mussel.

Mussel larvae are born as tiny specks – a populous wash of one to four million babies, released by the female and fertilized by the male. Only a few survive long enough to be inhaled by a host fish. Momentarily, they attach themselves to the gills of the fish and begin to feed on microscopic particles of nutrients as the scaly swimmer breathes and moves through the water. Mussels might take up residence in a Chinook salmon (*Oncorhynchus tschawytscha*), a rainbow trout (*Oncorhynchus mykiss*), a coho (*Oncorhynchus kisutch*) or a steelhead trout (*Salmo gairdneri*). All were once prolific residents of the Columbia/Kootenay River system and its tributaries. The mystery of how a mussel

Slocan Pool. Photo courtesy of Touchstones Nelson Museum of Art and History.

knows to attach itself to a fish early in that host's lifecycle, rather than just before it spawns and dies, may never be solved. Around a year later, the mussel is large enough to drop off its carrier and nestle in clean gravel or sand on an active streambed. It can live up to 100 years as it continues to filter and digest plankton from the moving water.

The Kootenay River canyon and its pool are silent and still as glass almost year-round now, the result of South Slocan Dam and the Kootenay Canal Generating Station upstream, and Brilliant Dam downstream. Only a few faint pit house depressions are visible above the shoreline in a modest-sized protected forest. These depressions hint at the large Indigenous population that once thrived here in year-round dwellings, feasting on many anadromous fish that ended their migrations at the pool. Moving water is essential to the survival of mussels, as it is to the health and well-being of the salmonids that host them. As the mussels eat and digest, they build up fine layers of calcium carbonate on the curved inner walls of their shell-homes, forming a smooth lining called nacre. The effort to smooth over larger particles of sediment caught in their soft systems leads mussels to create the nacre, the same substance that creates pearls. Scientists today believe that mussels actually clarify the water as they feed, benefitting other aquatic creatures and neutralizing some pollutants.

The ethnographer James Teit referred to the freshwater mussel in his research, calling it "famine food" for Salish tribes. Other accounts describe them being gathered by the Okanagan people through holes in the ice in the Okanagan River. In his 1981 study of a proposed heritage site on the Slocan River, archaeologist Gordon Mohs discovered discarded mollusk shell in concentrated deposits, recorded in his 1981 report. In 2009, Dr. Nathan Goodale, Alissa Nauman and their team discovered two small fragments of mussel shell in their own investigations of house pits at the Slocan River Narrows near Lemon Creek and Slocan Lake. According to Dr. Goodale, one fragment is cut-marked, suggesting that the mussel was consumed as human food. In the 1970s, Sinixt/Skoyelpi Elder Martin Louie confirmed that the mussels were gathered in the old times along the Columbia River and its tributaries.

Louie described the traditional harvest of another shell – one identical to the white, tusk-shaped creatures (*Dentalium pretiosum*) harvested and traded by Coast Salish people after being raked from the substrate below tidal zones. Before and after European contact, the tusk-shaped dentalia, open at both ends and known by the Chinook jargon term *higua*, formed an important part of Salish adornment practices. The shell is still highly prized by contemporary Indigenous bead artists. Multiple archaeological sites along the upper Columbia and its tributaries have contained dentalia. Archaeologists have always assumed that the dentalia in these burials were valued trade items, a shell originating from the Pacific coast. Martin Louie believed differently. He mentioned a place on the Colville Reservation called **Sn̓ ta?kín̓ tn̓**, located just below old Inchelium, near two small lakes. Here, Louie said, in the location of his Skoyelpi ancestors, a white, tusk-shaped shellfish lived in the clay. He described how his people once dug the shellfish up from the thick sediment collected on the lake bottom, boiled the soft insides out and used the shells for decoration. When he was shown samples of coastal dentalia by the ethnographer Randy Bouchard in 1978, Louie confirmed that they were identical to those once harvested at the two small lakes – from a thick, wet habitat not unlike the substrate below the tidal zone where the saltwater dentalia thrive. The fur trade explorer Alexander Ross encountered women at the mouth of the Okanagan River between 1815 and 1825, wearing hair "ornamented with double rows of the snowy

Dr. Nathan Goodale in an excavated house pit at Slocan Narrows archaeological site (numbers DkQi-1, DkQi-2 and DkQi-17). The site contains record of Indigenous occupation that spans at least the last 3,000 years. Ongoing archaeological investigations aim to understand human land use in the interior Pacific Northwest, as well as the socioeconomic organization of Indigenous Peoples in pit house village settings.
Photo courtesy of Mike Graeme.

higua." It's entirely possible that the *higua* adorning the hair of these Interior Salish women was not a trade item from afar but local shellfish found in fresh water. We don't have much to go on to support the theory; the lakes at **Sn̓ta?kín̓tn̓** where Louie says the shells were found, and the original settlement of Inchelium where many Lakes people migrated in the early 20th century following border enforcement, have both been destroyed by water backing up behind Grand Coulee Dam.

Louie's recorded memories of the upper Columbia River landscape have a precious value not unlike the dentalia – a resource that has been so overharvested as to be considered rare. The persistence of the western pearlshell in rivers and streams, despite the dramatic changes to the aquatic habitat of the upper Columbia region, is a delicate reminder of a time when host fish were abundant, and nobbly beds of bivalves spread thick across streambeds.

STRONG ARMS MAKE GOOD (HAMMERED) FOOD

Joe Bourgeois was born in 1928 and lived all his life in the upper Columbia region close to the Slocan River. When I met him in 2009, his short-term memory had begun to wobble, but he still had plenty to offer when it came to recollecting his childhood. Joe's face came alive when I asked him about his Depression-era upbringing on a dairy farm that was perched on an arid bench above the Slocan River. He described roaming the forests and the Slocan riverbanks as a child and shared a particularly vivid memory. One day, he and his brother were playing along the base of a bluff overlooking the river when they discovered several significant depressions in the ground, about 50 feet in diameter. One of them contained logs still buried as posts around the perimeter. Unaware that they had stumbled on remnants of pit house dwellings at an old Sinixt village site, they noticed a curious stone slab emerging from the gravelled soil beside one of the circular pits. Digging with youthful energy, they soon unearthed a large stone bowl. Further digging resulted in another bowl, and another. Joe and his brother dragged one of the bowls up the bluff to the farm to show their father. The boys had chosen to stop and play in a place identified by ethnographer James Teit as **Skt̓ək̓ʷla?xʷ**, near present-day Crescent Valley. The location of the village would have capitalized on sockeye salmon runs coming up the river every year. I asked

"Mr. Seward, one day while plowing, dug up many pestles and mortars and arrowheads."

—Recollection of R. Salstrom, Arrow Lakes Historical Society. Seward's orchard, now under water, was located at West Demars south of Nakusp, on the west side of the Columbia.

Author photo.

Joe what happened to the bowls. A shadow of confusion passed over his wrinkled face. After a few minutes, he shook his head. *I'm not sure.*

A year later, I heard a similar story about a stone bowl, this one unearthed more recently near Deer Park, on the Arrow Lake reservoir, during spring drawdown. While the property owner was digging a trench for a water line to a summer cabin, he was down over a foot and a half from the surface when his shovel struck a large stone with an unmistakable concave depression in its centre. He built the bowl into a rock wall.

How easily memories can slip through the grasp of history. Prior to European contact, stone mortars (bowls) partnered with hand mauls, or, pestles, to form the backbone of a woman's kitchen equipment on the Interior Plateau. She needed these tools to process and prepare many of the protein and plant foods for winter storage. Crushed and pounded food was so common in Sinixt culture that the language gave

Reservoir operations recently dislodged a lichen pounder from an eroding bank. Author photo.

it a special category of its own. **Ststaʔ**, they called it, "hammered food." In a culture where winters could be long and deep with snow, food preparation and processing were essential skills requiring strong arms and a deft, meditative rhythm with a stone maul striking against a stone bowl. Several collectors I know have an impressive array of mauls in various shapes and sizes. At least one archaeologist I have spoken with has expressed surprise at the great number of mauls found in private collections throughout the region, pointing both to the settled nature of the Sinixt lifestyle and to the intricacies of food preparation.

Salish hand mauls come in a variety of shapes and sizes. According to Grant Keddie, formerly archaeology curator at the Royal BC Museum, the nature of the geological material seems to play an important role in the ultimate shape. Flat, somewhat triangular, paddle-shaped mauls are often made of metamorphic schist or gneiss. Mauls with a broad, circular base are made of harder, igneous rocks, such as granite. These pounders vary in length, from less than eight inches to well over a foot. Stout mauls were handy for grinding wild hazelnuts and pine nuts to mash them with dried berries and bear grease before packing them into cleaned animal intestines for winter storage. Women also ground dried meat or salmon flesh with grease and fruit, to soften and flavour it before serving. The Sinixt used small mauls in small, ceremonial bowls, to grind and prepare the red ochre for painting pictographs. One of these small bowls, carved to resemble a frog, came into the hands of a local Nelson collector named A.E. Pickford. Pickford arrived in Nelson in 1910 at the age of 30, cresting a wave of British immigrants who came before the First World War. It's not clear why he was drawn to the upper

Columbia region, but in a letter he wrote to the Royal BC Museum in 1947, he recalled collecting many artifacts on the shores of Kootenay Lake and its West Arm, just after he arrived. He found several paddle mauls on beaches, calling them "spade-like stones" and explained that he had spoken to a "very old Indian whose English was not too good: from him I gathered their principal use was in the preparation of the well-authenticated moss bread prepared from the tree lichen."

Black tree lichen (*Bryoria fremontii*) was once a mainstay in the upper Columbia region's Indigenous food cupboard over a long winter. Men and women gathered the lichen late in the season with the help of long poles hooked or twisted at the end, and after all the other foods had been preserved. They pounded and washed the lichen with the paddle mauls, to leach out unpalatable flavours and help break up the fibres, so that it would cook and transform into something digestible, if not delicious. Sometimes, the lichen was combined with other roots, or fruits, for flavour. Next, the women wrapped lichen in clean leaves and placed it on a pile of vegetation that covered hot stones lying in the bottom of a pit. More vegetation, then soil, covered the lichen. Women poured water down a narrow passage that had been held open by a stick during the filling of the oven. This created steam. Finally, women tended a small fire on the top of the earthen oven, to maintain maximum heat. After a day or longer, the oven revealed dense cakes of baked lichen, the texture and colour of licorice. Some Plateau tribes preferred the lichen from pine trees, others from larch.

In 1916, Pickford met and married Rosina Gigot, his neighbour on Latimer Street in Nelson. They had a son in 1921, then moved to Victoria, BC, where Pickford eventually became assistant in anthropology at the provincial museum. He wrote articles about archaeology, taught and corresponded from 1923 to 1926 with Harlan Smith, an archaeologist with the Dominion Government of Canada living in Ottawa at the time. In the notes he sent to Smith, Pickford included a sketch of the zoomorphic bowl in the shape of a frog. Today's whereabouts of this frog bowl are unknown.

The beaches and shorelines all around Nelson that were once full of stone inspirations for Pickford are now empty of these sorts of memories. Most of the stone bowls, pestles and paddle mauls collected over the years rest in basements, on living room shelves or in permanent collections. Stone mortars and pestles express a symmetry and durability

Zoomorphic bowl. Courtesy
of the Canadian Museum of
History.

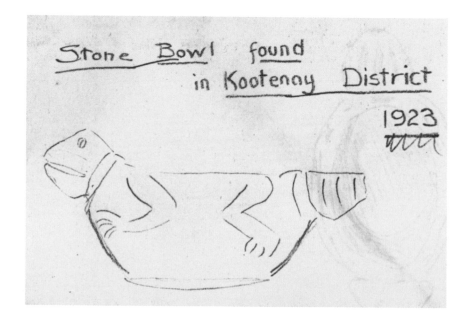

Stone Bowl found
in Kootenay District
1923

that has no equal in a modern tool. To hold such an object in one's hand, or to trace the size and heft of the stone food bowls themselves, is to connect with deeper layers of time in the upper Columbia River landscape. Over hundreds and even thousands of years of use, granite bowls developed depressions worn deeply enough to echo the curve of the Earth. The Royal BC Museum has several large, rounded bowls from Keith and Ellen Edgell's collection in storage. Touchstones Nelson's museum has one stone bowl in its display. It was donated to the collection in 2004 by a South Slocan church, where it had been serving as a baptismal font for decades. I have gratitude for A.E. Pickford, who cared enough to ask the right question of the right person to keep the story of the paddle maul's use in the region alive. The landscape is our first museum, and the story of these tools helps us understand more clearly the relationship between people and place, resources and their use. They are truly grounded in place.

DEAD AND BURIED

According to Elder Nancy Wynecoop, traditional Sinixt Interior Salish burial practices involved several steps. When a person's physical life came to an end, a family member placed the body in a loosely woven basket or bag and strung it in a tree, where it remained for several days in order to ensure that all of the life had left it. The house where the death had taken place was cleansed with the burning of juniper branches. The body was buried in a fetal position, usually in a gravel bed along the banks of a river. Wynecoop told Elmendorf that there was no belief in an afterlife as our culture would conceive it. Rather, the dead spirit would "merge with the entire body of nature like a bubble melting or bursting into a stream." This interpretation could partially explain why the dead were placed so close to water, in order to facilitate their merger with the larger cosmos. Water, an essential component of terrestrial life for any natural system, can be a powerful carrier for the spirit. Riparian burials practised by the Lakes people differ significantly from our own culture's burial in fenced graveyards. Gravel is, by comparison to clay, a shifting substance. Riverbanks can change shape over time, too. But that does not suggest that the Sinixt wished for their ancestors to be disturbed. Nor does it make the human remains of the pre-contact upper Columbia culture less significant as signposts of the landscape's narrative. Unfortunately, the streamside location for Sinixt burials has resulted in high levels of disturbance, especially from settlement activities in the last 100 years. In this region of narrow valleys, much post-contact development has also taken place close to shorelines, where Sinixt graves have been especially vulnerable. Road building, agriculture and development of towns and cities regularly disturbed burial sites until the 1950s, after which the construction of dams flooded the original shoreline.

"Archaeological investigations at DjQj1 [Vallican] have greatly expanded our knowledge of the local prehistory…. Aboriginal populations were in the Slocan Valley a considerable length of time and…the Vallican site was a popular settlement for a continuous succession of groups of hunters and gatherers."

—Gordon Mohs, 1981

In 1982, during the construction of a road and bridge, a double burial was partially exposed on an embankment along the Slocan River, downstream of Slocan Lake near the present-day site of Vallican. The Vallican site has been identified by more than one archaeologist as rich in significant findings and indicative of long, varied use over time. In this particular grave, archaeologists uncovered two tiny skeletal remains: one of a 7-month fetus and the other of a 2-year-old child. Buried with them were a large number and variety of small objects of a quantity not commonly found in other graves: leather shrouds, containers and clothing, fur trimming, sinew, plant cordage, human horse and deer hair, three hardwood arrows, 138 copper tube pendants, 2,102 assorted glass trade beads, brass rings and buttons, 595 dentalia shells and 52 elk incisor beads.

Not until 1989 did word of the disturbed remains finally reach the unofficial Sinixt headquarters in Inchelium, WA. Linda and Rick Desautel and over 50 other tribal members, including Yvonne Swan and her brother Coose, Jim and Margaret Swan, Meloni Burris, and Pat and Lucy Finley, packed up immediately and headed north. Linda is unflinching in her explanation of the seven-year gap. *The archaeologists knew we existed, but everyone involved blatantly went by government policy, that we were extinct. Until someone with a conscience let us know.*

For Linda, Rick and the others, the disturbance of remains was a moral issue. *My cultural upbringing is that you don't mess with other people's stuff*, she explains. *That place is sacred ground, because of all our burials. It's sacred whether it's paved or not. It's still hard to drive that road.*

Linda recalls the reburial that summer as a unique experience. *There was no sadness. We weren't saying goodbye. We were putting our ancestors back where they belonged. I felt immense gratitude. I'm glad we could help them rest.*

Archaeological reports are scientific in their language, attempting to maintain objectivity. Eldridge's discussion of the burial in his 1984 report refers to "osteological remains," "cranial elements" and "the lengths of longbones." There is little place for emotional musing. On the page following, a diagram shows the precise arrangement of the goods buried with the bodies as they were uncovered. I am unable to take horrified eyes off the drawing for several minutes. The array of beads and pendants over the skeletal forms have the look of scattered tears. They speak of grief's torn fragments, of emotional chaos and of maternal desperation. The story behind the two infants, one as yet unborn, one a toddler, cannot be known through scientific examination. Try as I might through an act of imagination, I am not able to hear their voices. But questions about their suffering still float through my mind as I trace the careful diagram, noting tube beads and bits of shell that may have come inland through trade. Did the fetus die within the mother or was it still-birthed with cries of anguish and loss? Was the 2-year-old a sibling? Were the beads and pendants the property of one family, or of a whole village? What happened to the father?

About a decade before the Vallican dig, a skeletal remain was exposed on an embankment of Gold Island, in the Slocan Pool on the Kootenay River just east of what is now Playmor Junction. Subjected to fluctuations in water levels due to the operation of Brilliant Dam, Gold Island's topography could no longer hold the partial skeleton to the shoreline where it had been placed. The remains came into the possession of Selkirk College, where they sat in a box on a shelf for many years. No protection of gravesites had been undertaken prior to the river being dammed by West Kootenay Power and Light in 1944, even though the federal archaeologist, Harlan Smith, had identified the island as containing burials, and the area around it as being culturally important, when he surveyed the region in the 1920s. The landscape had served up its own reminder of the spiritual significance of the island. Almost 20 years later, Selkirk College returned the skeletal remains exposed at Gold Island to the Sinixt People, so that they could be repatriated at the Vallican burial site.

The area all around Gold Island, like the area around the burial site in Vallican, is peppered with archaeological sites of villages and burials, many of them unrecognizable now, as in the case of Site DiQj8, a small group of pit houses on the high terrace between South Slocan Junction and Crescent Valley, destroyed by the construction of Brent Kennedy School. The peninsula east of Gold Island also contains many smaller cache pit depressions used for winter food storage. The landscape around the mouth of the Slocan River and the Pools, an important salmon fishing location for the Sinixt, sustained the lives and deaths of many souls over the millennia. Each of the pit house sites may have housed a year-round population of 50 or more.

While some riparian burials have been exposed by alterations to river water, others have been disturbed through excavation during dam construction and road building. Some of these disturbances resulted in responsible if limited archaeological surveys being done, as in the case of James Baker's report on the findings between Robson, the Brilliant Dam site and a proposed reservoir at Murphy Creek to the southwest. Many disturbances of burials went unrecorded, except through anecdotal recollections. There is an account by a settler in Trail, for instance, who had heard that a grave said to be of a Sinixt woman was located at Sandy Island. Apparently, the body had been buried in front of the face of a rock, on the beach near the Columbia River. In the 1950s, when the road to Sunningdale was paved, the rock was dynamited. No doubt the remains were splintered into unrecognizable shards, or buried further by the shattered rock and subsequent ribbon of asphalt. Another story tells of a grave being encountered during excavation for a house foundation in Castlegar. Still another describes how an early 20th-century settler in Needles, at the north end of Lower Arrow Lake, was digging out a basement for a new house on the knoll above the river when he "rolled out all kinds of skeltons [sic]," prompting the woman who had been planning to live in the house to (wisely) choose a new location. Known burials throughout the region were also subjected to grave despoilers, people who collected skulls or full skeletons as prizes, a common practice in the late 19th and early 20th centuries. In her 1964 book *Pioneer Days of Nakusp and the Arrow Lakes*, local historian Kate Johnson comments that the condition of remains exhumed by collectors at the burial ground at Arrowhead, near Galena Bay on the former Upper Arrow Lake, indicated that the grounds there had been used for a very long time. The particular gravesite Johnson describes experienced further degradation when reservoir waters rose behind Hugh Keenleyside Dam.

Can we excavate the landscape memory of this region's forgotten ancestors without disturbing any more graves? I am learning to walk with more reverence across this land than I have in the past, knowing that burials unmarked, unnoticed or even ignored may lie beneath my feet.

"The Kootenais River, as all know who have seen it, is a very rapid stream.... We had to make fourteen portages in that distance [fourteen miles, travelling east], one around what is known as the Bonnington Falls of a mile. I had one Indian with me called Peter, from Fort Colville. He was a very strong man, and packed my blankets, a sack of flour under each arm, his own traps, paddle and poles, and the canoe on top of it all."

—Edgar Dewdney, May 1865

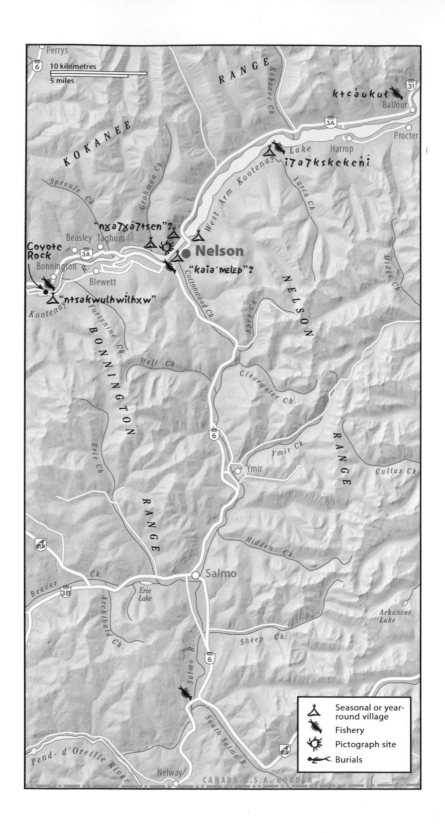

Perrys
6

10 kilometres
5 miles

KOKANEE   RANGE

Kokanee Ck.

k⁺cáukuⱡ
31
Balfour

3A
Procter

Sproule Ck.

Grohman Ck.

West Arm Kootenay

Lake Harrop

i7a7kskekeńi

Lasca Ck.

Midge Ck.

"nɣa7ɣá7ⱡsen"?

Beasley Taghum

Coyote
Rock
Bonnington
3A

Nelson

"kaia´ᴍᴇⱡɐ"?

Blewett

Cottonwood Ck.

Apex Ck.

NELSON

"nⱡsakwuⱡhwiⱡhxw"

Kootenay

Fortynine Ck.

Hall Ck.

Clearwater Ck.

BONNINGTON

Erie Ck.

RANGE

6

Ymir Ck.

Ymir

RANGE

Cultus Ck.

Hidden Ck.

Beaver Ck.

3B

Erie
Lake

Salmo

Archibald Ck.

Salmo R.

Sheep Ck.

Arkansas
Lake

6

South Salmo R.

3

Pend d'Oreille River

Nelway

CANADA U.S.A. BORDER

	Seasonal or year-round village
	Fishery
	Pictograph site
	Burials

Bonnington Falls to the West Arm & Salmo

iʔ əkɬkəkṅiʔ: "place of many kokanee." Seasonal village for root gathering, bear and caribou hunting, and trout and kokanee fishing. "Kokanee" is derived from the Sinixt word **kekeni (kəkṅiʔ)**.

Ṅx̌aʔx̌aʔčíṅ: "cave in the rocks." Seasonal village directly opposite Nelson, used for fishing trout and kokanee, and hunting caribou on the south side of the Arm.

Ky̓ʕamlúp: Nelson. Root digging in CPR flats. Pit depressions recorded in Rosemont neighbourhood.

Coyote Rock: Sinixt legend tells of Coyote (the trickster) placing the falls here to keep the ocean salmon from ascending to Kootenay Lake.

Grohman Creek: In the 1920s, archaeologist Harlan Smith identified evidence of pithouse depressions, indicating year-round settlement here. Gravel from dredging now covers the village site.

Sṅp̓ƛmip: "end of the pass" (village at Trout Lake; not pictured).

> "W.J. Astley...states that the Indians are fishing by the score at the mouth of the West Arm, every morning, and making big catches of char [burbot], occasional fish weighing 10–15 pounds."
>
> —*Nelson Minder*, May 4, 1910

MAP REGION 5: based on maps compiled by Randy Bouchard and Dorothy Kennedy in 2000 for the Columbia Power Corp. Map uses their practical orthography. Glossary uses linguistic symbols provided by the Salish School of Spokane.

7.
Bonnington Falls to the West Arm & Salmo

Shifting Geographies

TRAVELLING THE RIVER

Our modern understanding and use of the upper Columbia landscape is influenced by how we negotiate it: primarily in cars, on roads. The upper Columbia was not always laced with asphalt ribbons. To develop an understanding of these mountains and valleys as the Sinixt experienced them, we must park our cars, close our eyes and imagine the landscape topographically, to conceive spatially how the mountains sigh and heave, forming powerful barriers and creating natural passageways. To know which way a river flows across the tilt of terrain. To see how valleys are linked not only by roads but by geology's own, crafted openings. Perceiving the natural dictates of the region on a larger scale, as if I were a giant crawling on my hands and knees across it, increases my appreciation of the upper Columbia region's geographical challenges. The more I spend time in the region, the greater grows my admiration for the Indigenous People who found a way to live and flourish here. The mountains form obstacles, but they also feed countless streams, rivers and lakes, collecting on valley floors scoured deeply by glaciers and the gravels they once carried. The waterways provided the Sinixt with their own sort of highways, allowing circumnavigation around the otherwise daunting mountains. The Columbia River linked the more arid hills of the Interior Plateau at the southern reaches of Sinixt territory to the steep, thick rainforests of the Arrow Lakes, which linked to the Kootenay River, which linked to the Slocan River, which linked to Slocan Lake, creating a chain of aquatic beads, a sparkling liquid necklace linking one valley to another all the way north to the Big Bend in the Columbia River and east to Kootenay Lake.

The region's watercourses are often serpentine and rugged, with passage to some places in some seasons all but impossible. This is clearly evident in David Thompson's journals from the early 19th century. Like many of the region's colonial explorers, he was significantly challenged by the wild and impenetrable upper Columbia geography. Our ability to understand this landscape's aquatic chain as a primary method of access and transportation is undermined today by the fact that most of us travel behind the wheel of a car. And then there are the dams, which have broken the links in the chain with a perhaps irreparable permanence, making circumnavigation by water impossible. But whenever I am in a canoe or a boat on one of the lakes or rivers here, my perspective of this landscape opens into how the Sinixt would have seen it and used it in their travels. They travelled in canoes amid an expanding or contracting plane of liquid blue, with forested edifices rising on either side. They heard the rippling rumble of creeks and rivers, and followed the currents as they flowed. Their arms were sculpted with the strength required to paddle long distances. They spent winters most often on bluffs or well above the high watermark, where rising water levels could not flood them out in the spring. But they were never far away from a shoreline. Water absolutely defined their approach to terrain. It was their constant companion.

Consider a trip from present-day Castlegar to Nelson in pre-colonial times. A Sinixt canoe would have been set into the Kootenay River, beginning at its mouth, passing against the flow of water through a

Historian Jack Nisbet dates this map by David Thompson, circa 1826. After Thompson left the region in 1812, he appears to have used information gathered from other HBC explorers to add details to the base survey data. The misshapen north arm of Kootenay Lake, which he named McGillivray's Lake, and the perfect regularity of the twists and turns of the Kootenay River, demonstrate that Thompson only guessed the dimensions of these places, perhaps after looking into the distance or gathering scanty information from others. The writing on the map along the lower Kootenay River is that of a canoeist: "7 to 11 Carrying places according to the height of the water, when high quite unnavigable." Also visible on the map: a reference to "Painted rocks," an extensive panel of pictographs located near Cayuse Creek, recorded by several early explorers who came after Thompson. Courtesy of the National Archives of Great Britain, PRO 925-4622.

series of rapids. The canoe would paddle east past the mouth of the Slocan River and continue through Slocan Pools to Bonnington Falls, portaging several times over riffles in the shallow stretches of the river. At the falls, the traveller would lift the vessel from the water and carry it for about a mile, diverting around the noisy spectacle the Sinixt call N c̓akw̓ ławílxʷ, Bonnington Falls. The present-day path of the Kootenay Canal, siphoning river water for its generating station, more or less follows this ancient and important portage. At the upper end of the twin falls, the canoe and its passengers would return to the water for the short journey to Nelson, passing through two modest falls at Taghum and, finally, the last set of shallow rapids at Grohman Narrows, to reach the Nelson-area shoreline. The number of portages could decrease to three on a trip west, due to the ability of a canoe to run down over a riffle.

Today, the falls are frozen in concrete and dams block free access in many places. In prehistory, the Sinixt were able to circle the entire upper Columbia by foot or by canoe. Significant geographic barriers – cliff-bound rapids, waterfalls or especially narrow mountain passes – made some areas more difficult to reach. These impediments, most of them since overcome by our roads, rails and bridges, determined how and why certain locations were central to the daily lives of the Sinixt, and other places were not. It's important to unravel the surface effects of colonization to truly understand how they lived and thrived in the region.

The arrival of the combustion engine in the region, about the time of mining exploration, initiated a dramatic shift in upper Columbia geography. First, steamboats plied the rivers. Historical record indicates that Lakes Indians helped captains navigate the more challenging stretches of water, especially on the Arrow Lakes. Soon enough, train tracks and roads were forged. Trains, cars and trucks rather than boats became the primary method of travel. As such, we have a greater challenge to understand and respect the region's Indigenous pathways. Today, for example, Nelson is a hub and the north shore of the West Arm is heavily settled. But what we only glimpse as Lower and Upper Bonnington Dams out our car windows as we whiz along the highway was once a significant natural barrier between the West Arm and the lower portions of the Kootenay River. The falls impeded salmon as well as canoes, with the pillar of rock at the base of the falls a geological reference to Coyote, the trickster of Lakes tribal mythology who, they say, placed the falls there. Making sure that ocean salmon

Bonnington Falls prior to dams, with Coyote Rock visible on the right.
Photo courtesy of Touchstones Nelson Museum of Art and History.

"Not many specimens were secured [at Bonnington Falls], the site now being
an orchard and the best specimens having been picked up and scattered among
several collectors…. Round wickiup holes [house pits] marked the village sites,
these being so old, however, that no trace of the timbers could be seen."

—Harlan Smith, circa 1920s

were numerous on the down side, but non-existent on the up side, Coyote dictated that the West Arm above Grohman Narrows would be accessed seasonally.

The narrow valley running from Nelson south to Salmo is another example of a portion of this landscape accessed in a dramatically different way prior to roads being built. No ethnographic evidence supports heavy, year-round traditional use of the valley south of Nelson. Mountain terrain from Nelson to Whitewater links the Salmo to the Kootenay River through narrow, fast-flowing Cottonwood creek, a body of water too shallow and narrow to support a canoe, with a significant waterfall not far up from its mouth. The Salmo River, originating near Apex, widens and flows south rather than north from the more confined portion of the valley, into the relatively open place where the town of Salmo now sits. While there is record of an old Sinixt foot trail going south from Nelson toward Salmo, no surviving place names or known village sites have been recorded along this path. Considering the natural geography of the region, this makes sense. Accessing the Salmo River and its salmon was easier coming from the southwest than the northeast. Sinixt People returned seasonally to their Salmo River territory via the relatively broad and level Beaver Creek valley as recently as the early 20th century, trapping along Beaver Creek as they moved toward the salmon spawning grounds in the Salmo River.

Though Trout Lake may now seem a remote corner of the upper Columbia region, it was formerly accessed frequently by the Sinixt via the Staubert Lake valley portage/trail, south and east of Beaton. Lakes Indians told Hudson's Bay Company trader James Bissett in August 1868 that they journeyed from Upper Arrow Lake to Trout Lake easily in one day on horseback on "a good Indian trail" from which snow disappeared about the same time as at Fort Colville – many river-miles to the south. The presence of remaining large groves of cedar in that valley today testify to its milder climate. Another early explorer in the region, James Turnbull, commented on the sizable trout found in the aptly named Trout Lake, indicating plentiful fish resources. In fact, the Sinixt fished and dried the oversized "Gerrard" rainbow trout at a fishery there, as well as hunting caribou. They also appear to have regularly descended the Lardeau River and journeyed along the Kootenay Lake's north arm, taking advantage of annual freshwater cod spawning at present-day Balfour, before returning to the Arrow Lakes valley for winter.

The time when rivers and streams ran naturally, directing exclusively how people moved across and used this mountainous landscape, may be gone for the foreseeable future. Certainly the watery past of this region could not easily be recreated. The roads and rails constructed by colonial culture make certain areas more accessible than they once were and from our perspective generally make life here more pleasant. Yet, when I stop along the highway between Nelson and Castlegar to watch the water crash and spray as it releases from the narrow gate that has held it back, I think about the beautiful natural energy of water, about a stream's desire to flow freely again after having been sacrificed for one form of material prosperity. My interest in an earlier, wilder upper Columbia geography is perhaps driven by a wild corner of my own heart. Like all human hearts, mine knows what it is to be limited and held back. Sometimes my heart cannot imagine the intractability of concrete. It resists the seeming permanence of the ocean salmon's extirpation from the region, or the Sinixt People's "extinction" from their traditional territory. There can be a fury in the foaming water held back in a state of artificial stillness. Geography has shifted since European contact. The region's supernatural beauty is not always natural, nor is it necessarily uplifting.

> "Joe Paul and those of his tribe usually came to the Salmon River valley at Salmo by way of Beaver Creek, following roughly the route of the railway [circa 1900]. Sometimes they came up the Salmon [Salmo River].... By whatever route they came they were on familiar ground. This was the land of their ancestors; ancestors who knew not the restrictions of the white man's boundaries and his related laws."
>
> —Rollie Mifflin

SOPHIE GREEN BLANKET FEET AND THE POWER OF LOVE

In 1834, a baby girl was born in a Sinixt birthing hut, where the sound of a free-running Columbia River could be heard. She was the daughter of a Lakes/Sinixt Chief named Kee Kee Tum Nouse (Shadow-Top) and his Lakes wife Seeptza (Able One). This baby girl would one day grow up to be Sophie Green Blanket Feet, a woman with an astonishing story that unfolded within the turbulent times into which she was born. The Hudson's Bay Company Fort Colvile had been open for nearly a decade, with trade activities in full force. The tribal economy had begun to shift, to depend upon the efficient hunting and processing of beaver and other animal pelts valued by the trade. Tribes struggled with population decline due to the advent of waves of European diseases, after about 1780. The maternal grandfather of the new baby girl had been a great leader named Withered Top (Ski-Yaw-Tee-Kin), widely known as "the Blind Chief." Tribal stories told how his first four children had perished in the same measles epidemic that blinded him. The baby's mother, Able One, had been born in the year immediately following these losses. Her name reflected the Chief's hope that she would carry forward the culture and tradition of her tribe. She married a Sinixt leader named Shadow-Top, and the birth of this female child in 1834 was part of her effort to keep the tribe strong.

Able One was not Shadow-Top's only wife. He had five of them, a fact that demonstrated that he was both a very able hunter and a man of means. The twin forces of dramatic population loss from epidemics and the fur trade's hunger for mountains of processed furs may have increased the practice of polygyny – the taking of several wives. For the Indigenous culture, the practice had always been interwoven with the strength and solidity of tribal bonds and a healthy society. Women and their children were sometimes cared for, protected and fed by a Chief or Subchief, whose prowess as a hunter often attracted the wives in the first place.

Polygyny and its opposite twin polyandry – the taking of several husbands – had long been practised among the tribes, but only for specific reasons linked to survival and cultural care. Prior to the fur trade arriving in the region, a man might take more than one wife to strengthen the alliance between two families, especially in a very common form of polygyny, when a man married a wife's younger sister. Two of Shadow-Top's other wives were sisters: Touching Water and Blue Water. Sometimes, a man took another wife after that woman had lost her husband in warfare or to an accident. Doing so protected the children as well as the wife from trauma and poverty. Wives lived separately from each other, either in the same village or in different ones, to limit domestic conflict. Supporting more than one husband was far less common, in part because the domestic work associated with it could be overwhelming for one woman, who would have twice or three times as many hides to tan, as well as meals to prepare and moccasins to stitch.

By the time Seeptza (Able One) and Shadow-Top's new baby daughter was born, the less positive social effects of the fur trade had also become well established: disease, alcohol and endless demand for furs. Intermarriage with the colonial traders was more and more common, as tribes adapted and responded to the shifting social order, while attempting to maintain their sovereignty in the landscape. An existing tolerance for polygyny would have complemented the fur trade need for many hides to be processed for trade at the fort. The Indigenous culture had also experienced the practice of non-Indigenous traders taking "country" wives – women they married and lived with when they were in the Columbia District but left behind when they returned to "civilization." The arrival of Catholic missionaries in 1838 signalled yet another dramatic change in the social order of the upper Columbia tribes. The little girl who would grow up to become Green Blanket Feet was baptized Sophie Edwards in 1838, at the St. Paul's Catholic mission adjacent to the Fort Colvile trade centre. A new baby sister named Catherine was baptized that same year.

Different religious ideas took root, among them monogamy. Catholic priests frowned on the practice of polygyny. According to historian Larry Cebula, taking more than one wife was one of the greatest divides between the religion of the newly arrived culture and that of the Indigenous People. In the early days of the missions, Cebula says, some tribal men were willing to comply by giving away their multiple wives. Shadow-Top was one of them. One of Shadow-Top's granddaughters, Helen Toulou, described how her grandfather ultimately chose Able One as his only wife, in compliance with the Catholic faith. Yet, as the new cultural practices continued to fray tribal unity, and waves of disease continued to reduce populations, many other Plateau tribal leaders became instead increasingly resistant to monogamy. They knew that to eliminate the practice of taking more than one wife would likely speed the decline in the numbers of their descendants. They were suspicious of the impact of missionaries on their culture's health.

Sophie and Catherine faced a lifetime of uncertainty and challenge, as the Lakes tribes continued to adapt and respond to the effects of colonization. By the time Sophie had grown into a beautiful young woman, placer gold miners were moving into the region, bringing with them a particularly loose attitude toward marriage to Indigenous women. Tribal leaders testified to an Indian Affairs commissioner in 1873 that white men had been taking advantage of the cultural differences between marriage ceremonies, treating Indian women "in the light of cohabitation only." Antoine, Chief of the Skoylepi at the time, said that "white men have taken twenty of our squaws from us, and when they have borne children to them, the white men take all the property and leave the squaws and children." The abandoned women and children often had to be taken into tribal households already facing dwindling resources of food and shelter.

It is not surprising that – in an attempt to restore some social order – tribal leaders began to forbid marriages between Indigenous women and the white men. Their effort to do so was slowed by a deep-seated cultural habit of intermarriage with other tribes, including the new "white" tribe that had brought the fur trade. Those Indigenous People living near Kettle Falls had also begun to recognize that the American and British ways held undeniable power and prestige in the region, and were likely there to stay. Around 1860, despite tribal leaders having soured on marriage to settlers, Sophie married Robert Pelky, a dashing young lieutenant who had served in the US Army. The two were joined in marriage by a priest. Pelky appeared to be stable and loyal, initially. Sophie had paid a high price for her love, however: she was expelled from her tribe, by those who had decided marriage to white men must stop. It was an ominous sign.

Sophie bore two children with Pelky: Kitty, born in 1860, and Robert, likely born a few years earlier. As the children grew, Sophie's husband wished to return to his home in Missouri, to educate them. Sophie did not want to leave. There are, in the oral record, a few versions of what happened next. In one, her husband took the children as far as Spokane, at that time only a small crossroads for settlers. Here, that version says, Pelky waited two weeks for her to catch up to him. When she did not, he continued on alone with the children to Fort Benton in central Montana, where he caught a boat down the Missouri River. Another version describes how he tricked Sophie into going to Fort Benton with him, sold her into slavery to members of a tribe lingering around the fort (very likely the Blackfeet), and departed with the children on the riverboat.

Whether sold or abandoned, Sophie found herself forced to sleep in the teepee of a Blackfeet Chief by night and dig roots and process buffalo meat and hides by day. She soon met an old woman whose language was similar to her own. They began to talk in secret. The aging Salish woman had been plotting her own escape for years, though she had recently decided that she was too weak to pull it off. She had stashed away supplies: a large, green, woollen Hudson's Bay blanket, a sharp knife, sewing materials, several buckskin containers of pemmican and a traditional water carrier made of hide, complete with a sheep's horn cup. She urged Sophie to take these things with her and make her way west on foot. Knowing that the Blackfeet would chase after the young woman, the old lady shared one additional travelling tool that was to save Sophie's life: the root of a plant to make an acidic solution capable of blinding any dog who tracked her.

On the evening of a bright moon, Sophie listened for the imitation of a night bird before loosening the ties on her teepee door. Outside, she met a trusted young guide who led her away from the camp. Having prepared the acidic solution in advance, she was ready the next day when search dogs cornered her. The solution burned the dogs' eyes and sent them away. She wrapped herself in the green blanket and hid in some brush until the Blackfeet search party finally turned back. For weeks after that, Sophie travelled west through dense, mountainous country – crossing first the Rocky Mountains and next the Bitterroot Range. After she consumed all the pemmican, she used the empty buckskin bag to fashion new moccasins. By the time she reached the Kootenay River in northern Montana, she had already travelled over 300 miles, worn through the last of the buckskin, eaten all the food and was near the point of collapse. She stopped to build a raft, and when she had crossed to the other side, she wrapped her feet in strips of the green woollen blanket to protect them, carrying on into present-day northern Idaho.

Sophie progressed slowly west, surviving on berries and roots when she could find them. One day, she heard voices in the woods speaking a familiar language. She knew she was almost home. The band of Salish root diggers took her in to build her strength, so that she could complete the journey to Kettle Falls. She arrived home to Kettle Falls in the midst of the salmon harvest, a bedraggled, almost unrecognizable woman with feet wrapped in strips of green woollen blanket. Astonished by the remarkable journey of endurance, her people welcomed her back and gave her the name Quenquenchen – Green Blanket Feet.

Unfortunately, in the new era of social turmoil, there would be no happy ending for Green Blanket Feet. Soon after her return, she remarried, this time to Sheppard Bailey, a prosperous and hard-working Englishman who operated a riverboat system from Marcus, Washington, up the Columbia to the Arrow Lakes and southeast as far as Bonner's Ferry. She gave birth to a son named William Robert and all appeared to be well. But within a year, Sheppard Bailey's boat hit a snag in Kootenay Lake and he was drowned. After that, Quenquenchen moved from one relationship to another, snagged continually by her grief and the effects of a cultural shift in which white male settlers often viewed their union with Indigenous women as beneficial on practical rather than emotional or moral grounds. With Charles Brown, an entrepreneur, she had one son, Charlie Jr.; with Thomas Arcasa, a Iroquois-French man, she had one daughter, Mary; lastly, with a man named George Keating, she had two children: George Jr. and Joseph. There were reports that in her despair over the loss of her first two children and second husband Sheppard Bailey, she sometimes abused alcohol. This may have resulted in the Arcasa family taking her daughter from her, though some details of Quenquenchen's difficult life remain a mystery.

Just before Christmas 1877, when Quenquenchen was 43 and her youngest child was still in arms, and while she and her husband were visiting Marcus from Fort Shepherd for the holiday, she travelled on foot three miles through the snow to connect with the Arcasa family and her estranged daughter Mary. After three days, Sophie finally tore herself away from her beloved daughter to return to her husband on Christmas Eve. When she arrived George raged over her having stayed away too long, beat her to death and left.

Sophie Green Blanket Feet's daughter Mary Lloyd remembered the funeral as being "well like a dream: her head was bandaged so that she looked like a nun. In life as in death…beautiful." This tragic end spoke of a woman caught between worlds, grieving her children, struggling to survive, trying to reconcile the long-tested values of her tribal people with a newly arrived society. In Mary Lloyd's recollections of her mother, she described Green Blanket Feet's life as "a great love story told by a camp fire to the old and young ones, how Quenquenchen suffered for the sake of her first two children, whom she never saw again till she died."

This account of the life of Green Blanket Feet (Quenquenchen) is based upon the written and audio recollections of other Sinixt women: Mary Arcasa Lloyd (her daughter), Alyce Perkins Hallenius (her grand-niece), James Howath (her great-grandson), and Cull White, a close friend of her son, Charles Brown Jr. I am especially grateful to Quenquenchen's great-great granddaughter Patti Bailey for helping me stitch these accounts together into a whole. Patti is the latest in multiple generations of Sinixt women to carry with pride and meaning the name Quenquenchen. A fictionalized version of Sophie's story can also be found in Cogewea, *a novel by a Sinixt/Okanagan late 19th century descendant, Mourning Dove, who is also related to Sophie Green Blanket Feet.*

HALF-TRUTHS, MIS-TRUTHS AND THE FOUNDING OF NELSON

The discovery of silver and copper on Toad Mountain in 1886 is a human drama jammed with luck, secrecy and overnight fortune. The subsequent development of the Silver King Mine between 1887 and 1900 established the city of Nelson, putting it on the map across two continents as money and excitement flowed into the region. One minute Nelson was a natural shoreline of high cottonwood trees, cedar forest and seasonal wetland, and the next – it was boasting fortune seekers, hotels, opera houses, fine homes and a sternwheeler landing, all signs of a new culture springing up quickly and decisively, as if by magic. Hidden within this almost mythic tale of overnight riches is another, more complex narrative, a rabbit trick that has long been silenced by the busy and triumphant process of colonization. It's time to set the record straight.

Prior to industrial development of dams, the shoreline on which Nelson sits had a rich ecosystem fed by annual spring floods. This high water resulted from a rock cliff pressing itself into the riverbed of the Kootenay River just downstream, slowing water passage. The geological formation became known aptly as Grohman Narrows, for W.E. Baillie-Grohman, a settler who arrived in the 1880s to trophy hunt, and envisioned ways to alter the water's natural patterns that would support agriculture. Prior to the 1930s, the narrows forced spring snowmelt to rise high up the shores of the West Arm each year, forming a lake-like environment for months. Often, the water did not recede until early summer anywhere along Kootenay Lake, including from the rich soils at the south end of the lake, at present-day Creston.

The province of BC granted Baillie-Grohman permission to blast the rock and open up flow, but the results were minimal. More aggressive blasting and dredging of the riverbed and cliffs by West Kootenay Power and Light just before the Second World War freed up the flow of water, reducing flood levels. It also provided Corra Linn Dam downstream with more storage and a more consistent flow of water. The 1973 completion of Libby Dam upstream, on the Kootenay River in the United States, further controlled the spring snowmelt process. Today's citizens of Nelson experience greatly transformed water dynamics. These can obscure the memory of the natural shoreline and how the land was experienced by Indigenous People.

Stone tools found by local residents on Grohman beaches.
Photos courtesy of local residents.

"My father, William Ramsden, used to say that he had heard about Natives camping on the north side of Grohman Creek Narrows, on the east side of Grohman Creek mouth, though he had not seen them there himself."

—Alan Ramsden, born in Nelson in 1926

Dredging materials piled around the Grohman Creek riparian, burying pit
house depressions recorded by Harlan Smith in the early 1930s.
Photo courtesy of Touchstones Nelson Museum of Art and History.

For the Sinixt, the shoreline provided an abundant kokanee fishery;
plant foods growing in the marshes and flood zones once water had
receded; and autumn access to caribou hunting grounds on southward
paths that wound through the old growth and wetlands past Cottonwood Lake. A *Nelson Daily News* article titled "Hunting Stone Relics"
(published February 2, 1916) refers to an "exceedingly beautiful" arrow point of banded agate and other stone tools, all found on the CPR
flats. Archaeological reports from Harlan Smith (1920s) and Diana
French (1970s) record signs of a year-round Sinixt village nearby, below
Grohman Narrows at the mouth of Grohman creek, and more pit house
depressions found in Rosemont. Both signal Sinixt inhabitation in the
Nelson area across millennia, and across various stages of the river's
natural patterns.

The Sinixt knew well the mountain system that towered around
Kootenay Lake and the lower Kootenay River. Their sovereign travels
in the pre-contact era echoed the north-south direction of the natural
path of much of the water. Overland east-west mountain crossings by
the Sinixt and their neighbours – the Okanagan and Ktunaxa – were not
as frequent as a contemporary understanding of the landscape might
suggest. The future site of Nelson had always been more challenging

terrain to access from these directions. To better understand Sinixt presence in Nelson and area's landscape, the 1846 international boundary must be returned to what it is: an imaginary line that distorts contemporary understanding of the past. Even after fur trade activities waned through the 1850s, the Sinixt still travelled freely up and down the Columbia as they had for millennia. Complications around border access began in the 1860s, when gold seekers poured in to the still largely borderless region from across the continent, bringing with them a feverish desire to pan the rivers for fortune. A new economy built up around the frantic search for gold, with ferries and supply depots serving miners who travelled up the Columbia to the Pend d'Oreille River, where a good deal of gold was panned, and farther north, beyond Revelstoke, to the digs at the Goldstream River and the Big Bend. As they had with fur traders, the Sinixt, the Skoyelpi and other tribes in the inland northwest adapted, forming new alliances with these miners and suppliers, even as tax collectors from both countries worked to enforce the passage of gold.

One of the most significant alliances of the mining period was the romance between Justine Su-steel, born only decade after Green Blanket Feet, with a gold seeker and trader named Richard Fry. Justine was the daughter of Henricus, or, Ntsostiken. His base appears to have been **Ṅ k ʷlíla?**, a large village near the mouth of the Pend d'Oreille River. Not long after they were married, an 1861 dispute between miners and the Indigenous Sinixt and Skoyelpi resulted in Richard's life being threatened. The initial fracas involved a hunk of bacon, a dog and the tragic murder of Richard's brother, Alfred, who had recently come west to join him in the gold fields. The story of Justine, Richard and their children, like that of Green Blanket Feet, demonstrates the destabilizing colonial forces that continued to erode a sense of sovereignty and safety. The Sinixt found themselves more often on the defensive.

After Richard was taken captive, Justine's father stepped in to try to broker peace with some of the younger, more hot-headed members of his own tribe, who wanted to kill Justine's new husband. Her father's negotiations bought Justine enough time to quietly free the prisoner in the dark of night. With their young child on her back, she led Richard to safety over the mountains to the north. The next morning, the edgy tribal youths bent on retribution searched for Fry in vain by canoe on the Columbia. He had evaded capture by avoiding the most obvious route. There were others. Within a few years, the couple settled more permanently where they found opportunity, at the easternmost fringe of Sinixt territory where it overlapped with Yaqan Nukiy-Ktunaxa settlements, in present-day Bonner's Ferry, Idaho. Here, Richard opened a supply depot for miners and settlers and operated a ferry across the Kootenay River. Fry's ranch became a well-known way station. By the mid-1880s, his and Justine's children had come of age and were poised to integrate further with the newest wave of settlers to the upper Columbia region. In 1885, Justine and Richard's daughter Christina married Arthur Bunting, a farmer from New Brunswick, Canada. In summer the following year, a party of prospectors that included Sinixt men set out overland from the Colville valley, travelling north up the Pend d'Oreille River, then north and east up the Salmo and directly north again, deep into the Selkirk mountains, following streams into the peaks looming just behind and above the future site of Nelson.

The year 1886 had brought hard times to settlers around Kettle Falls. The expedition's leader, Winslow Hall, was a settler who had migrated west to the gold fields in the early 1860s. In the Colville valley, he married one of Green Blanket Feet's daughters, Catherine, with whom he had two daughters, and settled on a homestead along the Colville River. After she died, he married her sister, Adell Frazier, who gave birth to several sons through the 1870s. Hall had always wondered about unexplored streams in the mountains between the Columbia River and Kootenay Lake. His curiosity was now sharpened by economic reality. With the trans-Canada railway completed, farm produce was no longer being sold to construction crews in Canada. The gold rush of the 1860s had completely played out. Hall decided to take his five half-Sinixt young adult sons in search of more gold dust. Travelling with them were several other settlers and two Sinixt men who lived on the Colville Confederated tribal reservation – Narcisse Downey and Dauney Williams – who agreed to hunt for meat during the months-long exploration. William Brown, the father of Charlie, one of Green Blanket Feet's sons, provided the grubstake from his store near Marcus, Washington. Charlie operated the ferry that transported them upstream and across the boundary as far as the mouth of the Pend d'Oreille River, where Downey and Williams likely met the prospectors with horses to form the pack train. What happened next is a dramatic tale recollected by Charlie Brown himself in the 1950s.

Looking northeast from Toad Mountain, a contemporary view.
Photo courtesy of Mike Graeme.

After a long search prospecting through rugged country up the Pend d'Oreille, then the Salmo River and north into the Ymir valley, the prospectors found themselves close to the Kootenay River. Their supplies had run short and winter was not far off. Sent to round up horses, the two Sinixt hunters and some of the young Sinixt Hall brothers drifted up the flanks of a high mountain. There, one of them picked up a rock to throw it at a squirrel. Under the place where the rock had been, glistened a visible vein of precious metal. The story of their accidental discovery of the seam of copper and silver that became the Silver King Mine is well known today and has become the stuff of legend. What has been lost in the legend was the key role played by Sinixt men.

According to the September 25, 1897, Nelson *Tribune,* in early spring, 1887, the returning Hall party encountered deep snow as they tried to access the future mine site from the Salmo River valley to the south. They retreated and went east, overland, to Bonner's Ferry, in order to access the mineral strike by boat on Kootenay Lake. It was at that point that Arthur Bunting and his Sinixt wife Christina Fry appear to have left the Fry way station and joined the group. While the Buntings constructed the first cabin on a bluff above the shoreline, the prospectors began to map out the mine shafts on their claims high up the mountain. Word started to leak out across the transboundary region that an important discovery had been made, quickly putting the stretch of shoreline on the map. That year, Arthur Bunting filed in Victoria for a pre-emption of the land, so that he could sell lots. Almost overnight, a fabled land of fortune became an actual hot commodity. After hard rock mining began on Toad Mountain (assisted by a mule pack train and ferry system designed by Richard Fry), a BC gold commissioner named Gilbert Sproat arrived in the area. The standard written history of Nelson describes how Sproat founded Nelson. Bunting and his Indigenous wife disappeared almost overnight from the narrative, as a street grid was mapped out and lots went up for sale. But not everyone agreed early on with the account making Sproat Nelson's forefather.

"In claiming to be the 'founder' of Nelson, Gilbert Malcolm Sproat is in error," wrote the Nelson *Tribune* on March 31, 1894. "The town was founded by Arthur Bunting [and] established by the discovery of minerals on Toad Mountain." Again, on May 29, 1925, the *Nelson Daily News* reported that a written account of the founding of Nelson (a folio discovered gathering dust in an old house at the rear of the Royal Bank that had been occupied by the Svoboda family) told the real story. The author, Tom Collins, was correcting errors he said had been made in a version printed by Charles St. Barbe in the *Tribune*. Collins details

how, in 1887, the BC government had accepted Arthur Bunting's deposit, but that Sproat arrived and began declaring that the land was already in reserve. Bunting was no match for the brassy gold commissioner. His quiet claim on Nelson withered, and he returned to Bonner's Ferry, with his Sinixt wife.

Julia Fry Kane Peel.
Photographer unknown.

Cities were springing up all over the place, to meet the needs of set-tlers. That same year, George Kane, a millwright for Waterous Engine Works in Ontario, came west to install sawmill machinery at Canal Flats. On a visit to Kootenay Lake, he fell in love with its striking scen-ery, and also, eventually, with another one of Justine and Richard's daughters, Julia Ella Fry. According to family genealogy records posted online, Kane received a request from Sawyard Mill Company in Victoria to scout a location for a sawmill. He chose what became known as Pilot Bay. In 1891, he applied for pre-emption of 80,000 acres at and around the future townsite of Kaslo. By then, Julia's earlier marriage in 1889 to another settler named William Strong had ended after the birth of a son. The Kanes married early in 1892. Their daughter Christina was born in December. When baby Christina died, the marriage faltered, ending in divorce in 1901. Julia appears to have returned to her family at Bonner's Ferry. Kane married twice more, in 1905 and again in 1909, finding his way eventually to Prince Rupert, on the northwest coast of BC.

The era between the tapering off of the fur trade and the creation of cit-ies and towns as we know them today was a complex one during which Indigenous sovereignty was put to a severe test. A closer look at the his-tory of Nelson and a more careful understanding of tribal identity as it links to geography can clarify who was where, and why and when. Indigenous People had long survived through adaptability and resil-ience and were clearly positioned to integrate as community founders of the new city of Nelson, but the forces of fortune seekers and settlement could be fierce. Justine Fry's long and fruitful life in a unified family led by a settler and a Sinixt woman is an exception rather than a rule. Intermarriage of Indigenous People with the newly arrived culture was often not harmonious, setting in motion no small measure of cultural chaos and threatened identity. In particular, the record indicates how Indigenous women grappled with adapting to colonial expectations, as they sometimes entered into unions with men who were restless or on the move. Isolated from their web of Indigenous relations, these women likely endured what must have been an unstoppable current of racism, loneliness and failed expectation.

Was it mere coincidence that the names and stories of the Sinixt men who discovered the mineral deposits on Toad Mountain faded from the established record of the region's history? Why did it take so long to learn the important connections Justine Fry and Green Blanket Feet have to Nelson's founding? I have spent years untangling the knots in my own understanding, searching for valuable seams of continuing Indigenous presence in the region's history, a presence often silently embedded in the colonial story. Perhaps saddest is the fact that feverish settlement by whites had increasingly undermined a tribal system of intermarriage that had long been a tool of peaceful alignment between various Salish tribes. Intermarriages were not meant to dissolve Indigenous identity. Instead, they were an effort to strengthen the bonds between distinct peoples and promote a social harmony that was the underpinning of Salishan cultures throughout the Interior Plateau.

The final magic trick in the story of Toad Mountain may be the power of Indigenous survival. Through careful research in documents such as tribal rolls, genealogy records available online, early newspapers and even the cultural memoir of Green Blanket Feet's mother, *In the Stream,* it has been possible to piece together, map and trace the blurred lines between Indigenous Sinixt and settler identity, to erase the international boundary, and to restore the presence of Sinixt People in Nelson – right back to the first moments of colonial settlement. For a very long time before the discovery of minerals on Toad Mountain, the Sinixt lived their own settled life in this place, a place that, for them, had always provided many natural gifts to support survival. It was, without question, their home.

MAP REGION 6: Adapted from a map provided
by the Colville Confederated Tribes.

Confederated Tribes of The Colville Reservation
Traditional Territories

Confederated Tribes of The Colville Reservation Traditional Territories

ALBERTA

BRITISH COLUMBIA

Calgary

Columbia River

Kootenay River

Lakes

Nelson

Vancouver

Okanogan
Methow
Chelan
Entiat
Wenatchi

Okanogan River

Kettle River

North Half

Colville Reservation

Colville

Nespelem

Spokane Reservation

Sanpoil

Joint Use Areas

CANADA
USA

MONTANA

Spokane

Moses-Columbia

WASHINGTON

Palus

Chief Joseph Band of Nez-Perce and Palus

Chief Joseph Band of Nez-Perce

Snake River

Columbia River

Portland

IDAHO

OREGON

100 miles

200 kilometres

This is for informational purposes only. It does not represent an on-the-ground survey and represents only the approximate relative locations.

8.
Spokane, WA, to Sinixt Territory
Lines and Shaded Areas

WATER THAT MAKES A LOT OF NOISE

The more I have considered the natural and human history of the upper Columbia landscape, the less significant the lines drawn by colonial leaders have seemed. It takes time, and a willingness to defy these contemporary boundaries and the history that clings to them, to truly understand how Indigenous cultures long inhabited their upper Columbia River territories. The landscape will heal itself in direct proportion to the walls coming down. Walls that limit conversations between Canadians and Americans. Walls that limit knowledge and understanding of the whole river system. Walls that keep us all from knowing and loving each other and living in a renewed river system. The longer we stay in our minds, focused on defending various positions, the longer it will take. The sooner we get out there, to find and honour the truth of the land as it is shaped, the sooner we will find a broader and more inclusive way to work with natural systems.

One spring day in 2017, I diverged from my usual and well-worn path from the Spokane airport to Nelson, BC. Rather than travel directly north across the Pend d'Oreille flood plain and cross the border at Nelway, I headed west to connect with the Columbia River flowing south on its way to Grand Coulee Dam. My car rolled smoothly along a well-pressed asphalt ribbon laid flat through arid, fertile farmland. Fragments of the Selkirk Mountains rose faintly blue and expectant in the northern distance. When the farming community of Davenport, Washington, came into view, I turned north toward these mountains onto Highway 25, another black ribbon that undulates along farmland on the east side of the Columbia. Within an hour, I had wound my way into unculti-vated, swelling grassland and ponderosa pines to reach the remnants of the 19th-century military outpost Fort Spokane. Situated on the south side of the Spokane River's confluence with the Columbia, and not to be confused with Spokane House (a Hudson's Bay Company trade fort established in 1810 at the confluence of the Little Spokane and Spokane rivers), *Fort* Spokane was built by the US government in 1880. Then, as colonial settlement shifted from fur trade to agriculture, the fort housed four companies of armed soldiers. Their primary work was to restrain the Indigenous tribes around them, forcing them onto two new reservations established by the US government: the Spokane Reservation on the east shore of the Columbia and the Colville Reservation on the west shore.

I crossed over the imaginary line that marks the southern boundary of the Spokane Reservation. In spring, the confluence of the Columbia and Spokane rivers is fringed not by natural trees and cliffs but by un-natural dry, striated bands of reservoir silt. It was early April, and the annual drawdown of Lake Roosevelt was in effect. The highway had begun to steepen northeast through rising hills. Only an hour ago, they were faintly blue and distant. Now, they were straw-coloured, swelling and littered with pines. I was not yet in the geographically demarcated Selkirk Range, but the mountains had gently risen like a prayer. I pulled over to rest and stood under a tight grove of evergreens, listening to the wind pull at the feathery branches.

Maps of the traditional territory of the Spokane tribe mark out a broad landscape that encompasses the Spokane River watershed. Their homeland spreads north, south and east of their current reservation, continuing upstream along the Spokane and Little Spokane Rivers, past the falls that still animate Spokane (the capitol city of today's US Inland Empire), though they are artificially controlled. In 1881, an executive order from President Rutherford B. Hayes shrank the natural domain of the Spokane tribe from its approximately three million acres to the present-day 159,000, leaving them with merely 5 per cent of what had once been their sovereign lands. Parts of the Spokane Reservation are marked on some contemporary tribal maps as historically "shared use" area. The establishment of a military fort to enforce the movement of the tribal people was a heavy-handed decision that did not reflect the reality of their peaceful behaviour.

Even as they were oppressed and confined onto several reservations in northern Washington, Idaho and western Montana, these tribes did not engage much in armed resistance. Instead, they attempted to negotiate diplomatically with the US government, as they had with the officers of the fur trade, agreeing to release some portions of their traditional lands in order to maintain others that they valued most. This peaceful strategy based on principles of tribal sovereignty assumed that negotiators on both sides would keep their word, and underestimated the settlers' fierce sense of entitlement to land that was not, in the end, theirs. Under pressure from these settlement forces, the United States made many false promises and revoked some agreements by executive order. The whole process led to tribes being at once scattered and confined. To this day, the tribes throughout the inland northwest understand what has been left to them as the remnants of betrayal and deceit.

While the United States honours the Jay Treaty (an agreement that allows Indigenous People living on either side of the border to travel freely in parts of their transboundary territory), Canada does not. The Sinixt require up-to-date passports to cross the line, and once they do, they are only visitors. Their inability to freely access their homeland restricts them, though they persist in feeling the northward pull. This is evident in Judge Wynecoop's favoured huckleberry terrain, located in mountains that have a view of the boundary; and in Shawn Brigman nourishing hopes to access moister forests for canoe bark. I saw it alive in Shelly Boyd when she stayed with me for several weeks one autumn to harvest medicinal roots found more commonly in the moist or high mountains of her people's traditional lands above the boundary. When I pulled the car over at the edge of a logging road, close to a vague area a non-Indigenous herbalist had told us we might find it, she tumbled from the vehicle and disappeared immediately down a steep bank, calling out over her shoulder *I'll be back soon.* She knew she was home, and sure enough, much to my astonishment, she found the plant quickly and led us there to dig. For those few weeks she stayed with me, she was in avid and constant search for places to dig a root that I had never heard of before then, one that springs up streamside all over above 5,000 feet and, for most upper Columbia inhabitants, goes unnoticed. *The more places I have to dig, the more options I have. That way, the plant can recover.*

Over the past 70 years since the extinction declaration, tribal members have adapted their patterns of movement to remain below the boundary. They have found other places to pick huckleberry, dig bear root, harvest natural materials. But they have never forgotten who they are, or where they are from. Mike Finley, a Sinixt descendant and historian, explains how deeply rooted tribal identity is. *When I was a small boy, my grandma told me that I was Sinixt, before she died. She was part of the web of strong Sinixt families, the leaders who knew they were Arrow Lakes people deep in their bones. She taught me not to forget who I was. Our history is one of being displaced, relocated, pushed off of our land. We have struggled, but we have never given up. There's a pride in knowing who we are. A strength.*

The Colville Confederated Tribes (CCT) Reservation begins on the opposite side of the Columbia from Highway 25, with its southern boundary defined by a westerly dip and swoop of the great river as it heads toward Grand Coulee Dam. Despite what seems like a sprawling acreage, the original CCT reservation could not be large enough to serve as a forced homeland for the 12 different tribes in the region, including the Sinixt. All were told to move within its borders. As Sinixt scholar and historian Laurie Arnold will explain in the next section, the original Colville reservation boundaries were redrawn by the government more than once. Today, on its greatly reduced size, all the tribes who call it home are broadly referred to as "Colville," though, in fact, the word does not accurately reflect the diversity that exists within the CCT reservation boundaries. Yes, the reservation seems large. But when the traditional territories of the people are considered as context, it shrinks to a small side plate. This process has had a particularly outsized impact on the Sinixt.

The question of what to do about reconciling this troubling chapter of settler history – the forced removal of people from their lands and subsequent confinement – has long been unanswered. Reconciling that history grows even more complicated when a transboundary tribe rears its head, taking the BC government to court and reminding all Canadians of their existence. The Sinixt legal case has not made things easier, but it does offer a large opportunity to consider honestly and with a measure of justice the problem of colonial displacement. I have found that in the settler world, the question of what to do about the displacement of tribes is not even on the table among most Americans and Canadians. *It's too large to consider,* some say. *History is full of stories of conquest,* others say. *It's too complicated with that boundary.* Yet another evasion of the issue. *It's in the past.* Ah, but is it in the past, really? Spanning the transboundary region as I do, and have done, my head filled with stories from another time, I know that the present-day turmoil of climatic and ecological devastation reflects in its own way the story of Indigenous displacement and oppression. This issue is absolutely not in the past but, rather, lies at the heart of the work ahead. Displacement from land and its offerings is very much alive, and has merely changed clothes. The reconciliation of all people with place – settler and Indigenous – lies at the heart of our challenge to steer the planet and ourselves in a healthier direction.

I yearn to resolve the issue of Sinixt tribal exclusion from Canada with the same force that I yearn to live in a world that respects and knows the power of natural systems, a world that cares for and listens to this Earth, even as the anthropocene culture evolves and thrives. I am not a romantic. I don't want to live in the past and have no nostalgic belief that things were easier for land-based cultures. But I know that both economic security and thriving natural systems can co-exist, and I also have a gnawing hunger for harmony and truth. The entire system can exist in better balance, and when it does, we always know: beauty shows the way. The beauty of a wild-running river filled with salmon, whose bellies swell with the ache for home. Fields of camas and balsamroot sunflower filling open spaces that are shared by all. Gardens and fields left to fallow; cattle and deer grazing near each other; cities and forests intermingling. All this long century and longer, the effort to restrain and control the swelling beauty of natural systems has ended up merely limiting the physical world's unlimited blessings of beauty and godliness. It is always within our grasp.

Highway 25 continues north through the communities of Fruitland and Cedonia. Gifford and Rice. These last two are only vestiges of larger agricultural settlements flooded out by Grand Coulee Dam. Other settler communities that no longer appear on the map include Peach, Gerome and Harvy. Directly west across the Columbia River from Gifford sits Inchelium, the largest community of Sinixt refugees. In a late phase of their diaspora, they were welcomed by their sister tribe the Skoyelpi and settled in along the river. But that wasn't the end of it. A few decades later, they were once again forced to move uphill when the Lake Roosevelt Reservoir filled. Lawney Reyes's book *White Grizzly Bear's Legacy* explains that the tribal people received no formal notification from the government, until the water began to rise. The injustice of this afterthought, even the sheer lack of manners in the government's conduct, always eats away at me when I think about Inchelium, the compromised homeland of many Lakes people. Though it is not their homeland, they have made their adjustments, Mike Finley explains. *There is so much pride in this community. We know we are Lakes. It's so deeply rooted in our being, our tribe.* The highway on the east shore bent close to the Columbia again as I arrived in the settler community of Kettle Falls. Turning west on Highway 395, I crossed the Lake Roosevelt reservoir on the steel bridge that spans the river's confinement. Flat and expansive, the water shows no sign of the once audacious and beautiful waterfalls. The only memory is in the name of a contemporary way station on the west shore, owned and operated by the Colville Tribe. "Noisy Waters" gas and convenience store. **Sx̌ʷnitkʷ**. Water that makes a lot of noise.

Sinixt place names are scattered like pebbles across the upper Columbia river watershed from Kettle Falls, where their traditional territory begins, north along the Columbia and Kettle rivers and up into Canada. **Sx̌ʷnitkʷ**, their word for the audacious waterfalls that provided for rich salmon harvesting, is one of the few descriptive Salish language words for the Columbia River itself that have survived to the present day. It translates variously into English as "noisy water," "sounding water," "water that makes a big noise," "thundering water," and "Kettle Falls." But, really, there is no precise translation for the joyful cultural,

This 1915 view of Kettle Falls from Bisbee Mountain (4,964 ft.) shows
how the Columbia wrapped around the island where the Sinixt lived during
the salmon runs. Photo courtesy of Lake Roosevelt
National Recreation Area (LAR0 2550).

emotional and ecological significance of this part of the river, embedded
in the minds, hearts and DNA of the Sinixt.

Kettle Falls was the centre of the Lakes tribal world, Finley explains.
*Everything revolved around it. Everyone geared up for it. Trade, food,
diet, social relationships. Everyone at the falls – every member of our
tribe – had a role, and no role was more important than any other. Everybody had their purpose. When the Salmon Chief distributed fish evenly
among all, he was reflecting our belief that every single person there was
equally important, whether they were fishing, cutting and drying fish,
keeping a fire going, or hauling fresh water for cooking.*

No longer noisy, the falls have disappeared beneath the surface. The
contemporary Indigenous mind, tuned to memory more sharply than
my own, perceives them still as very much alive. This perception keeps
the loss fresh but also honours the natural river as it still wants to be.
At conferences I have attended, CCT tribal members proudly point
to recent sonar imaging, demonstrating scientifically how the agitated river currents flow, deep beneath the reservoir's artificial calm. We
can't hear **Sx̌ʷnitkʷ**, they say, *but it is still here.* The river continues to

Travelling shelter.

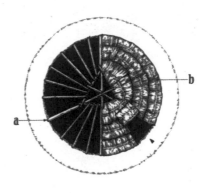

silently trace and honour the shape of the rocks that once supported a profuse salmon fishery. Things are still noisy, but the people are instead the ones being heard – verbal noise, drumbeat noise – about what was lost and what is still possible. They seem to know that the river's heart continues to beat for the salmon to return. They have a certainty about their responsibility to help the fish.

D.R. Michel's summary of what happened in the 1930s during dam construction is at once gentle and piercing in its honesty. *The salmon were taken away from us. We were never asked.* The long desire to bring the salmon back, he says, has spurred the tribes across a decades-long struggle to build capacity in legal and policy circles: fighting against the US government's mid-20th-century push to terminate Indian rights and reservations; hiring lawyers to press the government to honour agreements that had assured them cultural fishing rights; forming alliances with other tribes along the river system to lobby for co-management of fisheries below Grand Coulee and Chief Joseph. *We now have the legal and policy tools to make demands within the US system as sovereign nations. We've been here for thousands of years living beside the river and we're not leaving.* The proof of the rising power of the spirit of Salmon is in the recent, meteoric ascent of reintroduction efforts in the public consciousness.

For Finley, the salmon are genetically woven within the strands of his own tribe's DNA. The hatchery fish play a role, but the wild fish are most important. They are a bloodline to our people. We want

Indigenous fishermen
at the falls, circa 1930.
Photo courtesy of
the Upper Columbia
United Tribes.

that genetic connection from our ancestors, from the salmon that our ancestors harvested and ate. We make sure that the hatchery fish don't overwhelm the wild ones. Salmon, he says, demonstrate clearly what scientific experts have said for years was impossible. They carry the spirit of our people. We have a surviving sense of identity that we still carry – that has made it through so much colonial trauma. An example is the fishing that goes on at the base of Chief Joe. We are the ones who adapted and developed that three-way hook, to be able to keep harvesting in the dam's tailrace. We melt our own lead for the sinkers. Each Lakes family has its own hook. We are tied to that fish. We drive over three mountain ranges on the highway that takes us from Inchelium to Chief Joe. We do it to be able to keep fishing.

The Columbia River at Kettle Falls prior to being inundated by Grand Coulee Dam (looking north into Sinixt homeland). Photo courtesy of the Colville Confederated Tribes.

"And now, because I had built the falls in three levels, my people could fish at low, medium and high water…. I appointed the old man as Salmon Chief, and he and his descendants were to rule over the falls and see that all people shared in the fish caught there. All people must live there in peace, and no one should leave there unprovided."

—Aneas Seymour, assuming the voice of Coyote in the story
of the Kettle Falls fishery, told to Mrs. Goldie van Putman

In Finley's voice, I hear a raw energy and conviction that sweeps aside the chatter of my mind and wakes up my heart. He gives clear words to a great irony that I have observed frequently. In the colonial world, it always seems to take science to confirm what Indigenous People have always known from their lived experiences and Elder knowledge, passed on generation to generation. The memory written across their hearts and laced through their physical beings is not trusted by those immersed in contemporary science – until the rational mind catches up to the mystery.

Kelly Hill from the Sharpening Stone. Photo courtesy of Tina Wynecoop.

According to Finley, the ceremony to call up the salmon still occurs at Kettle Falls because the tribes know with deep conviction that the salmon were put in place by Coyote to serve the people. The ongoing ceremony, whether public or not, fulfills that responsibility as the tribes wait for the fish to come home again. The gift is not a one-way offering. The responsibility of the people – in exchange for abundance – is to take care of the fish.

Several miles upstream of the falls, Highway 395 forks left, to follow the Kettle River against its natural, southward flow. Before long, the highway has extended beyond the reach of the Lake Roosevelt Reservoir and the river returns to its natural self. Following 395 always allows me to connect with the least developed river landscape, a waterway that the Sinixt and Skoyelpi have called Ň x̌ʷiyałpítkʷ. No precise translation of the meaning of Ň x̌ʷiyałpítkʷ appears to have survived colonization. The Kettle begins in the Monashee Mountains north of Rock Creek, BC, tumbling down to the arid midlands around Grand Forks, dipping below the international boundary and back north of it again, before joining up with the Columbia. Salmon that did not fall into the traps at Kettle Falls, or did not continue up the Columbia to the Slocan, the Arrow Lakes and the Columbia's headwaters, found passage up this river to spawn, until they were stopped at Cascade falls, a natural barrier just above today's international boundary near Christina Lake. In my night dreams, I have been visited by a man standing in a dugout canoe, poling his way through shallow water, singing the word for the river over and over again, as if he was trying to get me to understand the meaning of something beyond language. I have woken with *neh-hoy-ull-pit-kew neh-hoy-ull-pit-kew* reverberating between my ears. On those mornings, I stepped into yet another day with my heart wearied by a mixture of mystery and grief. I longed for an interrelated time and way of living in the bosom of the world that has been largely lost, though the haunting sound of the Indigenous voice I heard remains. *neh-hoy-ull-pit-kew.*

While he served as the CCT's Arrow Lakes facilitator from 2013 to 2016, Virgil Seymour preferred travelling north on Highway 395 to access his people's "Canadian" territory. He told me he thought it was the fastest route, which made some of his tribal friends chuckle ironically. Shelly Boyd has told me that she travelled that way across the border when she first took over as facilitator after his death in 2016, because he had said it was quickest. She soon discovered, however, that he was wrong. The highway following the Columbia from Kettle Falls north through Marcus and Northport to the crossing at Patterson near Rossland, BC, is actually faster. Shelly's laugh was light and full of admiration. Virgil's love for the landscape of his ancestors shone true.

Virgil also told me that following highway 395 kept him close to his grandfather, Pete Seymour, as well as to other Sinixt ancestors who had been born and raised on the hilly triangle of land between the Columbia and Kettle Rivers. This may be the biggest reason why he travelled on 395. The hilly triangle that dominated the former north half of the CCT reservation, a place Lakes people refer to broadly as Kelly Hill, is still important to Lakes people. Here, in the southernmost reaches of their traditional territory, they congregated after they were pushed south out of British Columbia, but before they were forced to move farther south to Inchelium. Other north half families include the Stones, Toulous, Perkins and Arnolds. The Pia Mission's first Catholic masses were held in a log cabin belonging to a Sinixt woman named Josette, and the graveyard there is speckled with many Sinixt burials, including that of Chief James Bernard. Some Lakes families still own allotments, and contemporary tribal members often use "Kelly Hill" as a broader synonym for the entire North Half, one in a sequence of displacements that removed the Sinixt farther and farther from their homelands in British Columbia. There is an actual peak called Kelly Hill, a mountain that tops out at 3,303 feet, named for John Kelly, a settler who originally squatted on the Sinixt lands before they were opened to public domain. He was, according to Lakin, "good to the Indians and treated them with respect."

The Kettle River ruffles gracefully over cobbles and turns freely in its channel close to the boundary. It's easy to understand how the beauty of the pines and the softly rising mountains along this route north to Canada quickly wore a groove in Virgil's heart. I slowed to a stop at the Laurier border crossing, removed my sunglasses and prepared to show my passport. Still only sparsely settled, the lands of the North Half suggest the beauty and harmony the Sinixt and Skoyelpi and other tribes once lived with every day. The separation of the Sinixt from their homelands, a story holding timeless, even biblical resonance, is but one chapter in a deeply unethical narrative of land acquisition that underpins the entire settlement of the west. Most of the land was stolen, history now makes clear. According to historian Patricia Nelson Limerick in her masterful book *The Legacy of Conquest*, the colonial settlement of the west was driven by government policy decisions in far-away Washington, DC. The disconnection between the people in power and the distant lands marked on a map placed pioneers in an awkward position, one that standard historical narratives gloss over. While the pioneers believed that the land was free for the taking, it actually was not when boots hit the ground. My own ancestors participated in this process of taking, based on a paradox of heroic individual intention and government oppression. "Even when they were trespassers, westering Americans were hardly, in their own eyes, criminals; rather they were pioneers.... Innocence of intention placed the course of events in a bright and positive light; only over time would the shadows compete for our attention." (*Legacy of Conquest*, 36)

Ongoing Indigenous confinement reflects a wider conundrum about how to make things right. The irony always pierces me that an American

Pete and Lena
Seymour.
Photo courtesy of the
Seymour family.

Joseph Seymour
and his wife Rosie
(Camille) Seymour
lived on Kelly Hill to
the ripe ages of 87 and
117. "My father died
at a young age," their
son Pete Seymour told
historian Ruth Lakin.
"My mother lived
longer."

living in Canada has more entitlement to pass freely through Sinixt traditional territory than the Sinixt themselves do. With a legal status in both countries, as a resident of Canada and a citizen of the United States, I have been able to pass freely back and forth for many years, ranging like a literary coyote, following the scent of how things used to be even if my river was made of asphalt, and my canoe gasoline powered. There is deep injustice in that. But there has also been opportunity. That opportunity to defy the boundary and live geographically grows, expanding every day, every year, every decade. Over the past 20 years, the 49th parallel in the upper Columbia region has gradually dissolved. The result can be a richer understanding of land, especially, but also people and place, and a carefully nurtured hope that both settler and Indigenous can interweave their worlds to take better care of the planet Earth. Today's colonial shadows are undeniably long. It can get cold and uncomfortable, standing where the sun doesn't shine. But the shadows are worthy of our continued attention, until the light can finally touch the land again, to bring new life to the trees, the water, the salmon.

THE NORTH HALF OF THE COLVILLE RESERVATION

contributed by Laurie Arnold, PhD
(Sinixt Band Colville Confederated Tribes)

Colonial settlement made "Sinixt territory" difficult to define. Pre-contact, it was simple. The Sinixt knew their homelands and their neighbours recognized those lands, too. But Canadian settlement, industry and violence pushed Sinixt farther and farther south of their homes, until many Sinixt seemed to be living as liminal people, always on the threshold of the US or Canada. Eventually, the Sinixt were included in the confederation of the Colville Indian Reservation when it was established by an executive order from President Ulysses S. Grant in 1872, just months after the US Congress ended its century-old treaty-making practice. The first Colville executive order, signed in April, created a reservation that spanned roughly 3.5 million acres on both sides of the Columbia River all the way to the Pend d'Oreille River near present-day Idaho, including the new settlements in and around Kettle Falls and Colville, Washington. After howls of protest from non-Indian mill operators and shopkeepers who had arrived in the Colville area not long before, President Grant reduced the reservation by 400,000 acres, leaving the settler towns outside the reservation.

The new reservation encompassed 3.1 million acres, from the US–Canadian border on the north and following the jogs and turns of the Columbia River for its eastern and southern boundaries. The western boundary had less physical or territorial finality to it, but it ran along streams and lakes, and nearly reached the foothills of the Cascade range. The Colville Indian Reservation became home to the newly designated "Colville Indians" circa July 1872.

But as settler incursion into the Plateau increased in the last decades of the 19th century, and as the United States sought more land for Americans, Colville tribal people understood that their lives would continue to be disrupted. Their newly designated federal name likely created minimal changes in day-to-day lives for the people now known generally as Colville. They knew who they were and they retained their band and family identities. Having a recognized land base in ancestral homelands meant maintaining lifeways practised for generations, even if that land base was smaller than their traditional territories had been. But within two decades of creating the reservation, the US government reduced it again, bowing to pressure from settlers' requests for even more land, and Colvilles recognized that their lives would continue to change due to forces beyond their control.

In 1891, the government began negotiations with the Colville Indians to buy 1.5 million acres of the north half of the reservation (the North Half) and open it for settlement by 1900. The House Committee on Indian Affairs, a group charged by Congress to develop expertise on Native Peoples but that seemed to possess no direct knowledge of the Colville Reservation, characterized the reservation's vastness as "no less an injustice to the Indians themselves than a menace to the progress of the surrounding commonwealth" off the reservation. The committee, purporting advocacy for Colville people, argued that tribal citizens would learn from "well-ordered white communities" that could settle around them after the sale. Rather than acknowledging how a 50 per cent reduction in land base could destroy food sources and cultural practices, committee members asserted that Colvilles would profit from new market economies that would emerge in response to the newcomers' needs. The committee charged with serving Native Americans instead facilitated a land deal that would separate Colville people from their homes and homelands.

Based on the recommendation of the House Committee, Congress agreed to pay $1.5 million, one dollar per acre, for the land. According to an elder member of the tribe, "It was no more than a land steal and some of our teen-age boys were allowed to sign the so-called agreement between the Indians and the government."[1] But bills approving the sale of the North Half to the United States repeatedly died in Congressional sessions. The absence of a ratified bill did not preserve the reservation lands; the North Half opened for settlement in 1900, as scheduled by the 1891 "agreement." When Congress, 15 years after the original bill, finally passed the Colville Diminishment Act in 1906, it did secure the reservation along its present-day 1.4 million acre boundary downstream of Kettle Falls. However, the 1906 bill differed from the original agreement in a tangible way: it did not provide a cash payment for the North Half lands. Instead, the act mandated that allotment sale proceeds would go into a government fund for "the education and civilization" of the Colville Indians. The government would manage the funds and dispense them in accordance with government priorities. Not only did tribal citizens lose the land base and rights to live, hunt, fish and gather on the land, they also did not receive promised compensation and would have to appeal to the Bureau of Indian Affairs (BIA) to release any funds eventually paid into the account.

The 20th century progressed, but the loss of the North Half remained fresh for the Colville tribal members. The Sinixt were especially impacted by this loss; the North Half offered geographic continuity with their ancestral territories farther north. If the international boundary served as a barrier within their homelands, erasure of the North Half represented a chasm. Almost as soon as the Indian Claims Commission (ICC) was established in 1946, the Colville Business Council filed a bill for restoration of the North Half.[2] In 1934 and 1935, Secretary of the Interior Harold Ickes issued departmental orders withdrawing 818,000 acres of unallotted land on the North Half from further disposition until the matter of compensation and ownership was resolved.[3] The government clearly recognized an obligation in this matter, even though the parties could not agree on what that obligation entailed.

While awaiting review of the ICC claim, the Colville Business Council approached Congressman Walt Horan about co-authoring a Congressional bill to restore the unallotted lands of the former North Half of the reservation to the Colville tribes.[4] Horan served as US Representative for Washington's Fifth District, which encompasses most of eastern Washington, from 1943 to 1964 and had lifelong familiarity with land issues for Native communities in the Columbia Plateau region. Colville leaders believed he would assist them with restoration of the North Half, because they felt he understood what was at stake. This dialogue was well developed by 1953, when the topic of termination tied to restoration first emerged. The policy of termination sought to end federal recognition of tribes and finally assimilate Native peoples into mainstream American culture. House Concurrent Resolution 108, passed in 1953, characterized the legislation as an opportunity for Indians to become "subject to the same laws and entitled to the same responsibilities as are applicable to other citizens of the United States and to grant them all of the rights and prerogatives pertaining to American citizenship," as if Native people did not already possess citizenship and fulfill obligations associated with it.[5]

The Colville Business Council, the elected leadership of the reservation, began holding informal and community meetings to discuss restoration and termination, the first official one in 1954. The Colvilles' active pursuit of a policy that would destroy their nation is unlike any other termination experience, and the origins of this quest lie with the North Half. The main topic of the 1954 general membership meeting was restoration of the North Half, and how that restoration bill would be tied to termination. At this meeting, three traditional band leaders spoke. Chief Jim James of the San Poils, Chief Victor Nicholas of the Lakes Band, and Chief Cleveland Kamiakin of the Joseph Band of Nez Perce each opposed the bill. They did not support termination in principle, but told the tribal members they feared termination to be inevitable. Congressman Horan attended the meeting as well and reinforced to the membership that he doubted Congress would pass a restoration bill that did not include some kind of termination provision.[6]

As other tribes across the US fought termination and strived to retain federal recognition, some Colvilles accepted termination as inevitable not just for their tribe, but for all tribes. In this context, the Business Council prioritized restoration of the land base because they believed the Colville Confederated Tribes (CCT) could ultimately renegotiate this agreement with the BIA. Tribes were accustomed to the BIA and federal government changing their policies and their rules, as demonstrated by their previous capriciousness with Colville reservation boundaries. Congressman Horan assisted the Business Council in drafting a bill for restoration and termination, following his own instincts based on feedback he had gotten from Congressional peers. The council wrote a bill providing for the immediate restoration of the 818,000 acres. That bill included a promise from the Colvilles to draft a termination plan within five years of the land restoration.

The Colvilles were victorious in 1956 when Public Law 772 (P.L. 772) passed and the North Half lands were restored to the CCT. The victory was a qualified one: the reservation boundaries were not adjusted and the land is not included as part of the CCT's official landholdings. Instead, the CCT has rights to the land, such as hunting and fishing access, but the CCT does not own the land, and the reservation acreage and borders remain as they were in 1906 after loss of the North Half.[7]

Understanding the CCT's pursuit of North Half restoration also illuminates the signal importance of Sinixt recognition and the urgency of Colville participation in Columbia River Treaty negotiations. The US and Canadian governments and citizens may look at today's Colville Reservation boundaries and misunderstand the ancestral, cultural and geographic connections of Sinixt People in the US to Sinixt territory in British Columbia. If the North Half had not been severed from the Colville Reservation, or if it had been properly restored to the reservation and Colville people in 1956, today's maps would make visible and reinforce those connections rather than rendering them invisible through erasure.

SUBMERGED BY WATER AND TIME

In the fall of 1978, BC government archaeologist Michael Freisinger was surveying the Kettle River valley when he heard a story from a local fisherman about a dugout canoe that had been scuttled under the river's surface. Freisinger found the wet archaeology site just upstream of the international boundary and Cascade Falls. When he excavated, he discovered a set of log skids in the riverbed surrounding the boat, suggesting that the dugout had been intentionally submerged for storage. Though its sides had been partially smashed and broken by water surging through the falls, the 21-foot canoe was still 70 per cent intact. An Indigenous carver had shaped it out of a single ponderosa pine log, the butt end of the tree forming the bow. This, Freisinger observed, was a common technique for dugouts, to increase balance and buoyancy, making them "front-heavy" to keep loads balanced. The canoe had a sizable hole drilled through the top of the bow, suggesting that it might also have been towed when heavily laden, by people or a horse, from streamside.

Cascade Falls, a narrow rock canyon, forms an ecological boundary that restricted the lower Kettle River's annual ocean salmon run from ascending further. At the base of the falls, the Sinixt long had a productive fishery at a place called K̓ɬsax̌m̓ (end of fish going up). The river above the falls and its semi-arid valley could be counted on for deer, mountain goat and sheep, as well as the fresh green shoots of balsamroot sunflower and various other root crops. Today, the international boundary bisects the meandering upper Kettle River more than once, as it winds its way through ponderosa pine forest and bunchgrass

The canoe had been stored upstream of Cascade Falls canyon, pictured here at the lower edge. Photo courtesy of Mike Graeme.

prairie. Freisinger's report details dozens of places where Sinixt, Skoyel-pi and a third smaller band identified in the historical record as the **sn̓x̌ʷiya̱lpátkʷx** (Kettle River Indians) lived and processed resources, all the way from present-day Grand Forks, BC, to Curlew, Washington, and Midway and Rock Creek, BC.

On cliffs and bluffs rising around the upper Kettle River, Freisinger found plentiful archaeological evidence of meat-processing camps. Closer to the river's flood plain, he found intact storage or root-cooking pits. Just east of the confluence of the Granby River, in present-day Grand Forks, he found the remains of what had been a significant buri-al site. The site had already been thoroughly excavated by BC mining historian Bill Barlee in 1965. Barlee appears to have removed the fol-lowing contents of the graves he found: two human remains, buried in the flexed position common to the Sinixt, and covered by stones; 1,742 dentalium shells; a soapstone pipe; a quantity of red ochre (used for painting pictographs and ornamenting the body); and fragments of a wooden bracelet. By the time Freisinger did his survey, the skeletal remains of a total of 20 ancestral Sinixt had been disturbed and removed from the confluence of the Granby and Kettle rivers in present-day downtown Grand Forks. No doubt many other cultural items com-monly buried with these deceased also left their intended resting places.

Freisinger's summary report makes an effort to date the canoe. He quotes John Work, Hudson's Bay Company manager at Fort Colvile (adjacent to Kettle Falls) in the early 19th century: "Dougouts [*sic*] and sturgeon nosed canoes of bark were used on the numerous rivers and lakes of the district…. In many areas these craft provided the principal means of travel, even after horses came into use." Freisinger refers to the clear markings of a metal adze on the canoe's interior, and to a location nearby, marked as a campsite used by the 1860–61 British Boundary Commission. With these clues, Freisinger estimates the canoe's birth to be from the post-colonial period, at about 1875. Its discovery offers a clue about the Indigenous use of the middle and upper Kettle River valleys. Submerged near a portage route around Cascade Falls dating from antiquity, the canoe would have been ready and waiting for any-one wishing to transport dried salmon, or pick up stores of dried meat from successful upstream hunts and bring them back downstream, to be carried by water to larger villages along the lower Kettle River. By 1875, the international boundary had been established but was not yet

Michael Freisinger supervising
the excavation of the canoe.
Photo courtesy of the
Boundary Museum Society.

strongly enforced. The Sinixt
would have still passed freely
through the Kettle water-
shed, paying little mind to
the 49th parallel.

The Kettle River arcs back
below the boundary again
just west of Grand Forks.
There, it intersects with Curlew Creek, water that flows
out of Curlew Lake past the
town of the same name. Upstream of Curlew, Washington, the Kettle
River returns to British Columbia near Midway, BC, continuing past
Rock Creek toward Beaverdell and its headwaters. Freisinger surveyed
multiple sites along this winding, picturesque and still rural portion of
the Kettle, where he found a pictograph, multiple pit house depressions
and more evidence of food cache pits, bone fragments and fire-broken rock, all evidence of a deeply settled Indigenous culture. Though
Freisinger did not survey around Curlew, he corresponded with Washington State resident and researcher Madeline Perry, who confirmed
a dozen sites around the lake and more along the Kettle River. Place
names in the language shared by the Sinixt and Skoyelpi began to complete the picture of a prosperous valley.

Having been teased initially into reading Freisinger's report by the in-
triguing detail of a waterlogged canoe, I completed my journey through
the written pages of the Indigenous Kettle River region by looping back
around to the place where Christina Creek joins in after flowing out of
Christina Lake. Deep in the report, I found a brief reference to a foot trail

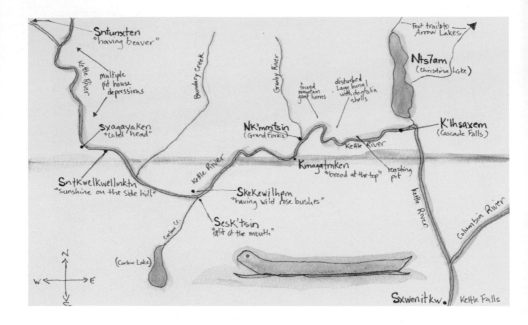

Map based on the work of Michael Freisinger. Created by author.

used by the Sinixt, connecting them overland from Christina Lake, east through mountains to the Arrow Lakes. New information, keeping me humble, revealing itself nearly two decades after I first learned of the Sinixt story. Poring over contemporary maps, I could only theorize about how the foot trail threaded through the Monashee mountain range to reach populous Sinixt territory in the Arrow Lakes valley. Choosing a pass that had the gentlest elevation change, my finger found a now abandoned rail line that follows the McRae Creek drainage north and east, to emerge on the west shore of Lower Arrow Lake considerably north of Castlegar. It was a decent guess, though guess was all I could do.

So much of what we could know about Indigenous use of the landscape is still submerged: place names, foot trails, portage paths, stories related to important geological formations, seasonal villages, root grounds. The international boundary, the development of smelters, sawmills, agriculture, gravel pits, housing developments, cities and highways, have all dramatically altered perception of the Kettle River's natural, Sinixt and Skoyelpi geography. Freisinger's report opens a portal into a nearly forgotten world of the foot trails and canoe transport, one ripe with imagining. The dugout canoe sheds fresh light on the rhythms of a different time, when no artificial lines on maps obscured the natural connections that free-running waterways always foster.

LINKS IN A JEWELLED CHAIN

"Customs officers…have been working hard to catch some Indians who smuggled horses across the line…. Your scribe can remember the time, only five years ago, when the 'Boston Man' [Americans] could take all the stock he liked across the line and not a question asked. Times have changed so much in the last few years that the 'old timers' cannot keep track of it, to say nothing about the Indians."

—*Northport News*, July 14, 1898

Looking west across the Columbia from a bluff upstream of Northport, Washington, I watch the sinuous wonder of the final run of Big Sheep Creek, tracing a braided path through the exposed reservoir silt. Each of the single strands of water glitters against the shoreline, hinting of a riparian habitat that once loosely laced all the creeks of the upper Columbia to the river's main stem. Just a few miles upstream of Big Sheep Creek, the international boundary decisively slices the Columbia in two. But history can still defy borders that have been so artificially set.

Immediately prior to Grand Coulee Dam's completion, archaeologists Donald Collier, Alfred E. Hudson and Arlo Ford worked all along the future reservoir from the new dam to the boundary, between the summer of 1939 and the autumn of 1940, rapidly surveying riverbanks and deltas. They found one of the richest and most complex sites at the mouth of Big Sheep Creek, a place they called No. 46. The Sinixt call it **Yumčn̓**. According to Mary Marchand, it was a winter village that extended from a large settlement of the Lakes people called **Sn̓k̓wil̓tn̓**, at and around present-day Northport. Researchers discovered many burials along the edge of a steep, sandy bank positioned about 30 feet above the river. They found more burials at the south end of a small island in the midst of the river, just upstream of the creek's mouth. This site they named No. 47.

All of the graves contained bodies in the flexed position that is traditional to Sinixt interment practices. All were oriented downstream, facing east toward the rising sun. Buried with the ancestral remains were numerous cultural items, ranging from obsidian knives and stone scrapers to granite pestles, pipes and ornaments. Precious or practical items buried with a deceased person are to assist and protect on the journey home. In particular, shells and horns have always offered special protection. Contemporary Sinixt language speakers and spiritual leaders describe death as a journey east "to the place of the bright land," the gleaming source of sun that lights our world.

The spiritual injury felt by Sinixt People and other tribes through the disturbance of ancestral burials is real. At the time Collier, Hudson and Ford did their work, the settler culture had little if any awareness about the significance of these tribal relatives. No connection was made in the report's findings between the Sinixt People's feelings and those feelings a researcher might have if his or her own family's remains were those that had been exhumed, itemized and studied. Over the many decades since the hasty survey, the Colville Confederated Tribes have gradually asserted more and more control over protecting the region's archaeological richness. Teams of archaeologists have grown more aware. Each year, when the water drops during drawdown, tribal members guard locations known to have remains or other cultural materials, to keep them from being further disturbed.

The investigations in 1939–40, and the discovered objects, were problematic for other reasons. The survey was an outsized, last-minute task in a race to understand several thousand years of archaeology before the record was drowned and destroyed. Beset by poor leadership, challenging weather and a short time frame, the work was recognized at the time as incomplete and inadequate. Yet, even in its inadequacy, even with the offensive cultural wounds it caused, the report has some value in what it reveals. It sketches an undeniable picture of a complex and successful Indigenous culture that thrived on the upper Columbia. Illustrations of the precious and beautiful items found in the burials serve to stir the human imagination and evoke a once-graceful, riverside world.

At burials located in sites No. 46 and adjacent No. 47, the archaeologists found several intricately carved digging stick handles, fashioned from deer antler. Smoothed to a fine sheen, each of the handles had a

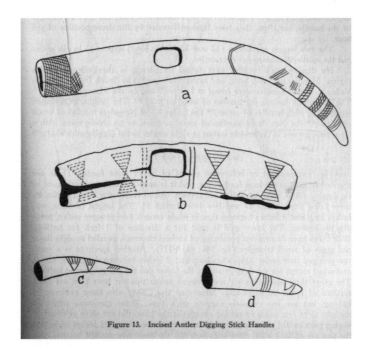

Figure 13. Incised Antler Digging Stick Handles

Digging stick handles. From Donald Collier, Alfred E. Hudson and
Arlo Ford, *Archaeology of the Upper Columbia Region,* 1942.

tapered hole in the centre, through which the digging stick would be
passed, forming a crosspiece near the top. Downward pressure from a
woman's hands increased the secure fit of the handle. After loosening
a good number of roots with her hands firmly on the carved handle,
a woman would crouch to sort the roots by size. She would pull them
gently, replanting the largest (for future new roots) and smallest (to gain
size and strength) and shaking away the mid-sized ones to place them
in her gathering bag or basket.

The exhumed digging stick handles bring more light to the significance of plant foods dug up from the ground, commonly known in the
Indigenous world as "roots." For over a century, mostly male and non-Indigenous archaeologists and ethnographers concentrated on studying
hunting and fishing practices more than gathering activities, reflecting
a broader, unconscious gender bias against "women's work." Buried
wooden digging sticks and woven carrying bags and baskets often rotted

quickly in the upper Columbia's moist, acidic soil. When interviewing Elders and surveying archaeological sites in the first half of the 20th century, experts had a tendency to see and value sharpened spear points and hide scrapers. Gradually, however, awareness of the significance of food and medicine plants has dawned outside the tribal world. Researchers now understand what Indigenous People already knew: how much nourishment plant foods could and did provide, and how much the tending practices of women gardeners gently shaped the landscape. According to anthropologist Lillian Ackerman, the diet of Interior Salish Plateau people such as the Lakes was "approximately half vegetable and half animal," a fact that Ackerman believes reinforced unique gender equity among Interior Plateau tribes. The various forms of what is loosely called camas (*Camassia quamash,* and in dryer locations, *Lomatium canbyi*), along with bitterroot (*Lewisia rediviva*), were staples of the Plateau diet, as essential to survival as meat and salmon. For Sinixt women, tiger lily, Indian potato and glacier lily widened options.

Site No. 47 revealed a nearly flat, four-sided piece of red abalone shell, with a hole at one end. Likely used as a pendant, the shell was resting among glass trade beads, horned spoons and surviving fragments of woven basket. Red abalone (*Haliotis rufescens*) is a large, edible sea snail that feeds exclusively on kelp and clings to rocks in cold Pacific sea water. Its habitat ranges along the coast of western North America, from British Columbia to California. The ear-shaped shell's exterior is rough and brick red and grows up to 12 inches in diameter. Secured to a rock by a large, sucking "foot," the creature moves slowly, taking its nutrients from sea kelp suspended in the crashing tidal waves. Inside, the creature secretes a glistening mother-of-pearl substance that builds up over time into a rainbow of hues. Reflective and smooth, the interior abalone shell glows with swirling and luminous hues of pink, blue, gold and green.

Historically, abalone flesh was for some Pacific coastal Indigenous People like salmon was for the Interior Salish: a prolific, delicious and reliable seafood, a dietary keystone upon which a culture could be constructed. This seemed to be true in particular for the Chumash of the central California coast near Santa Barbara, who left enormous abalone middens on the Channel Islands. Abalone middens have also been found among the traditional lands of the Ohlone, Pomo, Karuk, Hupa, Yurok and Wiyot people of northern California. In British Columbia, the shellfish was treasured by the Nuu-chah-nulth, Nuxalk, Tsimshian, Manhousat and many individual tribes of the Kwakwaka'wakw-speaking peoples of the inner south coast. All of these tribes revered various species of the snail for food, and for the beauty of its shell.

To transform abalone shell into an ornament for use in celebratory regalia and jewellery was a time-consuming, careful process. Artisans cut or broke the reddish, rough shell into pieces and gradually shaped them by patient scraping against rough rock. More smoothing and cutting, then careful drilling of holes, resulted in pendants of refined quality that showcase the shell's luminous interior. These abalone disks still feature in dance regalia for many California tribes. The clacking and clicking of dozens of pendants sewn to skirts in rows or fashioned into collars continue to fill the air with the spirit of Abalone Woman, whose own story winds through the life of the giant shell and the people. Members of the nobility class of British Columbia's Kwakwaka'wakw speakers, those who have achieved status through exceptional personal character and social behaviour, have long worn abalone as a form of jewellery. They inlay it into their dance masks and sew it onto hereditary robes.

We will likely never know the exact coastal origin of Site No. 47's abalone pendant. Its discovery so far from the ocean nonetheless confirms that Columbia River water once linked tribe after tribe to each other, all through the Northwest, from high, snow-laden mountains, across a vast sagebrush desert, to the foggy, forested coast of Oregon and Washington. Morsels of abalone shell once travelled as people did, always close to water, reaching well beyond the sea creature's natural range, finding their way slowly into a freshwater mountain culture. One thriving on the banks of the upper Columbia River.

Because it is the 21st century, and much has changed in the landscape since colonial contact, I have to ask myself if the glistening path of this water takes some of its shine from deposits of mining slag. Emptied into the Columbia River by an upstream Canadian smelter for a century, the slag by-product contains silica, calcium, iron, zinc, lead, copper arsenic and cadmium. The dark, glass-like grains do not know political boundaries, and neither do the smelter's liquid discharges containing toxic levels of mercury and cadmium. Slag and contaminated sediments roiled along on currents for decades, coming to rest on beaches, within the riverbed and on shorelines in the state of Washington. Deposits within the boundaries of the current reservation, as well as those around Northport, Washington, have long been the focus of the Colville Confederated Tribes' drive to hold Cominco (today known as Teck) responsible for having allowed pollutants to flow freely across the international boundary and cause harm to the Columbia River as far south as Grand Coulee Dam.

To that end, in 1999, the Colville Confederated Tribes petitioned the US Environmental Protection Agency to investigate toxicity in soils from upstream smelter discharges in Trail, BC. According to Patti Bailey, a Sinixt descendant and key CCT staff member, the initial investigations found that sediments near the boundary were over 53 times greater than the CCT standard for zinc. Levels were many times over other standards or guidelines set by tribal, state and federal governments that seek to protect sediment-dwelling organisms. A similar situation exists, she points out, for the other toxic metals and mercury common to Teck's present and historical discharges. The petition began a 20-year-long, transboundary legal battle waged by the CCT, joined by the State of Washington on behalf of non-tribal residents, only a few years after it began. The case highlights both the expansive nature of the CCT's sense of responsibility to water and land, and the ironic reality that the Columbia River, despite its having been dammed and a boundary slapped into place, still connects everyone in the region beyond nationality. The ten million tons of slag intentionally dumped into the river upstream – in Canada – have caused harm downstream – in the US. In 2019, the CCT finally reached the end of the long legal road with a ruling in the State of Washington's Ninth Circuit Court holding Teck responsible for all damages and mandating cleanup efforts. This, despite Teck's efforts to argue in court that EPA rulings in the US should not apply to Canadian companies.

From a distance, parked on a bluff south of the border crossing, I know that what glitters is not always gold. But I make an effort to trace an analogue for beauty in the water carving its way. Big Sheep Creek – lit by the strengthening springtime sun – is like the abalone disk removed from its resting place. Despite all that we have done to harm the water, it can still be reflective and graceful, aqueous and appealing. The spiritual protection offered by that fragment of ocean unearthed at Site No. 47 is a reminder of what the river, and all those who live beside it, need from us. Protection from harm. The twists and turns of cultural geography can form a surprising arc of meaning, one that connects the far-off crashing waves of the Pacific coastal sea with the continental interior's steep rainforest mountains, all the while tracing a persistent stand for transboundary ecological and political justice for the Sinixt People. We are all connected, across time and across places. Each act, each decision, affects us more than might appear on the surface. All of us, in one way or another, live downstream of each other.

9.
Gathering It All In

Landscape is the common thread that binds human beings from one era of inhabitation to another. Though attitudes and values about land use might not be shared, love of place – love of land and water – is universally experienced by the human psyche. Our minds, hearts and bodies are built to appreciate natural beauty, to form a relationship with a source of wild and worldly energy that is non-human, even if a contemporary lifestyle can eclipse these tendencies. Despite the significant changes that have occurred in the upper Columbia since David Thompson arrived, the mountains have not moved, the sky has not shifted. The moon still floats above a high ridge to cast its soft light into an inky sky. The burnished spires of the larch still rise sharply from the fur of evergreen hillsides each autumn. These are continued testimonies to the wild potency of this beautiful and inspiring landscape. Flames of possibility.

An expansive view of the contemporary natural world where we live emerges when we follow a common thread stretching between the settler culture back to the Indigenous one. In my research over two decades, I have sensed within many contemporary upper Columbia residents, and even within myself, a shred of wily fibre spun and twisted together with the modern mind. This wily fibre is especially noticeable today in the recreational hunter, fisher or gatherer of wild foods. Being "out there" searching for wild plants and animals seems to call on a very old part of ourselves that knows how to satisfy hunger with a natural searching, one that finds great satisfaction in wild places. The enthusiasm and respect for the land that I hear in the voices of some hunters or fishers sharing their stories, the humming, meditative heat surrounding me during an afternoon picking berries, all these experiences are linked to the untamed upper Columbia landscape as it naturally wants to be. Despite the divide that seems to exist between hunters and "environmentalists," the hunters I have talked with know, admire and value the landscape greatly. They also respect the wild animals they seek. In attempting to satisfy basic hunger with landscape, a feral love takes hold. At the same time, a connection to land frees itself from domestic restrictions, growing unpastured and more mysterious. Hunting and fishing, as well as their gentler counterpart, gathering of berries or roots, all encourage a deeper knowing and valuing of place. This is an Indigenous way of knowing, whether those who search the wild landscape for food are of Aboriginal descent or not.

Gathering upper Columbia berries was once an essential activity for the Sinixt. In traditional times, women gently caressed the curving branches of many shrubs to remove the delicate globes of ripe fruit. Today, many of those wild fruits of the upper Columbia region that once formed an important part of the Sinixt diet fall largely uneaten to the forest floor: soopolallie, Oregon grape, kinnikinnick, gooseberry, red osier dogwood, hawthorn, elderberry, wild rose hip, mountain ash. Even though they are not poisonous, their tart or bitter flavours, their sometimes mealy and seedy flesh are perhaps too wild, too unbidden for most settler taste buds. Groomed by a culture that adores sweet things and rejects bitter or extremely tart ones, I found it easy to appreciate the succulence of wild strawberry, saskatoon, huckleberry and wild raspberry, all of which were also gathered and enjoyed by the Sinixt.

A common berry ripening in June is also often ignored by contemporary settler gatherers. Thimbleberries are not very cooperative in how they ripen: one at a time on each plant. Only a sprinkling at any time may be ready, across a large patch. It may be why Lakes people once treasured

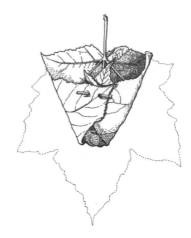

Thimbleberry plant and leaf basket.
Photo and sketch from author's collection.

the berry. They may also have prized it because the berry's flesh was too delicate to dry or preserve easily. Picking and keeping a thimbleberry intact requires soft, nimble fingers. One needs a large swatch of plants to accumulate enough to stir into yogurt or ice cream and stain it pink, or simply to enjoy the tart and sweet flavour one by one. The thimbleberry's most ingenious contribution is in the leaves. The Sinixt developed a way to fold a thimbleberry leaf into a temporary basket for those berries or even others discovered unexpectedly. When I see a group of plants on a walk, I know I will always have a berry basket for picking.

Another common edible fruit for the Sinixt, the soapberry, has not been so esteemed as the huckleberry in settler culture, though it has always been by the Sinixt. The small, red-orange, translucent fruit of *Shepherdia Canadensis* has unique chemical properties, a high iron and vitamin C content and an extremely bitter taste. The Sinixt call it **sx̌ʷusm̓** (foam). Its English common name derives from the Chinook jargon term: soop (soap) alallie (berry). Both the Sinixt and Chinook jargon terms refer to how the berries and some water can whip into a pale pink foam. In traditional times, the foam was relished and prepared as a special treat, sweetened with dried saskatoon berries and huckleberries. Its transformation from berry to pale pink cloud had an air of magic, and still does. Today, the Sinixt continue to whip up what they also call "Indian ice cream," a meringue-like dish that they sweeten with huckleberries or white sugar as a treat for winter dances. They also eat soopalallie berries fresh, or dry them later for use. Some contemporary Sinixt People I know love the berry and pick it avidly.

In interviews with Indigenous gatherers across British Columbia, ethnobotanist Nancy Turner has recorded tribal knowledge of how to encourage productivity in many berry species. Tribes regularly burned to maintain clearings and generate nutrients to feed shrubs, making them more productive. They pruned and even transplanted bushes. The continual management of berry grounds may well persist in the high concentration of soapberry bushes I have noticed growing around the Kettle Falls Interpretive Center, adjacent to the flooded falls. "That's always been the best place to pick **sx̌ʷusm̓**," Shelly Boyd told me recently. My own first taste of a soopalallie berry took place on the fringes of a hot gravel road in late July. I quickly spat it out, driven by a conditioned belief that something tasting that bitter was likely poisonous. But I knew then and still do that the soopalallie is no more poisonous than sorrow. Embarrassed at my lack of courage, I popped another into my mouth, trying to allow the sharp, acrid juice to roll wildly around on my tongue. I have gradually learned to enjoy the mix of bitterness and sweetness, and particularly like the berries crushed and added to lemonade to stain it pink. One year, camping overnight along Wilson Creek in the Slocan valley in mid-July, I discovered two bushes growing out of thin, hot soil beside the water, loaded with the ripe red berries. I picked a pile of them and took them home to dry into tiny, maroon raisins. Whenever I eat soapberries, I marvel at the ability some cultures have to value the bitter tastes of the natural world as well as the sweet ones. Bitterness is a tonic for the heart, I have been told.

Many contemporary upper Columbia hunters have a locally adapted living room survival skill that berry pickers have not had to develop: they keep very quiet about being hunters. They are almost secretive and seem reluctant to demonstrate their passion for stalking deer, elk, bear and mountain goat, unless they recognize that judgment about what they do has been suspended. Then their faces open and the stories of their experiences in the bush begin to pour out. They know that their hunting activity is often frowned on by our contemporary culture; that conservationists, animal lovers and even vegetarian eaters are eager to empty all the rifle barrels in the region of their bullets. So they

Bear trap.

"Martin Louie told us [in the 1970s] that after a black bear was killed, the hunters would immediately sing a traditional song for the bear, and that he had seen some old aboriginal people, including his grandfather, cry when singing the song. Mr. Louie also recalled that many years ago, after the bear's head was skinned to be eaten, charcoal had first to be placed on its forehead, in accordance with the bear's legendary 'make-up.'"

—Randy Bouchard and Dorothy Kennedy, 2000

privately display their love of place. They slip into their trucks at dawn to head out to track a bear. They hike quietly to a remote cabin on a high ridge to eat, sleep and dream a mountain goat. They shoulder elk into the back of their enclosed truck to drive it home for their freezers. In today's landscape, hunting is not nearly as acceptable as berry picking. Hunting is perceived to involve an aggressive impulse that modern culture does not always feel comfortable embracing. But like berry picking, hunting calls on a deeply embedded ability to take a wild product from nature as food. Hunting requires a direct relationship with place. The hunter as well as the gatherer must possess knowledge of terrain, a sharp, intuitive eye and great patience for the rhythms of the wild.

Given the importance of meat in the Sinixt traditional diet, hunting skills were a central part of pre-contact Sinixt cultural training and practice. According to Nancy Wynecoop, young boys began spending large amounts of time exclusively with their fathers and other men sometime after they could walk, so that they learned the intricate techniques necessary to stalk and kill game. They watched men fashion spear and arrow points from various stone materials. They learned to carve arrow and spear shafts from **məc̓ mc̓ iłp** (ironwood, *Holodiscus discolor*). Just before large seasonal hunts such as took place in autumn, they watched the men remove themselves from women for days, fasting, praying and cleansing their "scent" in sweat lodges. The Sinixt followed seasonal rounds, pursuing deer, mountain sheep and mountain goat in spring; deer, sheep, elk and bear in fall; deer and caribou in mid-winter and sheep again in spring. Early 19th-century explorers described the upper Columbia region as being rich with mammals. Extensive trapping, especially in autumn and winter, took place throughout the region after the arrival of trade forts. Trade fort statistics indicate that the Sinixt were adept trappers of marten, fisher, beaver, wolverine and mink, though these mammals may not have been as heavily pursued in traditional times. Groundhogs were certainly a favoured small game both before and after European contact, with many of them obtained by the flooding of holes. Snowshoe hares, too, were taken from their holes or caught with snares. The traditional methods for hunting larger mammals varied. Most often, deer were seized in communal drives during their natural autumn migration. Beginning at night, groups of hunters drove them into channels and over bluffs or toward a river, where men would be waiting to take them down with bow and arrows. Caribou might also be hunted in this way, with the animals being driven into the lake and speared from the side of a canoe. The Sinixt used deadfall traps baited with fish or venison for both grizzly and black bears. Sometimes, they killed bears with a bow and special long arrows that could double as spears if the bear charged the hunter. They drove mountain goats to the edge of cliffs, prodding a fall with the use of long poles.

Hunting was not a hero's pursuit to be boasted about but was undertaken for the common good. Nancy Wynecoop describes the importance of modesty in a hunter's demeanour. Success was a product of spiritual preparedness and training, not individual prowess. She explains how each village had a central area where fresh kill would be deposited. Once it was placed there, the meat became the property of the whole group and was shared out equally in much the same way that salmon are distributed at the major fisheries on the Columbia, and even upstream of the dams through the sharing of downstream tribes. In this way, the hunter-fisher-gatherer society expressed an inherent aspect of

"The Lakes pursued [mountain] goats over the cliffs with a long pole until they got them in a place from which they could not escape. They put the pole under them and pried them off the cliffs.... The Lakes hunted for mountain goats considerably; they liked the meat."

—Allan Smith, 1950

healthy communities, that of sharing and equal use of resources. Waste was frowned upon. The Sinixt used every part of the animal, including the bones, pulverized to extract marrow. The skins and hides of the animals became blankets and clothing. Men and women wore tanned deer hide tunics, pants and dresses, often decorated with porcupine quills or disks of shell. Women stitched moccasins, slightly pointed at the toe, from deer or caribou hide, stuffed with goat hair or dried leaves and moss for the colder months. In winter, they wore pants of bear hide, fur-side-out, for leggings. The teeth and claws of various mammals became necklaces. Antlers and bones became hunting horns, needles, handles for digging sticks and ornaments. For occasional hauling overland, the Sinixt fashioned parfleches of heavy deer or buffalo hide, the latter acquired through trade. Women wove blankets from cord spun from mountain goat hair. Even animal intestines had another use, storing bear grease, deer tallow or a paste ground from wild hazelnuts.

RICK DESAUTEL, CEREMONIAL HUNTER

When he was small, Rick Desautel's Sinixt grandmother Madeleine Paul Desautel taught him about God. She led him outside and pointed up to a tree growing on her farm just west of Inchelium, Washington. *If you don't believe there's a god, then think about this tree. Watch how a tree matures from a very small seed to become very large and complex. This is the work of the Creator.* Born in 1888 and removed from her family at the age of 6 to be educated in the Catholic tradition at the St. Regis Mission residential school in the Colville valley, Madeleine Paul Desautel became a devout Catholic. She took Rick and her other grandchildren to weekly mass – whether they wanted to go or not. She was, at least on the surface of her life, an unlikely person to provide Rick with the guidance he needed to emerge as a ceremonial hunter for his people. But under that surface she was still a Sinixt woman, one who knew the old ways. She passed some of these old ways on to her grandson, helping him transform into a man with enough strength and certitude to test Canadian Aboriginal law.

Rick recalls seeing Sinixt Elders visiting his grandmother often, men like the great storyteller Pete Seymour and an old friend from school days named Dora, who wore traditional clothing and headscarf. Rick recalls hearing Dora and her grandmother talk in their language. *They got together and when they laughed it sounded like two old hens cackling.* These and other old-timers had strong links to the traditional ways. Madeleine's own grandfather, August Paul, was a Salmon Chief who helped distribute the fish at Kettle Falls. Another Paul family descendant, Celia Smith, told historian Ruth Lakin that Madeleine's grandfather long resisted the pressure to be baptized. Rick heard those visiting and talking with his grandmother speak of a different sort of religion, a Sinixt spiritual practice based on the acquisition of a guardian spirit power. Intrigued and curious, Rick asked his grandmother when he was about 10 years old if he, too, could get that power. He laughs lightly, remembering his childhood. *I guess you could say that my brother and me, we just wanted to stay in the woods and play. We didn't want to go to church. So we really started quizzing her about all that. We wanted to find the spirit outdoors. We wanted to know and it took us quite a while to convince her.* Recalling the spiritual journeys of her own parents, Annie and Old Paul, and their parents before

Madeline Desautel.
Photo courtesy of the
Desautel family.

them (including August Paul), she agreed to help Rick and his brother try to access their spiritual power.

During his testimony for the 2016 trial, *R. v. Desautel,* Rick detailed the process. He had learned from his grandmother that not everyone achieved what he wanted. Some people, she told him, went out over and over again into nature and never found their song, their connection to a part of the natural world that would give them strength. The strength in a song, she explained, could turn a life around. It always gave those who received it a sense of purpose. She sent him and his brother across the field from the farmhouse, to a bluff where they had to wait, without food or water, until the song came. But that, she said, would not be the end of it. Once the song came, Rick would need to have it so deep inside him that he would never forget it. Remembering it the next day, the next week, the next year – this meant that the song was truly his.

Rick described how he ran with his brother back into the land behind her house and sat on the bluff in spring sunshine. He sat all day long, dreaming of pancakes. His brother sat with him and together they stayed all night long, without getting much sleep. Temperatures dipped to freezing, and they had only a thin blanket. The next morning, his brother snapped to attention and said he'd heard his song. Rick watched his brother run back down the hill, across the field to the house. He remained alone on the bluff all day long. Waiting. Hungry. Tired. Wanting pancakes. *I was praying really hard all day so that I didn't have to spend another night out there. It was cold.* The following afternoon, as he sat still waiting, a ladybug landed on his arm. He watched the insect as it walked all the way up his arm. He felt it walk across his shoulder, his neck, his other shoulder, then down the other arm, before it flew off into the spring sunshine. His spirit burst through with its certainty. In a flash, he was down the hill, back in the kitchen eating pancakes, the song lodged in his heart.

In the courtroom, I watched, holding my breath, as the lawyer representing Rick Desautel asked him to sing his song. The lawyer for

Rick Desautel.
Photo courtesy of Mike Graeme.

the BC government leaped to his feet, requesting an official court translator. Testimony could not be entered into the record, he said dramatically, without us knowing what it means. Everyone turned to the judge, whose reply was direct, calm and emotionless. *I don't think that will be necessary, Mr. Thompson. Sing your song, Mr. Desautel.* And so, Rick sang his song. The courtroom filled with the sound of a spirit, held in the body of a man. I set my pen down as the hair rose on my arms. An intense feeling flourished in the air. I could hear the sound of the spirit of the land, of a man who knew where he came from, and of a tribe grounded in purpose.

When I asked Rick a few years later how he could have sung something so private, personal and spiritual in a public courtroom, his answer got right to the point. *If you're afraid to sing your song, then you're not proud to be a human being. I didn't have any problem with all that. Singing my song is just like praying in church. People do that all the time out loud. I can talk to my spirit through my song. That's what's going on. It's a good thing.*

Rick's tribal members consider him to be a ceremonial hunter, a man who hunts not only for his own interests but also to distribute meat to others. The work of a ceremonial hunter is always to bring the game to people who need it, to share it widely. In the process of developing the test case that led to *R. v. Desautel*, Rick took several trips north of the international boundary into traditional Sinixt territory to hunt on behalf of his people. His expeditions between 2009 and 2011 had a larger purpose: to let the BC government know that he had hunted without

Grazing elk. Photo courtesy of Alistair Fraser.

a licence, based on his Aboriginal rights. If charged with an offence under the Wildlife Act, he would plead not guilty, triggering a legal case to test the rights of the Sinixt to access their territory. *It took three times to get them to charge me,* he said. He laughs. *They had a hard time tracking me down and I think they had a lot of other stuff going on.* The first hunt resulted in a small bull elk and a buck white-tailed deer, both of which were distributed to Elders. The second hunt produced an elk, distributed to various tribal members as Rick drove home across the reservation. A third hunt produced an elk whose meat went into the Colville Confederated Tribes' food distribution system. Finally, he was cited under the BC Wildlife Act. The case testing his Aboriginal rights under the Canadian Constitution had begun.

Listening to traditional stories told by his grandmother over the years, Rick wondered to himself why they always involved animals and insects: chipmunk, grouse, wood tick, coyote, mosquito, bear…no people. *I asked her one day: Where were all the people in the stories? She says to me: They were the people. The animals were the people.*

A foundation of Lakes cosmology rests in the account of life on Earth before people. In Mourning Dove's preface to *Coyote Stories,* she explains that "the Animal People were here first." She calls these First Animals *Chip-chap-tiqulk,* also the name for the stories themselves.

The interrelationship between people, animals, insects and other living things emerges from this wise tap root: a cultural understanding of the interrelationship of all forms of biological life. Even life energy that is not overtly "alive," such as a rock, or a tree, can be filled with spirit. Mourning Dove's version of the traditional stories often describes Coyote, the transformer, as the agent for change, one who carries spirit everywhere. Spirit power can come from any animate or inanimate natural being: wind, rock, water, tree, even smoke. The animals. The people. Fire. Water. Forest. Rocks. All filled with spirit. Listening to Rick, watching the trial, hearing his song, learning more about why he does what he does, I gradually came to understand that the elk, the ladybug and the man are all of the same origin.

I guess it's in my DNA, being in the woods hunting and trapping. My father died when I was young. I was mentored by great hunters, my brothers. I learned where to place the shot. To know where an animal was wounded by the colour of the blood it dropped. That wounded animals always travel downhill. Lots of stuff my brothers taught me. And yeah, there's a couple of young ones learning and doing it now. The whole thing keeps going.

Beneath the surface of the Sinixt cultural material and practices I have been drawn to write about resides a continuity of dignity and patience, humility and grace, and acceptance and respect – for all nature gives the people. The BC appeal courts twice confirmed the original 2017 decision supporting Rick Desautel's Aboriginal right to hunt. It landed at the highest court in Ottawa. About that time, it dawned on me that the delicate spirit of a ladybug had brought down the BC government for colonial and deeply unjust policies. A ladybug quietly confronted a government that refused to change, refused to admit a mistake, refused to confirm what the historical record makes very clear. A small, seemingly inconsequential insect can still float on the spring air, lodge itself in the heart of a boy and support the development of a ceremonial hunter. This man, Rick Desautel, carried the ancestral link between people and land across the flimsy, invisible line, into the mountains where it all began.

"The hair, horns and hoofs are sometimes thrown away as useless, but no other part of the animal is suffered to be lost even the bones are pulverized to extract every particle of fat from them."

—John Work, Hudson's Bay Company clerk, 1829

R. V. DESAUTEL: RECLAIMING SINIXT IDENTITY

contributed by Mark Underhill, lead counsel for Rick Desautel

"Mr. Desautel, I hereby acquit you of these charges."[1]

Those were the last words spoken by BC Provincial Court Judge Lisa Mrozinski on March 27, 2017, as she delivered her reasons for judgment in the Nelson courthouse in the case of *R. v. Desautel*. For anyone in the courtroom that day, the memory of those words, and the wave of raw emotion that followed, will not soon be forgotten.

On April 23, 2021, just over four years later, a similar wave of emotion swept through the crowd of **sṅ ʕaẏ́ ckstx** (Sinixt[2]) people gathered on the shores of Kettle Falls (**Sx̌ ʷnitkʷ**), the major fishery that the Sinixt governed and managed for millennia, prior to its inundation by the Grand Coulee Dam. Young and old were gathered there in the early morning hours to receive the news of the judgment from the Supreme Court of Canada, the final stage of the journey of Rick Desautel and the Sinixt through the Canadian court system. Their victory that morning confirmed that the Sinixt were an Aboriginal People of Canada with constitutionally protected rights to hunt in their traditional territory in Canada.

In the space I have been given in this important book, I want to share some thoughts on the development of the case, and the important lessons it has taught us all about the impact of colonialism on Indigenous Peoples, and the enduring power of the connection between Indigenous identity and land. Like this book, the *Desautel* case has been able to shine a light on the often dark history of a people whose culture, traditions and very identity were pulled apart over the last 150 years, but who endured to experience those extraordinary moments in Nelson and Kettle Falls.

The hunting charges against Rick Desautel (hunting without a licence and as a non-resident) were first laid in 2010. The decision to send Rick to Canada to conduct a ceremonial hunt, and notify the provincial wildlife authorities, was years, if not decades, in the making, and I know it weighed heavily on the minds of a number of leaders within the Colville Tribes. "Everything" was at stake: if Rick's case failed, the result would be that the Sinixt would never be able to establish constitutionally protected rights in Canada, and in turn meaningfully carry out their culture in their traditional homeland north of the border.

When the case started to move forward in 2013, I sought advice from as many people as I could from the legal community, and more than one senior member of the Aboriginal law bar in British Columbia told me that *Desautel* was an "unwinnable" case; no Canadian court was ever going to find that a group of "American Indians," largely resident in Washington State, were an "Aboriginal People of Canada" with constitutionally protected rights.

My trepidation increased to some degree as we began to work up the evidentiary foundation for the case. I was fortunate to be able to travel around the Colville Reservation with the late Virgil Seymour, then the Sinixt cultural coordinator (a position now held by Shelly Boyd, the author of the foreword for this book), to interview a number of Sinixt Elders. We were both struck by the consistency of the evidence we heard (and that Virgil had also personally experienced in his younger days): specifically, that the parents and grandparents of the Elders had all been very reluctant to talk about the "move" to the reservation in the late 19th century, the reasons for it, and, more generally, the ways and culture of the Sinixt.[3]

Virgil believed that a number of factors were likely at play, perhaps the most important of which was that a collective trauma, and associated guilt and depression, surrounded the forced dislocation of the Sinixt from their homeland in Canada. The story of that dislocation is complex, and was not fully told in the *Desautel* case. But for me, the strength of the forces working against the Sinixt, and in turn the strength of their resiliency, is best captured by the amendments to the BC Game Act (now the Wildlife Act) back in 1896. In that year, a provision was added to the legislation that made it illegal for "non-resident Indians" to hunt in British Columbia. As the Crown's expert witness, Dr. Dorothy Kennedy, acknowledged during cross-examination at trial, that provision was passed by the legislature in Victoria on Vancouver Island specifically because of the conduct of the Sinixt in the West Kootenays. That is, despite the involuntary move south, and the establishment of the Colville Reservation in 1872, the Sinixt continued to return to Canada to hunt to such a degree that the local settler population in BC raised a hue and cry sufficient to get legislation passed hundreds of miles away. As Dr. Kennedy testified, it certainly demonstrated the importance of hunting – and hunting in Canada – to the Sinixt.

That testimony directly undermined a key thesis in her expert report – namely, that the Sinixt had voluntarily left their Canadian homeland to "enthusiastically embrace farming" on the Colville Reservation. It is important to note that, at that time, Dr. Kennedy, along with her colleague Randy Bouchard, was widely considered to be the leading scholar on the Sinixt, having embedded herself in the community many years before, and co-authored, among other publications, the Sinixt chapter in the prestigious *Smithsonian Handbook of American Indians*.

How, then, did the Sinixt overcome all of this, including Dr. Kennedy's troubling thesis, to prevail in *Desautel*?

It is first important to acknowledge the contributions of Dr. Andrea Laforet, who authored what the trial judge described as a "masterful" review of census documents and Oblate and Jesuit sacramental records to compile genealogies of 21 Sinixt families, including the Desautels, tracing them back to families living in British Columbia prior to 1830. That unprecedented work, which revealed the descendants of those families living in both Washington State and British Columbia (some among the Okanagan First Nation communities), was instrumental in shaping our thinking and approach to the case. It also helped overcome the systems imposed on both sides of the border that attempted to redefine Sinixt identity through a non-Indigenous lens. South of the border, the "blood quantum" system for confirming tribal identity is in use on the Colville Reservation, and in Canada, the much (and properly) maligned Indian Act dictates who can or cannot be a band member. Dr. Laforet reminded us that Indigenous identity is not defined by a government-issued card but by the familial and cultural connections that bind together a people.

In my view, however, the most important contribution came from the Sinixt People themselves, whose evidence went in entirely unchallenged, and left the trial judge with "no doubt as to the veracity of their belief." Among others, Rick himself spoke of the "chills that went up and down my spine" when he had the opportunity to hunt in Canada where his ancestors had hunted since time immemorial. Perhaps the most powerful evidence came from Shelly Boyd:

[Nsyilxcen spoken]. This land is so sacred. This is – this is – when I say we come from this land, I mean we come from this land. We come from the animals of this land. We come from the water of this land. We come from this place. And it doesn't matter what people say. This is – the truth is this is where we are from [.....]

It's, like, people talk about, like, never having gone to Ireland, and then they go and it changes their life. And for us, it's like we know. We know. And, like, my friend Insinkalink [sp?] Virgil [Seymour] would say is, like, we never left this river. We never left this water. Even being part of that Confederation of Tribes. We are Sinixt first. And all I can say is this is sacred, and it hurts. It hurts when I hear things like – that we – I can't remember the thing about, like, enthusiastically leaving. People can say that – whatever they want, you know, about us being farmers or school councillors or whatever, but every one of these Lakes people, they have deer meat in their freezer, and that's what they live off of, and that's – it wouldn't even matter if they did have a cow or – I don't know how many cows it takes to be a farmer, but the thing is they know. They know how to hunt. And it's not – you don't go out with a gun and shoot something. That's not hunting, you know. Hunting is much different than that.

If you talk to Ricky, you know what, he can tell you about what it takes for a deer or any of those four-legged animals to live for a year. It's part of who we are. And I don't think I have the words to really explain that. In our language it is so much more connected. Our language doesn't say random things. It says [Nsyilxcen spoken]. It doesn't say how are you. It says what is your heart like. How is your heart. You know, it says specifically what we are. Like, haa-haa ^ [sp?]. You know, that's sacred. It's, like, you can hear it. But I couldn't say what this means to me. Maybe – you know, maybe that's why we have a winter dance. We can sing it.

In my view, this evidence confirms why Dr. Kennedy's abandonment thesis, a doctrine that British Columbia continues to advance in litigation to this day, is offensive and has no place in Canadian law. Indigenous identity is defined by an enduring and unbreakable connection to land. To be Sinixt is to be from their **tm̓ xʷúlaʔxʷ** in Canada. There has never been, nor will there ever be, a "voluntary" abandonment of Indigenous territory by those who have stewarded it for thousands of years, and who have a sacred obligation to continue to do so for future generations. It betrays a complete lack of understanding of the Indigenous perspective to even suggest the contrary, let alone to pursue it aggressively in litigation.

When thinking about this issue, I am always reminded of a conversation I had during the trial with the sister of one of our Sinixt witnesses, who approached me to thank me for our team's work on the case. She said she had struggled through depression and addiction in the past, but sincerely believed that the case could make her and all Sinixt People "whole again." The Supreme Court of Canada has now confirmed that the Sinixt People are indeed whole again, such that they can finally embark on the long overdue process of reconciliation in their Canadian homeland.

> "They [the Lakes Indians] are under the jurisdiction of the Indian authorities of the United States and therefore the status of the nomadic marauders on Canadian territory becomes an international question that should be settled between the two governments. They should be made to understand by the United States Government that they have no rights to land north of the boundary line."
>
> —*Kootenay Mail*, April 13, 1895

IN CLOSING

The pursuit of wild food forges a unique relationship with landscape. In hunting or gathering local nourishment, we encounter directly the unique aspects of our bioregion: its abundant patches of berry, its patterns of animal migration, its rhythms of swimming fish. Nature transforms from an outdoor museum that we carefully wish to preserve, or place of adventure that we sometimes selfishly consume, into a terrain with which we form a basic, direct relationship: nourishment. By baking a huckleberry pie, grilling an elk steak or gutting a kokanee, we are temporarily released from the idea of food as a purchased commodity grown in an out-of-sight land, or even as the product of our careful labours in a garden. We are transported momentarily back into a wilder aspect of human existence, when meat and fruit arose directly from the immediate world around us. When the offerings of the natural world were paid for not with currency, or even with the effort of a shovel and seeds, but with intuitive ingenuity, with gratitude and with care. Wild food has its own price, of course. It requires persistence and patience to seek it out, a willingness to accept different flavours, and the ability to face directly the role of being taker at the top of the food chain. In return, a more complete relationship with the natural world develops, one with a foundation of interdependence between human beings and nature. In the role of participant, human beings can counteract the tendency in many contemporary societies to value human needs over all others in a natural system. What is our collective responsibility?

"At the height of land I was in hopes that we had struck an Indian trail when suddenly our guide informed me that we had been traveling for the last half hour, not upon an Indian, but a carriboeuf road.... Carriboeufs frequent this part of the country [the Pend d'Oreille and Salmo River valleys] in large numbers, as the woods are traversed by their beaten track)."

—John Sullivan, Palliser's expedition, September 1859

Twenty years ago, the common way to refer Indigenous culture and lifestyle in studies by anthropologists and archaeologists was "hunter-gather." This category, like so many created by those in the colonial world where people stand outside the Indigenous culture and look in, does not fully capture the intricacy of Indigenous relationship with natural systems. The publication of *Maps and Dreams* (1982), and then *The Other Side of Eden* (2000), by Canadian anthropologist Hugh Brody, reflected an increased understanding of the rich relationship Indigenous People have with place. More recent work of ethnobotanists and Indigenous knowledge keepers has spent more time listening, helping to translate to the settler culture a distinct perspective on plants and animals that considers all elements of natural systems to be alive, and all plants and animals to be relations. While it is true that Indigenous People hunted and gathered in traditional times, they also *managed* or cared for the resources in their territories, connecting as they still do through their hearts. Their science was – and still is – to acquire knowledge through intensive observation over thousands of years; to know the landscape, its plants, animals, seasons and resources intimately. Sinixt People have always depended to one degree or another on the seasonal rhythms of these resources in a way that even contemporary berry pickers, fishers or hunters can only imagine. Their millennial relationship with the upper Columbia can be better understood by listening to all the ripening wild berries, even the less palatable ones. It can inform issues related to wildlife management, as modern science makes attempts to partially restore balance to the habitat for the region's once-abundant mammals, birds and fish. The once-prolific resources echo across the lives of beings that struggle to survive in a contemporary landscape greatly altered by dams and electricity: sturgeon, bull trout, giant rainbow trout, kokanee, caribou, beaver, mountain goat and others.

The miraculous return of the kokanee each autumn urges all of us toward a greater revaluing of the wild, and a stronger sense of responsibility. So close to being extinguished in the early 1990s, kokanee populations have increased again simply because we, the colonial human inhabitants, began to think sensitively about the needs of the fish, not just our own interests. We recognized in time the importance of substituting nutrients that had been trapped and depleted by dammed water. And while the artificial feeding of water systems is not an ideal solution, it is an example of how everyone can form a more reciprocal relationship with the places where we live. We have further to go in the protection and fostering of caribou habitat, not to mention sturgeon, Gerrard rainbow and many others.

In September, I watch the **kəkn̓ iʔ (kokanee)** struggle valiantly upstream with their red skirts flashing in the current. I revel in their miraculous, cyclical return. The ocean sockeye salmon, saltwater sister to the kokanee, wants to come home to join them. What are we willing to exchange for rivers to bulge with that marine life again? Can we give as well as take? The stories of the Sinixt are like fish eggs, released into the gravel for rebirth. They have been long enough embedded. I wish for them, like the swimmers themselves, to spring to life and re-enter the wild streams of time, participants in a renewing cycle of wisdom and respect for the landscape. The spirit of a place and its First People can enrich the present and inform the future of this landscape.

"A good honest man would distribute [fish] to everybody, and sometimes not keep any for himself."

—An unnamed Sinixt informant to Verne Ray, 1930s

Appendices

Mountain Goat and the Origin of Huckleberry

~~~~~~~~~~

Note: This is a transcript of a story told to anthropologist William Elmendorf by Sinixt Elder Nancy Wynecoop, in 1935–36. During that time, Elmendorf's fieldwork on the Spokane Indian Reservation resulted in the surprise discovery of a Lakes woman who carried in her heart and memory a rich trove of cultural information about her people. This is an exact transcription of the myth as it appears in Elmendorf's field notebook, with paragraph breaks added for legibility. Wynecoop, fluent in her own Lakes dialect, the Spokane language and English, appears to have provided her own translation.

"Myth times" was also called "the time when they made things" and refers to the creation period in Lakes Indian oral history. Eagle, person who lived at Kettle Falls; she was a very beautiful creature; in myth times; her teachers decided to give her to the best runner; report was sent all over and competitors come to Kettle Falls; course led over rough ground and precipice; one precipice hung directly over the Columbia; Mountain Goat lived far up north in the mountains; he sent his sons; the eldest had already come to Kettle Falls to court the Eagle; she despised him and so did all the people; their legs, big horns, thick body;

Old Goat decides to send rest of his sons and restore his honour; they brought huckleberries as their contribution to the doings; When they got to Kettle Falls the people all said: "here are some of those ugly creatures coming; how can they ever run a race with their thick bodies"; all the racers were out there with their contributions; the goats were so unpopular that their contribution was set aside and not grouped with the others; the other brother goat was sitting by himself despondently; the brothers planted a huckleberry bush they had brought from home in front of this brother; he ate all the berries off it and felt all spruced up and recovered his self-respect after this act of kindness;

The people finally decided to let the goats run although nobody thought they could win; at the beginning of the race the goats all grouped together while running and everybody laughed to see them do this; after running they came to the cliff and raced right across the face of the rock; none of the other animals could do that, so they won the race by a long way; At the beginning the old grandmothers went over and were going to throw the huckleberries in the river; when they saw them go across the face of the cliff, they won the people's esteem; the grandmothers then brought the choice basket of berries over to the girl for her to taste and name; she named it the "sweet berry"; from the bush the goats had planted come all the huckleberries now in this part of the country;

The goats after the race did not force themselves on the people or Eagle; they just set out for home; Eagle followed after them: Eagle said that when she saw the goats in her home at Kettle Falls she thought them very shabby; but as they traveled toward home their coats became white as snow and she saw how they nibbled only the dewy tips of fresh grass; she tended carefully Old Goat and was able to accompany the goats about the mountains. So Old Goat adopted her and she married the eldest son and stayed in the mountains; she builds her nest there still. Fish Hawk, Buzzard, Water Snake, Mountain Magpie; all natives of the place all followed after the goats to marry them.

Watersnake never got as far as the mountains where the sna'itskstx [Sinixt] live, just to where the Kootenay hits the Columbia. Eagle married the oldest goat. Some of the girls followed the goats when they got up to where the old man lived. The Fish Hawk [osprey] saw Jack Rabbit ("Long ears"); Rabbit was sitting in the corner and every time he moved his head his ears flopped and made her giggle; she also laughed at the old chief goat because of his appearance; instead of attitude of reverence; the boys didn't like this at all so they sent her away; she came down out of the mountains into the Columbia River Valley; can be heard screaming as she fishes there yet.

SOME COMMON WILD FOOD PLANTS OF THE SINIXT/ ARROW LAKES INDIANS

COMMON NAME (PART EATEN)	BOTANICAL TERM	SINIXT DIALECT
black tree lichen	*Bryoria fremontii* *Bryoria fuscenscens* *Alectoria fremontii*	**sqʷí̓ip**
western larch (pitch)	*Larix occidentalis*	**čiqʷí̓x**
ponderosa pine (cambium, seed, pitch)	*Pinus ponderosa*	**sʔatqʷłp** (tree) **c̓íxʷiʔ** (cambium; also refers to sap running) **sq̓aw̓q̓w̓** (seeds) **t̓ič̓** (pitch)
*blue camas (bulb)	*Camassia quamash*	**ʔíʔtx̌ʷaʔ** (bulbs) **ṅʔíʔtx̌ʷaʔm̓** ("patch")
yellow glacier lily (bulb)	*Erythronium grandiflorum*	**sxʷixʷ** (also used for rice)
yellow bell (bulb)	*Fritillaria pudica*	**x̌aʔtímṅ**
tiger lily (bulb)	*Lilium columbianum*	**stx̌čiṅ**
false Solomon's seal and star-flowered Solomon's seal (shoot, rhizome)	*Smilacina racemosa and Smilacina stellata*	**t̓xay̓ápaʔ**
**cow parsnip (flower stalk, leaf stem)	*Heracleum lanatum*	**x̌ʷəx̌ʷtiłp**
chocolate tip (young shoot)	*Lomatium dissectum*	**ʕ̓ayúʔ**

little white camas (bulb)	*Lomatium farinosum*	**túxʷaʔ** (with white "camas" being understood to be biscuit root [lomatium])
yampa (root)	*Perideridia gairdneri*	**sƛ̓ukʷm̓** (used for both wild caraway [Perideridia gairdneri] and desert parsley [*Lomatium macrocarpum*])
arrow-leaved balsamroot (root, shoot, seed)	*Balsamorhiza sagittata*	**smúkʷaʔxn̓** (root), though commonly used to refer to the plant **smkʷaʔxnílp** (plant) **miktúʔtn̓** (seeds and the name for the month of June)
tall Oregon grape (fruit)	*Berberis aquifolium*	**sc̓r̓siłp** **sc̓r̓siłəmíx** (common name for all Oregon grape) **sc̓əc̓ris** (berries)
hazelnut (nut)	*Corylus cornuta*	**q̓íp̓xʷaʔ**
blue elderberry (fruit)	*Sambucus cerulea*	**c̓kʷikʷ**
red osier dogwood (fruit)	*Cornus stolonifera*	**stikčxʷ**
soopolallie (fruit)	*Shepherdia canadensis*	**sx̌ʷusm̓** (foam berry)
kinnikinnick (fruit)	*Arctostaphylos uva-ursi*	**skʷlis** **skʷlsiłəmíx** (kinnikinnick vine/bush)

COMMON NAME (PART EATEN)	BOTANICAL TERM	SINIXT DIALECT
mountain huckleberry (fruit)	*Vaccinium membranaceum*	sťxałq sťxłqiłəm̓ lx (bush)
dwarf blueberry (fruit)	*Vaccinium caespitosum*	səsapt
gooseberry (fruit)	*Ribes irriguum*	ṅt̓it̓m̓lps
Canby's lovage/ bear root (root)	*Ligusticum canbyi*	x̌asx̌s
western spring beauty (corm)	*Claytonia lanceolata*	sk̓ʷṅk̓ʷinm̓
bitterroot (root)	*Lewisia rediviva*	sp̓iƛ̓m̓
saskatoon (fruit)	*Amelanchier alnifolia*	słaq (berries) síya? (berries) skəksáła?q (seedy variety of berries) slhkilhp (bush)
black hawthorn (fruit)	*Crataegus douglasii*	sxʷa?ník sxʷa?ṅkiłp (bush) stm̓uqʷ (red hawthorn berries)
wild strawberry (fruit)	*Fragaria virginiana*	tq̓im̓tq̓m̓
chokecherry (fruit)	*Prunus virginiana*	ləx̌ʷłax̌ʷ
blackcap (fruit)	*Rubus leucodermis*	mčakʷ (blackcap wild raspberry) məčk̓ʷiłəml̓x (bush)
thimbleberry (fruit)	*Rubus parviflorus*	pal̓p̓lqṅ (berry) pl̓p̓lqniłəm̓l̓x (bush)

*Careful identification required. Not to be confused with highly poisonous death camas (*Zigadenus* spp.).

** Careful identification required. Not to be confused with highly poisonous water hemlock (*Cicuta bulbifera*).

Shelly Boyd with freshly harvested x̌ʷəx̌ʷy̓ iłp (devil's club/*Oplopanax horridus*) from the Laird Creek drainage. "It's a really good medicine for auto-immune issues." Photo courtesy of Mike Graeme.

Notes:

1 This list is not comprehensive. Royal BC Museum ethnobotany books and notes on ethnobotany found in the region's botanical standard *Plants of the Southern Interior* do not identify the Sinixt specifically. Their identity in these resources has been qualified as "Okanagan," based on a language rather than tribal grouping. The most authentic source of Sinixt ethnobotany remains Nancy Wynecoop's interview notes by William Elmendorf, or the Royal BC Museum's *Ethnobotany of the Okanagan-Colville Indians of British Columbia and Washington State*, currently out of print but available in PDF format through ResearchGate.net.

2 Sinixt place names often associate with the plants growing there. They also identified seasons for the food plant available then, at that time. Plants having flower or fruit are considered to be "male," while those having only leaves are "female." In traditional times, the Sinixt dissolved the pitch of čiqʷɫx (western larch) in hot water to make a

Shelly Boyd translates bog orchid (*Habenaria dilatata*)'s Sinixt name, **sqəqi̓qíla?xʷ**, as "a bunch of little Indians." This plant has a strong spiritual aspect. Author photo.

syrup and also ate it right off the tree like candy. They chewed the pitch of **s?atqʷłp** (ponderosa pine) like gum. They crushed the roots of **sƛ̓ukʷʷm̓** (yampa), mixed it with cooked **sqʷłip** (black tree lichen) and then formed it into balls for winter food. **N̓t̓it̓m̓łps** (wild gooseberries) were a staple – eaten green (May/June) and ripe (July/August). They crushed **skʷlis** (kinnickinnick berries) and pressed them into cakes to serve with salmon eggs as ceremonial food. The fruit of **sc̓r̓siłp** (Oregon grape) was considered by the Lakes Indians to be too tart to eat raw, but they juiced them in hot water. The Lakes also juiced elderberry, gooseberry and wild raspberry in this way. They crushed **q̓íp̓xʷa?** (hazelnuts) and mixed them with preserved meat and berries to form cakes that were then dried by the fire. All food prepared this way was called **ststa?** ("hammered food"). **Stikčxʷ** (dogwood berries) were eaten raw, as a kind of relish. **Paɬ̓pɬ̓qn̓** (thimbleberries) were highly prized among the Lakes.

3 This table is based on information provided by Sinixt Elder Nancy Wynecoop (granddaughter of Able One), recorded in the field notes of William Elmendorf and extracted from Nancy J. Turner, Randy Bouchard and Dorothy Kennedy, *Ethnobotany of the Okanagan-Colville Indians of British Columbia and Washington State.*

A collage of various pictograph images from around the Sinixt homeland.
From tracings by John Corner, courtesy of the Corner family.

"THINGS WISHED FOR OR DESIRED" –
UNDERSTANDING PICTOGRAPHS

On a rainy, cool, late-summer day in 2014, I joined a group of Sinixt
People from the United States on a boat ride across Slocan Lake. Then
Sinixt facilitator, Virgil Seymour, had arranged the trip. It was made
possible by a local New Denver man's long, broad canoe, fitted with
an outboard motor. We headed across the agitated water from the east
shore of the lake, with brisk winds swirling around us. Our destination
was a series of granite bluffs on the lake's west shore where a cluster of
pictographs are still clearly visible. Pictographs have been documented
in many places across Sinixt territory, and also exist in other places not
yet formally documented: Trout Lake, Kootenay Lake, the West Arm
of Kootenay Lake, the Kootenay River upstream of Brilliant Dam, the
Arrow Lakes valley, etc.

Virgil Seymour with Joanne Signor. Photo courtesy of Shelly Boyd.

For some on the journey, it was their first time at this ancestral location of Slocan Lake, even their first time across the border into Canada. No one, other than the local man piloting the boat and me, had yet seen the pictographs. As we crossed, I talked about pictograph research, mostly things I had read in books. I was not aware that my intellectual knowledge was soon to be decisively overruled – by a tribal sincerity, integrity and spiritual understanding that humbled me entirely. There is still so little I understand about life lived close to water in traditional Indigenous times. There is even less I can know about how that tradition informs the characters of the people who know they are Sinixt.

We approached the west shore. The local man slowed his boat, a signal that we were drawing near to one of the pictographs. As the tribal members began to fix their gazes on the rock cliffs, I realized then that my words were irrelevant to their experience. Embarrassed, I finally went quiet. We drew in close to one panel of rock paintings. Shelly Boyd began to sing softly and sweetly in the Sinixt language. The beauty of her feminine voice curled around us as the motor idled and the boat swelled gently over the waves stirred by the late-summer storm. I bowed my head. It was a few years before I could ask Shelly what she had been singing that day. Her answer was simple and pure. *I was greeting the pictographs. Telling them we were all so happy to see them again, after so long. Telling them how much we loved and cared about them.*

In 1968, John Corner self-published *Pictographs in the Interior of British Columbia*, a survey of all the pictograph sites he had seen and mapped in the BC Interior Plateau – from the Okanagan to the Rocky Mountain trench – during eight dedicated years of exploration and inquiry. Having spent his childhood in the West Kootenay region, Corner imbued his book with an obvious affection for the scenic valleys and waterways of the mountains north of the border, those places inhabited in traditional times by the Sinixt. Corner's book reflects the author's strong affinity to "the mystery of the unknown" that he believed pictographs represented.

Though he did not record every pictograph in existence, his lovingly crafted and important work preserved the memory of many pictograph sites before they were degraded by time or destroyed by settler development. His careful tracings of what he discovered are works of art themselves. The same year he published his book, the province of BC allowed several of the sites he had identified in the Arrow Lakes valley to be destroyed – by road building or being flooded behind Hugh Keenleyside Dam (then known as the High Arrow Dam). As other pictographs throughout the upper Columbia and Interior Plateau regions have continued to degrade naturally over time, Corner's work takes on more value. The reproductions are a window into another world.

Pictograph sites are a strong signifier of Interior Salish culture. According to ethnographer James Teit, by spending time at these sites, tribal "novices" in the Salish world could gain power and knowledge "to help them in after years." Positioned in places where the mysterious forces of nature were believed to be in greater abundance and strength, the sites offered seclusion, inspiration and open expanses of granite on which to record extraordinary visions or experiences, or the acquisition of a spirit-song. Almost always, these sites are beside rivers or lakes. Sometimes, they are located along trails or important crossroads. Indigenous People sometimes painted pictographs on rocks whose shape suggested metamorphosed animals, gods or human beings. With pictographs, people could record "things wished for or desired" – such as the strength to be an able hunter, a shaman or an excellent basket weaver. Men as well as women might cultivate personal power or a central

The aptly named Paint Lake, near Mount Symons on the west side of upper Arrow Lake. Photo courtesy of Arrow Lakes Historical Society.

purpose for life in this way. They could share their inner experiences with their community by painting on rock.

Pictographs locate themselves and their rituals firmly in the landscape, recognizing and respecting the often unacknowledged and yet mysterious power embedded in the natural world. Corner's book observes that almost all of the 105 panels of pictographs that he surveyed in BC's Interior face south or west, as do the panels I witnessed that day with Sinixt People. As well as orienting pictographs toward the sun, the Sinixt buried their dead to face the rising sun in traditional times. According to Teit, they also enlisted a tribal Elder to pray for the sun to return before dawn each morning.

The great bulk of BC Interior pictographs are painted in red. This colour, according to Teit, was, for the Salish, "symbolic of life, goodness, [and] good luck." The paint was made either from the mineral hematite (in its pure form, a deep red), or limonite (a vibrant yellow mixed with water and baked by the fire, after which it, too, would turn a beautiful red). The Sinixt ground these minerals to a powder, mixed them with clay, bear grease and other ingredients, and then applied the colour with a finger or the tip of a bird's feather to the granite canvas. Formulas for the paint varied, with families or tribes guarding the privacy of certain ingredients. The raw red mineral was a popular Indigenous trade item throughout the interior, and the upper Columbia region appears to have had a good supply. In 1810, David Thompson was told by a Kalispel guide that downriver of present-day Metaline Falls, rich deposits of the mineral existed in the steep canyons and mountains around the lower Pend d'Oreille River. Known deposits also exist along the Lardeau River north of Kootenay Lake, in the shadow of Vermilion Peak (2649 m), in the East Kootenay, and beside Mount Seymour at Paint Lake, high above the west shore of the former Upper Arrow Lake. Likely there are more.

Much can be made of the meaning of various pictographs. Relying on Teit, who relied on his Nlaka'pamux (Thompson Indian) wife and her relations, Corner's book includes a large table identifying common images – from insects to snakes, stars to bighorn sheep, tule mats and bark canoes. Teit commented that anyone who tried to interpret the images "would know nothing of certainty" beyond their obvious literal meaning, though he added that an image of an animal might, for example, reflect a wish to be good at hunting, or one of an unfinished tule mat, a wish to weave them successfully for the tribe. It seems important when viewing the pictographs not to overinterpret with too much confidence, but to maintain a measure of curious awe and respect.

The cosmology pictographs represent is important for all of us, Indigenous or non-Indigenous, to contemplate. The Salish tribes, the Sinixt among them, perceive a raw power in the natural world. They strive to relate to natural power directly, as Shelly Boyd did that day with her respectful and loving song of praise. The tribes also respect unseen, internalized experience as valid and true, even if there is no rational explanation for a vision, a desire or a dream that comes to them. In the right circumstances, they believe that these internal experiences are worthy of sharing, linking the world in which they live day to day with their rich inner tapestries.

How old are the pictographs? I'm not sure it really matters. Their beauty is timeless and graceful. Speculating about dates does not seem relevant. Teit himself may have asked the same question of those he learned from. Several Salish Elders explained to him that the pictographs had been painted "since time immemorial." Corner believed that a relatively recent period of painting, as little as 500 or fewer years ago, "started spontaneously, flourished and then ended as quickly as it began." Any upsurge of pictograph art across time may have been related to times of food abundance, social security or the strong leadership of a Chief who could bring spiritual prosperity and happiness. It may also have been related to experiences of collective spiritual crisis. Many unanswered questions about these rock paintings remain. Really, that is just fine. We can be grateful for Teit's unpublished notes and Corner's book, as well as for the relatively enduring quality of ochre and granite, all of which connect us to an upper Columbia Renaissance, when mystical art flourished. Of the field trip across Slocan Lake that day, Shelly Boyd describes it years later as "one of my favourite memories in my life." For the contemporary Sinixt, with easy access to sites of traditional meaning having been severed by a boundary for over a century, "things wished for or desired" takes on far more meaning than Teit ever could have imagined. The losses they experience sharpen the meaning and significance of precious moments when the work of their ancestors can be viewed.

Teit's original *Notes on Rock Painting in General, Spences Bridge* is at the Glenbow Archives (mss. M3689), and as a typescript on file at the Touchstones Nelson Museum. Corner's book is out of print, but may be available at some regional libraries.

PREHISTORICAL AND HISTORICAL TIMELINE

Note: Due to the small number of archaeological excavations that have taken place in the upper Columbia, this timeline can only suggest the depth and accuracy of prehistoric inhabitation. Knowledge of prehistoric upper Columbia culture will remain extremely limited and theoretical until more archaeological work can be done. Though archaeologists have named prehistorical phases by geographical region, cultural practices of these periods are not limited to those locations. All prehistoric dates are measured in relation to the present (b.p.: before present)

10,000 b.p.–3500 b.p. Big-stemmed points found at Deer Park north of Castlegar are consistent with the cultural inhabitation of the Interior Plateau dating back 10,000 years. Very little is known about this period of earliest settlement of the upper Columbia, which began shortly after the warming of the climate and retreat of glaciers between 13,000 and 9500 b.p.

3500 b.p.–2450 b.p. The Winlaw Phase. The Winlaw Phase is the earliest period archaeologists have been able to define cohesively. Archaeological finds associated with this phase: "stemmed and shouldered" projectile points, unmodified flake tools and pit house dwellings, usually centred around areas of salmon resource.

2450 b.p.–1250 b.p. The Vallican Phase. This period of inhabitation demonstrates an increase in the complexity of tools and a continued use of pit house dwellings. Archaeological finds associated with this phase: "corner and basally notched" projectile points, scrapers, "key-shaped" perforating and scraping tools, ground stone or bone tools and mammal bones of great variety.

1250 b.p.–250 b.p. The Slocan Phase. While pit houses remain in use, some excavations appear as oval and some as rectilinear. Shallow rectilinear depressions suggest the possible growing use of rectangular mat lodges at this time. Archaeological finds associated with this phase: "side notched" points, a wide variety of stone materials used in tool making, "flexed" skeletal burials, food cache pits, roasting platforms and fire pits.

1770 A.D. The first of several epidemics dramatically reduces Aboriginal populations in the upper Columbia through the arrival of smallpox passed from intertribal trade.

1811 David Thompson arrives in the Arrow Lakes valley as he searches for a navigable route to the Pacific.

1825 Hudson's Bay Company (HBC) establishes "Fort Colvile" (later spelled "Colville") near present-day Kettle Falls, Washington, at the sight of a traditional Aboriginal trading centre.

1830 Sinixt People from the Arrow Lakes valley winter for the first time at Fort Colvile, when ice impedes their return north.

1838 Quebec (Oblate) Mission Jesuits baptize 17 Lakes children at HBC "Fort of the Lakes," constructed that same year near Arrowhead.

1846 Catholic missionary Pierre-Jean De Smet visits the Arrow Lakes and converts more Sinixt living near Arrowhead, at a traditional village site now under water. The International Boundary Treaty is signed, marking the 49th parallel as the dividing line between the colony of British Columbia and the United States of America.

1850 The Sinixt continue to make seasonal use of as many as 28 traditional village sites in the upper Columbia.

1852 Findings of gold are reported at Fort Shepherd, initiating a rush to "49 Creek" in the 1860s.

1856 The HBC constructs "Fort Shepherd" on the west side of the Columbia River just under a mile north of the international boundary.

1861 Gold Commissioner W.G. Cox arrives at the confluence of the Columbia and Kootenay rivers to settle conflicts between miners and Indigenous inhabitants and marks the area "Indian Reserve." Miners trapped by weather are helped through the winter by Aboriginals living just south of Revelstoke.

1865 Walter Moberley (of the Columbia River Exploration Expedition) passes through the upper Columbia, recording some Indigenous trails settlement.

1870 Fort Shepherd closes, signalling an end to the fur trade era in the upper Columbia.

1871 British Columbia joins the confederation of Canadian provinces.

1872 Fort Colville closes. The US Government establishes an Indian Reservation stretching from the international border to central Washington.

1882 The Bluebell Mine is staked, prompting large numbers of miners to begin entering the upper Columbia in search of their own motherlode.

1885 Completion of CPR at Revelstoke. J.C. Haynes purchases land for a townsite at the mouth of the Kootenay River that had been previously set aside by Gold Commissioner Cox as "Indian Reserve."

1886–88 The Silver King Mine outside Nelson begins exploration for hard rock mines.

1892 The US Government purchases from the Colville Confederated Tribes the northern portion of the Colville Indian Reserve.

1894 Sam Hill shoots and kills Cultus Jim at Hill Creek.

1896 One source reports that 60–70 Sinixt who still inhabit a traditional village site at the outlet of Slocan Lake must move south in response to the explosive growth of Slocan City.

1902 The Canadian Government establishes the Arrow Lakes Indian Reserve at Oatscott on Lower Arrow Lake.

1909 Ethnographer James Teit conducts fieldwork among Sinixt living at the mouth of the Kootenay River.

1912 Peter Verigin purchases traditionally occupied Sinixt land at the mouth of the Kootenay River from the estate of J.C. Haynes.

1914 The Christian family moves south to the US. Alex Christian relocates his cabin to the mouth of Syringa Creek.

1920s Alex Christian dies of old age.

1928–31 Archaeologist Harlan Smith corresponds with local collectors and eventually travels west to explore the upper Columbia region.

1934 Last known salmon caught near Nelson at Slocan Pools.

1935–36 Ethnographer William Elmendorf conducts fieldwork among Lakes Indians living in Washington State.

1948 The "1948 Flood" causes extensive damage in communities on the Columbia River, from Trail, BC, to Astoria, Oregon, initiating international negotiations for the Columbia River Treaty.

1956 The Arrow Lakes Indian Band is declared "extinct" by the Canadian Government. The rolls of the US Indian Reservation of the Colville Confederated Tribes list 257 Aboriginals of Lakes ancestry that year.

1961 The Columbia River Treaty is signed, initiating a national controversy in Canada. The US Senate immediately ratifies the agreement.

1964 Canada ratifies the agreement. Planning and construction of flood-control dams (Mica, Keenleyside and Duncan) begins.

1961–62 Archaeologist Peter Harrison conducts a four-month archaeological survey of the Arrow Lakes valley for the BC Government prior to inundation.

1968 Water rises in the Arrow Lakes valley after the completion of the Keenleyside Dam. Of 152 recorded cultural sites, only 12 remain above water when inundation is complete.

1970s–80s Ethnographers Randy Bouchard and Dorothy Kennedy conduct interviews with Lakes Indians living on the Colville Indian Reservation.

1980s Human burials are unearthed during road building near Vallican. Archaeological work results in Vallican being declared a BC Heritage Site.

1989 Sinixt People travel from Washington State to occupy the Heritage Site in order to protect burials and begin a long process of repatriating remains.

1990s Robert Watt, appointed by the tribe to caretake the burial site, contests a Canadian Immigration order of deportation. The order is quashed, but without a ruling on Aboriginal rights.

2016 *R. v. Desautel* finds for Desautel and confirms Sinixt Aboriginal rights in Canada.

2017 *R. v. Desautel* decision upheld on appeal by BC Supreme Court.

2018 *R. v. Desautel* decision upheld on appeal by BC Court of Appeal.

2020 *R. v. Desautel* decision upheld by Supreme Court of Canada, 7–2.

Notes

Parting the Veil of Time

For more on government policy related to Indigenous People in BC in the mid-20th century, see Wilson Duff, *The Indian History of British Columbia: The Impact of the White Man*, Rev. ed. (Victoria: Royal BC Museum, 2014).

The Canadian policy of denying transboundary rights related to ownership of allotments on the North Half is detailed in "In the Matter of the Indian Act, Being Chapter 149 of the Revised Statutes of Canada, 1952, and in the Matter of the Inquiries Act (Part 2)," RG 10, Indian Affairs, vol. 8215, 1954, Library and Archives Canada.

For a detailed account of the Vallican blockade, see "Remembering the 1989 blockade in the Vallican," *Tribal Tribune*, October 24, 2016. See also Laura Stovel, *Swift River* (Revelstoke, BC: Oregon Grape Press, 2019).

Robert Watt's legal case is referenced in Greg Boos, Heather Fathali and Greg McLawsen, "The History of the Jay Treaty, and Its Significance to the Cross-Border Mobility and Security for Indigenous Peoples in the North American Northern Borderlands and Beyond," in *The North American Arctic: Themes in Regional Security*, ed. D. Menzies and H. Nicol (London: UCL Press, 2019), 35–66.

For more on the oral agreement between HBC Governor George Simpson and the Salmon Chief at Kettle Falls, see Eileen Delehanty Pearkes, *A River Captured: The Columbia River Treaty and Catastrophic Change* (Victoria, BC: Rocky Mountain Books, 2016).

Henricus and the Priest's Pen

With particular thanks to Andrea LaForet for detailed genealogical research, and input on this essay.

See also Chad S. Hamill, *Songs of Power and Prayer in the Columbia Plateau: The Jesuit, the Medicine Man and the Indian Hymn Singer* (Corvalis: Oregon State University Press, 2012); The Joset Papers, quoted in Sister Maria Ilma Rauffer, *Black Robes and Indians of the Last Frontier* (Milwaukee: Bruce Publishing, 1966); and Noah Elia, Colton Clark and Jeff Doolittle, "Fashioning Identity by Reduction: Jesuit Influence on the Coeur d'Alene Culture," https://www.sutori.com/story/fashioning-identity-by-reduction-jesuit-influence-on-the-coeur-d-alene-culture--E2KiiLmgPmxVEScDZYdmvuN9.

Andrea LaForet, "Sinixt (Lakes) Familial Connections to British Columbia," February 2015, an expert report available to the public through supporting documents and evidence filed in the provincial court of BC, for *R. v. Desautel* (2016), 2017 BCPC 84, [2018] 1 C.N.L.R. 97 (Mrozinski J.).

Dead and Buried

Further details about the incident involving the Sinixt burial grounds at Needles can be found in the Olds-Flick interview, on file with the Arrow Lakes Historical Society.

Swimming Upstream

Technical and cultural information for this section was provided by Joe Peone, director of the CCT Department of Fish and Wildlife, and D.R. Michel, executive director of Upper Columbia United Tribes (UCUT). The natural capital report by Earth Economics can be downloaded from https://ucut.org/habitat/value-natural-capital-columbia-river-basin/. The Colville Confederated Tribes maintain a website with information on Chief Joseph Hatchery and the sockeye restoration, as well as their adaptive management and selective harvesting approach to mitigate the impact of hatchery fish on wild stocks. Much of the analysis of this important foundational period in salmon restoration comes from my own witness, in attendance at meetings and conferences between 2012 and 2019.

Half-Truths Mis-Truths and the Founding of Nelson

More details of the story of Nelson can be found in "What Happened to Richard and Alfred Fry," *Spokesman-Review*, July 11, 1954; "The Dramatic Story of the Silver King Mine," *Spokesman-Review*, November 30, December 7, 14 and 21, 1958; or in *My Home: Collected Writings of Goldie Van Putnam Author & Historian*, as gathered and privately printed by Crystal A. Putnam Lawson, circa 2007. With special thanks to Sinixt Elders Nancy Michel and Gary Kohler for tracking tribal affiliations and lineage, and to West Kootenay historian *par excellence* Greg Nesteroff. See also file no. 19, "The Hall Family and the Silver King Mine," by Pauline Battien, located on file in the Shawn Lamb Archives, Touchstones Museum of Art and History.

The North Half of the Colville Reservation

1 "Tribe Debates Termination," *Spokesman-Review* (Spokane, WA), March 4, 1964; John McAdams Webster Papers, cage 145, container 2, folder 5, Washington State University's Holland and Terrell Library Special Collections (hereafter WSU HTSC), "Interrogation of Chief Barnaby of the Colville Reservation by John M. Johnson, Clerk and Acting Agent of the Colville Agency," October 16, 1906; "Letter from John McAdams Webster to The Commissioner of Indian Affairs, July 8, 1907"; Laurie Arnold, *Bartering with the Bones of Their Dead: The Colville Confederated Tribes and Termination* (Seattle: University of Washington Press, 2012), chap. 1.

2 The Indian Claims Commission grew out of the old Court of Claims, created in 1855. President Harry Truman signed the ICC into law in August 1946.

3 National Archives and Records Administration Washington, DC, branch (hereafter NARA DC) Record Group 75, Colville 054, Central Classified File 2 (hereafter RG 75, Colville, CCF 2), box 21, folder 00-1953-054, part 1, Colville, "Colville Agenda Colville Business Council With Commission Glenn L. Emmons Yakima, Washington," p. 2.

4 The Business Council began pursuit of restoration by the late 1940s, but the process became formalized in the early 1950s.

5 House Concurrent Resolution 108, introduced by Senator Henry M. Jackson and passed during the 83rd Congress, August 1, 1953 (H. Con. Res. 108), 67 Stat. B122.

6 "3 Old Indian Chiefs Join in a Discussion of New Plan," *Spokane Daily Chronicle*, June 28, 1954.

7 Congress, House Committee on Interior and Insular Affairs, Subcommittee on Indian Affairs, *Restoring to tribal ownership certain lands upon the Colville Indian Reservation, Washington, and for other purposes*, 84th Cong., 2d sess., 1956. The victory was qualified in another way as well. As Congressman Horan predicted, Congress tied the land restoration to termination, and the CCT had five years to draft a plan to end federal recognition. However, it turned out that the Business Council was ultimately correct, too; the government changed its mind about termination and renounced the policy before the CCT became subject to it.

Submerged by Water and Time

The Kettle River excavation is detailed in Phase I Report of the Boundary Archaeological Survey September 25, 1978–June 1, 1979, Permit no. 1978-27, and in Phase I Supplemental Report of the Boundary Archaeological Survey July 1–September 21, 1979, both by Michael A. Freisinger.

After excavation, the canoe came to rest in the basement of the Grand Forks city hall. Later renovations meant that the canoe could not be removed intact. It had to be cut in half for removal and display in the Boundary Museum and Interpretive Center in Grand Forks, where it sits today. Special thanks to museum coordinator Owen Cameron for help with this story. For more see Freisinger's report, on file in the Selkirk College local collection in Castlegar. The report's extensive bibliography provides many primary sources for a further understanding of the upper Kettle River's human history.

Links in a Jewelled Chain

Sinixt descendant Patti Bailey led the legal effort on behalf of the entire CCT for nearly two decades, and has hiked extensively in the Big Sheep Creek area.

According to family genealogical records, Justine Fry's second son George was born at Sheep Creek, in about 1861. A full summary of the archaeology team's findings can be found in Donald Collier, Arthur Hudson and Arlo Ford, *Archaeology of the Upper Columbia Region*, University of Washington Publications In Anthropology 9, no. 1, pp. 1–178 (Seattle: University of Washington

Press, 1942). For more on gender equity, see Lillian Ackerman, *A Necessary Balance: Gender and Power among Indians of the Columbia Plateau* (Norman: University of Oklahoma Press, 2013).

R. v. Desautel

1. 2017 BCPC 84, para. 187.

2. For ease of reference, I will use the term Sinixt throughout, but much is lost in that translation – see para. 22 of Judge Mrozinski's Reasons for Judgment, at 2017 BCPC 84, [2018] 1 C.N.L.R. 97.

3. At trial, Dr. Michael Marchand, then Chairman of the Colville Tribes and a direct descendant of Sinixt Chief Aurapahkin, told a powerful story of his own father's reluctance to share the reasons why he hung a deer heart up in their yard after a hunt, and his regret at never having had that conversation before his father's death.

Contributor Bios

LAURIE ARNOLD is an enrolled Sinixt member of the Colville Confederated Tribes. She is an associate professor of history and director of Native American Studies at Gonzaga University. She has previously held positions at the D'Arcy McNickle Center for American Indian and Indigenous Studies at the Newberry Library in Chicago and at the University of Notre Dame. Her family has deep connections to Kelly Hill, the North Half and what is currently British Columbia.

LADONNA BOYD-BLUFF is a Sn̓ʕayckstx (Lakes) member of the Colville Confederated Tribes. She is very connected to her community, family and people. Ladonna has worked for many years in tribal health and wellness and is an advocate for spiritual and cultural revitalization. Ladonna and a team of consultants are developing an integrative healing model for Indigenous People. She's very proud of this project.

SHAWN BRIGMAN, PhD, is an enrolled member of the Spokane Tribe of Indians and descendant of the Sn̓ʕayckstx (Sinixt), sənpʕʷilx (San Poil), and tk'emlúps te secwepemc (Shuswap). As a northern Plateau recovery artist for 15 consecutive years, he has practised ancestral recovery efforts in Washington, Idaho, Montana and British Columbia. He aims to educate and transform the way Indigenous and settler people read Plateau architectural space by celebrating the physical revival of ancestral art and architecture.

LARAE WILEY is **Sn̓ʕayckstx** (Sinixt), Arrow Lakes Band. She is a proud grandmother of five grandchildren and is one of the new fluent speakers of the highly endangered Sinixt language. She is the executive director and a founder of Salish School of Spokane. Salish School of Spokane is a non-profit organization that operates two Salish immersion childcare/preschool centres, a Salish immersion private elementary school, a Native Youth Empowerment Center for Grades 8–12, a Salish language teacher training program and community Salish language classes.

Judge in 1972.

JUDGE WYNECOOP is one of seven sons. His mother was the first enrolled Spokane tribal member to achieve teacher certification. His father, Cil-speelya, was born on a blanket of five coyote pelts. His grandmother worked with linguist William Welcome Elmendorf during two summers of fieldwork on the reservation in 1935–36, when she shared Sinixt traditional ways and language, instilled in her by her mother Ellen and her grandmother Sepetza (Able One).

MARK UNDERHILL is a partner with Arvay Finlay LLP in Vancouver, British Columbia, where he maintains a general civil litigation practice, with particular expertise in Aboriginal, administrative and environmental law. He represented Rick Desautel in all four levels of court through to the Supreme Court of Canada.

Selected Bibliography

Note: Many reports and scholarly surveys that detail Sinixt ethnography and archaeology are now available online, including scanned copies of the Elmendorf notes from his important interview with Nancy Wynecoop, and her own remarkable memoir, *In the Stream*. James Teit's original field notes are at the BC Archives in Victoria. *The Ethnobotany of the Okanagan-Colville*, a Royal BC Museum book produced in 1980 by Nancy Turner, Randy Bouchard and Dorothy Kennedy, is the best resource for specific information on the use of plants by the **Sṅ ʕayckstx** (Sinixt). Although RBCM publications have been slow to acknowledge the Sinixt as the distinct tribe that they are, and this publication's particular misnaming of tribal identity as "Okanogan-Colville" was in error, the information in it is invaluable.

Ackerman, Lillian. *A Necessary Balance: Gender and Power among Indians of the Columbia Plateau*. Norman: University of Oklahoma Press, 2003.

Baker, James. Murphy Creek Project/Heritage Resource Detailed Impact Assessment. BC Hydro, January 1983.

"Being on the Land: Histories at the Confluence." *Symposium on the People of the Kootenay and Columbia Rivers*. Mir Centre for Peace at Selkirk College. June 19, 2007. Available through the Mir Centre for Peace.

Belyea, Barbara, ed. *Columbia Journals: David Thompson*. Montreal and Kingston: McGill-Queen's University Press, 1994.

Boos, Greg, Heather Fathali and Greg McLawsen. "The History of the Jay Treaty, and Its Significance to the Cross-Border Mobility and Security for Indigenous Peoples in the North American Northern Borderlands and Beyond." In *The North American Arctic: Themes in Regional Security*, edited by D. Menezes and H. Nicol, 35–66. London, UK: UCL Press, 2019.

Bouchard, Randy, and Dorothy Kennedy. First Nations' Ethnography and Ethnohistory in British Columbia's Lower Kootenay/Columbia Hydropower Region. Castlegar, BC: Columbia Power Corp., 2000. Reprinted 2005.

———. *Indian Land Use and Occupancy in the Franklin D. Roosevelt Lake Area of Washington State.* Report prepared for the Colville Confederated Tribes and the United States Bureau of Reclamation, 1984.

Collier, Donald, Alfred E. Hudson and Arlo Ford. *Archaeology of the Upper Columbia Region,* University of Washington Publications In Anthropology, vol. 9, no. 1, pp. 1–178. Seattle: University of Washington, 1942.

Corner, John. *Pictographs in the Interior of British Columbia.* Vernon, BC: Wayside Press, 1968.

Duff, Wilson. *The Indian History of British Columbia: The Impact of the White Man.* Rev. ed. Victoria: Royal British Columbia Museum, 1997.

Eldridge, Morley. *Vallican Archeological Site (DjQj1): A Synthesis and Management Report.* Victoria, BC: Heritage Conservation Branch, 1984.

Elmendorf, William. [Field notes of Lakes Indian Culture and ethnography recorded from Lakes informant Nancy Wynecoop]. BC Archives. Accession no. 934888.

Franchère, Gabriel. *A Voyage to the Northwest Coast of America.* Edited by Milo Qauife. New York: Citadel Press, 1968.

Freisinger, Michael. *Phase I Report of the Boundary Archaeological Survey: September 25, 1978–June 1, 1979.* Permit no. 1978-27.

———. *Phase I Supplemental Report of the Boundary Archaeological Survey: July–September 21, 1979.*

Geiger, Andrea. "Crossed by the Border: The US-Canada Border and Canada's 'Extinction' of the Arrow Lakes Band, 1890–1956." *Western Legal History* 23, no. 2 (2010): 121–53.

Harper, Russell J. *Paul Kane's Frontier, including Wanderings of an Artist Among the Indians of North America.* Toronto: University of Toronto Press, 1971.

Hart, E. Richard. "Maps Showing Sinixt Territory, 1811–46." *Cartographia* 55, no. 4 (2020): 219–40.

Hobrook, Stewart H. *The Columbia.* New York: Rinehart & Co., 1956.

Johnson, Kate. *Pioneer Days of Nakusp and the Arrow Lakes.* Naskup, BC: Self-published, 1951.

Keddie, Grant. "Social Patterning in 'Rock Art' and Other Symbolic Objects of the Interior Salish." Victoria: BC Provincial Museum, 1974.

Kennedy, Dorothy, and Randy Bouchard. "Northern Okanagan, Lakes and Colville." *Handbook of North American Indians,* vol. 12: Plateau. Edited by Deward E. Walker Jr., Washington, DC: Smithsonian Institution, 1998.

———. "Utilization of Fish by the Colville Okanagan Indian People." Copy of an unpublished manuscript in possession of the BC Indian Language Project, Victoria, BC, June 1975.

Lakin, Ruth. *Kettle River Country: Early Days along the Kettle River.* Orient, WA: Self-published, 1976.

Limerick, Patricia Nelson. *The Legacy of Conquest: The Unbroken Past of the American West.* New York: W.W. Norton, 1987.

Mohs, Gordon. Archeological Investigations at the Vallican Site (DjQj1), Slocan Valley, Southeastern BC, 1982.

Mourning Dove. *Cogewea, the Half-Blood.* Lincoln: University of Nebraska Press, 1981.

———. *Coyote Stories.* Edited by Heister Dean Guie. Lincoln: University of Nebraska Press (Bison Books), 1990.

———. *A Salishan Autobiography.* Lincoln: University of Nebraska Press, 1990.

Parish, Roberta, Ray Coupé and Dennis Lloyd. *Plants of the Southern Interior.* Vancouver: BC Ministry of Forests and Lone Pine Publishing, 1996.

Pryce, Paula. *"Keeping the Lakes' Way": Reburial and the Re-creation of a Moral World among an Invisible People.* Toronto: University of Toronto Press, 1999.

Putnam, Goldie Van Bibber. *My Home: Collected Writings of Goldie Van Bibber Putnam, Author and Historian.* As gathered by Crystal A. Putnam Lawson. Privately printed in the USA, *ca.* 2007.

Ray, Verne. "Native Villages and Groupings of the Columbia Basin." *Pacific Northwest Quarterly* 27, no. 2 (1936): 99–152.

Reyes, Lawney. *White Grizzly Bear's Legacy: Learning to Be Indian.* Seattle: University of Washington Press, 2002.

Schlick, Mary Dodds. *Columbia River Basketry: Gift of the Ancestors, Gift of the Earth.* Seattle: University of Washington Press, 1994.

Stovel, Laura. *Swift River.* Revelstoke, BC: Oregon Grape Press, 2019.

Teit, James. "The Salishan Tribes of the Western Plateaus." In *Forty-fifth Annual Report of the Bureau of American Ethnology, 1927–28*, edited by Franz Boas, 23–396. Ms. no. 171, National Anthropological Archives, Smithsonian Institution, Washington, DC, 1930.

———. *Fieldnotes on Thompson and Neighboring Salishan Languages* [circa 1904–13]. Copy held by the BC Archives and Records Service, Victoria. Add. Mss. 1425, Microfilm A-262.

Turner, Nancy J. *Ancient Pathways, Ancestral Knowledge: Ethnobotany and Ecological Wisdom of Indigenous Peoples of Northwestern North America.* 2 vols. Montreal: McGill-Queen's University Press, 2014.

———. *Food Plants of Interior First Peoples.* Vancouver: UBC Press/Royal BC Museum, 1997.

———. *Plant Technology of First Peoples in B.C.* Vancouver: UBC Press/Royal BC Museum, 1998.

Turner, Nancy J., Randy Bouchard and Dorothy Kennedy. *Ethnobotany of the Okanagan-Colville Indians of British Columbia and Washington*. BC Provincial Museum Occasional Papers Series, no. 21, 1980.

Turner, Nancy J., and Dawn C. Loewen. "The Original 'Free Trade': Exchange of Botanical Products and Associated Plant Knowledge in Northwestern North America." *Anthropologia* 40 (1998): 49–70.

The Value of Natural Capital in the Columbia River Basin: A Comprehensive Analysis. Earth Economics, for the Upper Columbia United Tribes, Spokane, WA, 2017. https://ucut.org/habitat/value-natural-capital-columbia-river-basin/.

Wah, Fred. *Pictograms from the Interior of B.C.* Vancouver: Talonbooks, 1975.

Weir, Craig. "Written in Stone: Exploring Kaslo's Prehistory." N.d., n.p.

Wong, Rita, and Fred Wah. *Beholden: A Poem as Long as the River*. Vancouver, BC: Talonbooks, 2018.

Wynecoop, Nancy, with N. Wynecoop Clark. *In the Stream: An Indian Story*. Spokane, WA: Privately printed, 1985.

Acknowledgements

Many Sinixt People, living and ancestral, have inspired me with their stories, songs and cultural practices over the years. In particular, I'd like to thank Able One, Eva Orr, Virgil Seymour, D.R. Michel, Michael Finley, Rick Desautel, Shelly Boyd, Patti Bailey, Nancy Michel and Judge Wynecoop.

Randy Bouchard and Dorothy Kennedy provided important academic expertise, linguistic ability and editorial input in the first edition. Special thanks to Alan Ramsden for his memories of the pre-dam landscape around Nelson, and for the folk and academic knowledge of Janis Palmer, Charlie Maxfield, Gary Birch, Peter Jordan, Dale Anderson, Tom Braumandal, Ursula Lowrey, Ted Antifeau, Nancy Turner and Paula Pryce. To the institutions and individuals who safeguard our region's colonial cultural heritage; the Colville Confederated Tribes, departments of wildlife and history and archaeology, who have been responsive and supportive; Grant Keddie, archaeology curator at the Royal BC Museum since 1972; Romi Casper, Heritage Resource Centre; Nakusp Museum; Kyle Kusch and the Arrow Lakes Historical Society; Revelstoke Museum and Archives under the leadership of the indomitable Cathy English; Touchstones Nelson Museum of Art and History (especially Shawn Lamb, who retired in 2009, and archivist Jean-Philippe Steinne); and last but not least, the Nelson Public Library.

Bob Price started it all when he said *let's do it* and published the 2002 edition. Don Gorman and the staff at Rocky Mountain Books have helped the second edition grow gracefully and reach a wider audience. Peter Enman paid care and attention to the Sinixt language and other editing details. Mike Graeme and the Corner family both generously shared visual materials for this edition.

More than I could measure, I appreciate my loyal family and community, those who have supported me in sustaining an independent voice as a writer all these years.

Index

abalone, 196–97
abandonment thesis, 215
Able One, 82, 108, 155, 156
Ackerman, Lillian, 83, 196
Adeline (wife of Cultus Jim), 55, 57–58,
    60–61
adzes, 33, 80, 102, 190
alcohol, 155
Allard, Jason, 106
Antoine, Chief, 156
Arcasa, Thomas, 159
archaeological collecting, 62–66
Arnold, Evelyn, 34
Arnold, Laurie, 22
Arrowhead, 20
Arrow Lakes
    archaeology of, 62–66
    basket-makers of, 98
    flooding of, 56–59, 68
    LaRae Wiley on, 60–61
    narrows, 62
    natural history of, 16, 45
    navigation, 151
Arrow Lakes Indians. See Sinixt People
Arrow Rock, 68
assimilation, 186–87
Astley, W.J., 147
avalanche lilies, 129
baby boards, *51*
Bailey, Patti, 97–99, 103, 159, 198
Bailey, Sheppard, 158, 159

Baillie-Grohman, W.E., 160
Baker, James, 69, 71, 144
Balfour, 153
balsamroot sunflower, 70, 87–89, 174, 188
Barbe, Charles St., 166
bark
    for baskets, 99, 100–103, 107
    for canoes, 25, 29–31, 33, 34–35, *38*,
        40–41, 55, 172, 190, 231
    food for hares, 47
    harvesting, 33, 36, 102–3
Barlee, Bill, 190
Barr, William, 91
baskets, cedar, 97–103, 195–96
BC Game Act, 213
bear grass, 102
bears, 12, 55, 107, 130, 138, 147, 203, 204,
    205, 206
bear traps, *204*
Beaver Creek, 153
Beckwith, Brenda, 85, 87
Bernard, Chief James, 15, 95, 182
berries, 107–12, 201–3
Big Bend, 163
Big Sheep Creek, 193
birchbark, 100
bitterroot, 12, 70, 196
Blackfeet people, 157
Blanchet, Reverend, 50
blankets, 47, 48

"blood-quantum" system, 214
Blueberry Creek, 74
Bluff, J.R., 80
Boaz, James, 101
Bonner's Ferry, 158, 164, 165, 166, 167
Bonneville Dam, 115
Bonneville Power Administration
    (BPA), 113, 114
Bonnington Falls, 145, 151, *152*
border, Canada-US, 20–5, 53–54, 60–61,
    76–77, 78, 163, 170–71, 172–73, 183,
    190–91, 209–10, 212–13, 216
Bossburg, 108
Bouchard, Randy, 2, 3, 14, 43, 134, 204
Bourgeois, Joe, 136
bowls, 136–41
Boyd, Agnes Christian, *78*
Boyd, Harry, 78–79
Boyd, Jim, 3, 79
Boyd, Shelly, 4, 82, 95, 172–73, 181, 203,
    213, 214–15, *225*
Boyd-Bluff, Ladonna, 78–81
Brigman, Shawn
    about, 33–34
    basket fish traps of, 39–41
    paddles of, 41
    sturgeon-nosed canoes of, 34–38
    tule lodges of, *35*, 41
Brilliant, 24, 69, 70–75, 133, 143, 144
Brilliant Dam, 70, 74, 133, 143, 144
British Boundary Commission, 190
Brody, Hugh, 217
Brown, Charles, 159, 164
Brown, William, 164
Bunting, Arthur, 165–66
Bureau of Indian Affairs (BIA), 186, 187
burial sites
    Arrowhead, 145
    Big Sheep Creek, 193
    Brilliant, 73, 74
    Castlegar, 144
    disturbance of, 141–43, 144–45
    Fauquier–Castlegar (map), *67*
    Gold Island, 143–44

Grand Forks, 190
grave contents, 194–95
Lower Arrow Lake, 24
Needles, 144
No. 46, 194–95
No. 47, 193–95, 196, 198
Revelstoke–Fauquier (map), *42–43*
Rossland–Omak (map), *90–91*
Sandy Island, 144
Slocan Lake–Slocan Pool (map), *125*
traditional practices, 141
Vallican, 27, 142–43
burning, controlled, 129
Burris, Meloni, 142
Burton, 59, 63, 98

camas, 81–87, 129–30, 196
Cameron, William, 49
Campbell, Bob, 47
Campbell, Lola, 108
Canada–US border, 20–25, 53–54, 60–61,
    76–77, 163, 170–71, 172–73, 183,
    190–91, 209–10, 212–13, 216
canoes
    archaeological finds, 188–92
    design and construction, 25, 29,
        30–33, 34–37, *77*, 188
    in hunting, 205
    last known traditional, 31
    paddles, 41
    Salmon Ceremony and, 119
    sturgeon-nosed, 31, 34–38, 40–41, 45
    travel by, 31, 33, 45, 70, 71, 149–53, 190–91
caribou, 15, 153, 205, 217
carving, 41, 138, 188, 194–95, 205
Cascade Falls, 181, 188, *189*, 190
Castlegar, 11, 16, 69–71, 73–75, 76, 82, 85,
    94, 144, 232
Cawston, Rodney, 121
Cayuse Creek, 150
Cebula, Larry, 156
cedar, 12, 33, 97–103, *119*
Charles St. Barbe, 163
Chief Joseph Dam, 113–14, 115, 117, 118,

120, 121, 177, 178

Chinook jargon, 55–56, 202

chokecherry, 102

Christian, Adeline Augusta, 78

Christian, Alex ("Indian Alex"), 74, 75, 76, 78–81

Christian, Baptiste, 31, 72–74, 76, 78

Christian, Marie (Mary), 78

Christian family, 24, 73

Christina Lake, 16, 108–12, 191–92

Chumash people, 196

Circling Raven, 50

climate change, 48–49, 116–18

cod, freshwater, 153

Coeur d'Alene tribe, 50

Collier, Donald, 193, 194

Collins, Tom, 166

Columbia Mountains, 7, 9–10, 15–16, 19, 44–45

Columbia River
    Chief Joseph Dam, 113–14, 115, 117, 118, 120, 121, 177
    confluence with the Kootenay, 69–75, 77, 82–84
    geography of, 149–54
    governance of, 115
    importance to Sinixt, 70–71
    Keenleyside Dam, 57, 59, 62, 145
    narrows, 62
    natural history of, 45, 46, 48–49, 81–82, 83, 87–88, 92–93, 96–97
    as a "person," 119
    polluted by Teck, 197–98
    Sinixt north-south travel on, 149–51, 162–63
    in Sinixt story, 127–28
    See also fisheries; salmon

Columbia River Treaty, 26, 57, 115–16, 118, 119–20, 188

Colville Confederated Tribes (Skoyelpi)
    attempted assimilation, 186–87
    care for burial sites, 194
    diet and food practices, 88–89
    fighting pollution by Teck, 197–98

Fish Accord, 113–14
    language, 16
    relations with settlers, 145, 172, 184–88
    relations with Sinixt People, 18, 95, 111, 175
    restoring salmon, 118, 120, 121–23
    traditional territories, 169, 172, 209–10

Colville Indian Reservation
    author's visit to, 5
    "blood-quantum" system on, 214
    establishment of, 213–14
    forced migration to, 60–61, 78–79, 80, 181, 184
    "North Half" of, 25, 52, 60–61, 181–82, 184–88

Comaplix, 43

Cominco, 197–98

controlled burning, 129

Corra Linn Dam, 160

"country wives," 155–56

Cox, W.G., 70–71

Coyote Rock, 147

Coyote the trickster, 96, 147, 151–52, 179, 180, 211

Crescent Valley, 136–37

Cultus Jim, 54–60

dams
    archaeology and, 63, 68
    Bonneville, 115
    Bonnington, 151
    Brilliant, 70, 74, 133, 143, 144
    camas destroyed by, 85
    camas fields eliminated by, 83
    Chief Joseph, 113–14, 115, 117, 118, 120, 121, 177
    Columbia River Treaty and, 25–26
    Corra Linn, 160
    Grand Coulee, 93–94, 96, 97, 113–14, 115, 117, 120, 121, 136, 175, 177, 179, 193, 212
    harm to wildlife, 96–97, 218

Keenleyside, 57, 59, 62, 70, 145
Kootenay Canal, 133
Libby, 160
South Slocan, 133
Waneta, 104–5
dancing, 18, 32, 61, 129, 197, 203, 215
deer, 205
Demers, Reverend, 50
dentalia, 134–36
Desautel, Linda, 142–43
Desautel, Madeleine Paul, 207–8, 210
Desautel, Richard
    ancestry, 52
    R. v. Desautel, 53, 76–77, 208–15
    spirituality of, 207–8
    Vallican burial site and, 142–43
De Smet, Father Pierre-Jean, 51
Dewdney, Edgar, 71, 145
digging sticks, 85, *86*, 87, 88, 194–95, 206
diptheria, 20, 50
disease, 19–20, 50, 52, 89, 154, 155
Douglas, David, 45, 83
Doukhobors, 73–75
Downey, Narcisse, 164
dreams, 5, 78
Durrand Glacier, *11*
dyes, 102

Edge, Eli, *56*
Edgell collection, 66, 141
Edwards, Catherine, 156, 164
Edwards, Sophie (Green Blanket Feet),
    154–59
Elders, 3, 36, 48, 53, 78, 96, 99, 104, 121,
    185, 196, 207, 210, 213
    See also names, e.g., Wynecoop,
    Nancy
Eldridge, Morley, 126, 143
Elmendorf, William, 32, 34, 39, 127, 131, 141
Environmental Protection Agench
    (EPA), 198

Fabi, Sylvain, 119–20
Finlay, Jaco, 83

Finley, Lucy, 142
Finley, Mike, 113, 117, 177–80
Finley, Pat, 142
fisheries
    decline on the Columbia, 22
    freshwater cod, 153
    Kettle River, 103–4, 177–80, 188–90
    kokanee, *90*–91, 130, *146–47*, 162
    locations, *42–43*, *67*–68, 70, 82, *90*–91,
        94–96, *125–26*, *146–47*
    restoring, 97, 113–24
    sturgeon, 41, 82, 118, 218
    trapping, 39–40, 94–95
    trout, *42–43*, 82, *125–26*, 130, 132,
        146–47, 153
    See also salmon
fish traps, 39–40, 94, 95–96
Flat Creek, 60
Flathead Nation, 53
Ford, Arlo, 193, 194
Fort Colville, 20, 22, 53, 145, 153, 154, 190
Fort of the Lakes, 20, 43, 54, 233
Fort Shepherd, 22, 53, 104, 106
Fort Spokane, 171
Fort Steele, 71
Fosthall Creek, 14, 50
Franchère, Gabriel, 46
Frazier, Adell, 164
Freisenger, Michael, 188–93
French, Diana, 162
Friedlander, Randy, 123
Frog Mountain, *128*, 131
frogs, 127–28, 139, *140*
Fry, Alfred, 163
Fry, Christina, 164, 165–66
Fry, Julia Ella, *166*–67
Fry, Richard, 91, 104, 163–64
funnel basket traps, 39–41
fur trade, 20, 22, 23, 43, 50, 71, 83, 94, 104,
    105, 130, 135, 155, 157, 163, 171, 172

Galbraith, May Etue, 108
Galbraith, R.L.T., 73
Galena Bay, 55–59

game laws, 24–25, 212–13
    See also R. v. Desautel
Geiger, Andrea, 23
Gigot, Rosina, 139
glacier lilies, 196
Gold Island, 143–44
gold rushes, 19, 70, 89, 156, 163–66
Goldstream River, 163
Goodale, Nathan, 134, *135*
Grand Coulee Dam, 93–94, 96, 97,
    113–14, 115, 117, 120, 121, 136, 175,
    177, 179, 193, 212
Grant, Ulysses S., 184
graves. *See* burial sites
Green Blanket Feet (Sophie Edwards),
    154–59
Gregoire, Chief (Kessewilish), 22, 51
Grohman Creek, 16, 147, 161, 162
Grohman Narrows, 151, 152, 153,
    160–62
groundhogs, 205

Hall, Winslow, 164–65
Hallenius, Alyce Perkins, 159
hares. *See* rabbits, snowshoe
Hayes, Rutherford B., 172
Haynes, J.C., 71, 73
Haynesville, 71
hazelnuts, 206
hemlock, 29
Henricus, 52, 53, 156, 163
Herridge, H.W. "Bert," 26–27
Hill, Sam, 55, 57–58, 60–61
Horan, Walt, 186, 187
horses, 89, 190
House Committee on Indian Affairs
    (US), 185
houses, 16–17, 22, 45, 104–5
Howath, James, 159
huckleberries, 107–12, 202–3, 219–20
Hudson, Alfred E., 193, 194
Hudson's Bay Company (HBC), 20, 22,
    53–54, 83, 95, 154, 190
Huff, Valerie, 85, 87

hunting
    attitudes to, 201, 203–4, 205, 211,
        214–15
    bears, 55, 75, 130, 147, 203, 204–5
    caribou, 15, 153, 205
    ceremonial, 207–15
    commercial, 130
    deer, 205
    elk, 205, 210
    groundhogs, 205
    mountain goats, 68, 205, 206
    sheep, 205
    traditional, 204–5
    war about, 18
    See also R. v. Desautel
Hupa people, 196

Ickes, Harold, 186
Inchelium, 52, 60, 134, 142, 175, 182, 207
Incomappleux River, 6, 43, 55, 56, 107
Indian Act, 214
Indian Affairs, 73–74
Indian Alex (Alex Christian), 74, 75,
    76, 78
Indian chocolate (camas), 81–87
Indian Claims Commission, 187
"Indian ice cream," 202–3
Indian potato, 196
influenza, 20
inoculation, 52
Interior Salish people, 16
invasive species, 88

James, Chief Jim, 187
Jay Treaty, 172
Johansson, Eva, 85
Johnson, Kate, 145
Joset, Father, 52
Jr, Charles Brown, 159

Kalispel Tribe, 36, 53, 82, 109, 111, 231
Kamiakin, Chief Cleveland, 187
Kane, George, 167
Kane, Paul, 95

Karuk people, 196
Kaslo, 167
Keating, George, 159
Keddie, Grant, 62
Keenleyside Dam, 57, 59, 62, 145
Kelly Hill, 60, *180*, 181–82, 183, *183*
Kennedy, Dorothy, 2, 3, 14, 43, 204, 213–14, 215
Kettle Falls
    archaeological finds at, 16
    celebration of *R. v. Desautel*, 212
    as core Sinixt territory, 16, 88, 91, 94, 176–77
    David Douglas exploring, 83
    fishery, 18, 22, 23, 45, 88, 94–96, 188, 212
    Green Blanket Feet (Sophie Edwards) in, 157, 158
    Hudson's Bay Company at, 20, 22, 83, 95, 190
    inundation by Grand Coulee dam, 176–77, *179*
    missionaries at, 50
    natural history of, 82, 87, 203
    place name, 95, 175
    Salmon Ceremony, 41, 103–4, 118–19, 121–23, 176, 180, 207
    settlers of, 157, 164, 184
    sharpening stone at, *117*, 180
    significance to the Sinixt, 176, 177–78
    Sinixt village near, *67–68*
    Sinixt villages near, 67–68, *90–91*
    in story, 219–20
Kettle Falls Interpretive Center, 203
Kettle River, 16, 175, 180–81, 188, 190, 190–93
Kettle River Indians, 190
Kohler, Joyce, 103
kokanee, *10*, 55, 58, *90–91*, 130, *146–47*, 162, 218
Kootenay Camas Project, 85
Kootenay Canal Generating Station, 133
Kootenay Lake
    archaeological finds at, 139

David Thompson exploring, 19, 150
    natural history of, 16, 45, 149, 160
    Sinixt legend about, 147
    Sinixt use of, 16, 19, 153
Kootenay River
    confluence with the Columbia, 69–75, *77*, 82–84
    dams, 24, 69, 70–75, 133, 143, 144, 160
    geography of, 149–54
    Grohman Narrows, 151, 152, 153, 160–62
    natural history of, 70, 82, 132, 145
    salmon weir at, 68
Kreps, E.H., 47
Ktunaxa people, 18, 24, 36, 70, 162, 164
Kuskanax, 43
Kuskanax Creek, 26
Kutenai people, 18
Kwakwaka'wakw people, 197

Laforet, Andrea, 50, 51, 52, 53, 214
Lakes Indians. *See* Sinixt People
Lakin, Ruth, 182, 183, 207
lamprey, 118
land claims, 26, 187–88
land sales, 185–86
larch, 29
Leighton, Caroline, 82, 83, 87
Libby Dam, 160
lichen, 138–39
Limerick, Patricia Nelson, 182
Little Ice Age, 45
Lloyd, Mary, 159
Louie, Martin, 88, 134, 136, 204
Louis, Jerry, 38
Lower Kootenay Band, 36, 164
Low Pass, 108
Lum, Alvina, 93

Manhousat people, 197
maps, *13*, *21*, *42*, *67*, *90*, *125*, *146*, *150*, *169*, *192*
Marchand, Mary, 104, 194
Marcus, 74, 82, 108, 158, 159, 164
marriage, 155–59, 163, 164, 167

Marshall, Clark, 43
Mason, Virginia, 34
matrilocal society, 17, 83
mauls, 137–41
Maxfield, Charlie, 62–66
McDonald, Angus, 95–96
McDougall, Rev. John, 73
McKay's House, 20
McRae Creek, 192
measles, 20
medicine, 50, 61, 78–81, 89, 99, 172, 196
Megraw, A., 74
Michel, D.R., 113, 115, 118, 120, 121, 177
Michel, Nancy, 103
Mifflin, Rollie, 154
Mir Centre for Peace, 34, 35, 38, 75
missionaries, 22, 50–51, 53–54, 156, 214
Mohs, Gordon, 65, 134, 142
Morin, Jessica, 34
Mosquito Creek, 59
mountain goats, 68, 130, 205
Mourning Dove, 88, 159, 210–11
Mrozinski, Lisa, 212
Murphy, Harry, 59
mussels, 132–35

Nakusp, 26–27, 43, 80
Nauman, Alissa, 134
Needles, 24, 144
Nelson
    archaeological finds in, 139, 141
    change since pre-colonial period,
        149–53
    founding of, 160–68
    Sinixt villages, 146–47, 162
Nez Perce Tribe, 95, 122, 187
Nicholas, Chief Victor, 187
Nisbet, Jack, 150
"non-resident Indians," 213
"North Half" (of Colville Reservation),
    25, 52, 60–61, 181–82, 184–88
Northport, 60, 194
Northwest Museum of American Arts
    and Culture, 39

Nuu-chaah-nulth people, 197
Nuxalk people, 197

Oatscott reserve, 24, 71, 72, 73
Ohlone people, 196
Okanagan First Nation, 16, 53, 88–89,
    122, 134, 162, 214
Okanagan Nation Alliance, 53, 114
Okanagan River, 113, 114, 115, 134
Omak, 52, 93
Orr, Eva, 93, 97, 108
oxeye daisy, 88

paddles, 41
Palliser's expedition, 217
Palmer, Janet, 64
Paul, August, 207, 208
Paul, Joe, 153
Pearkes, Eileen, 112
Peel, Julia Fry Kane, 166
Pelky, Robert, 156
Pend d'Oreille River, 3, 53, 82, 94, 104,
    163, 164, 184, 214–15, 217
Peone, Joe, 113
Perry, Madeline, 191
Pia Mission, 60, 181
Picard, Edouard, 43
Pichette, Louis, 89
Pickford, A.E., 138–39, 141
pictographs, 18, 42, 67, 90–91, 125–26,
    150, 190, 191, 227–31
pit houses, 16–17, 22, 45, 49, 73, 104–5,
    134, 135, 136, 144, 162, 191
Playmor Junction, 143–44
polyandry, 155
polygyny, 155–56
Pomo people, 196
Public Law 772, 187
Putman, Goldie van, 179

Quenquenchen. See Green Blanket Feet
Quigg, Jimmy, 84
Quintasket, Charlie, 2, 27

rabbits, snowshoe, 47–48
racism, 4, 58, 167
Ramsden, Alan, 161
Ramsden, William, 161
Ray, Verne, 24
reconciliation, 4, 6, 75–77, 124, 174, 216
religion. *See* missionaries; spirituality
reservations (US), 2, 22, 23, 54, 60,
    171–72, 184–88
    See also Colville Confederated
    Tribes; Colville Indian
    Reservation
reserves (Canadian), 11, 23–24, 70–72
Reyes, Lawney, 75, 175
rheumatism, 89
Robson, 84
Rosemont, 162
Ross, Alexander, 68, 94, 134–36
Ross, John, 83
Royal BC Museum, 66, 138, 139, 141
Royal Commission on Indian Affairs, 74
R. v. Desautel, 53, 76–77, 208–15

Salishan sturgeon nose canoes, 37–38
Salish language, 4
Salish people, 16, 88
salmon
    about, 120–21, 124
    of the Columbia River, 18, 22, 45,
        90–97, 103–5, 130, 132
    hatcheries, 41, 113–15, 120, 122, 177–78
    Kettle Falls ceremony, 41, 118–19,
        121–23, 180
    of the Kootenay River, 132, 133
    mussels parasitizing, 132–33
    of the Pend d'Oreille River, 104–5
    reintroduction, 97, 113–24, 177–78
    significance to the Sinixt, 124, 177–78
    tracking, 120, 123
    traps, 39–41, 94, 95–96, 103–4
Salmon Chiefs, 22, 95, 103–4, 176, 179,
    207
Salmo River, 152–53, 154, 165, 217
Sandy Island, 144

Sanpoil people, 122
saskatoon bush, 91, 100, 107, 201, 202–3
Selkirk College, 37–38, 143
settlers
    burial sites and, 144–45
    marriages with Sinixt women, 163–68
    relations with Colville Confederated
        Tribes, 145
    relations with Sinixt People, 19–20,
        22–24, 45, 70–75, 106, 130, 151,
        156–57, 159, 182, 213
    value system of, 80, 130–31, 179, 194
Seymour, Aneas, 179
Seymour, Lena, *183*
Seymour, Pete, 181, *183*, 207
Seymour, Virgil, 5–6, 33–34, 181, 213, 215
Shadow Top, Chief, 154, 155, 156
sharpening stone, the, *117*
Shuswap people, 24
Silver King Mine, 160, 165
Simpson, George, 22
Sinixt People
    abandonment thesis, 215
    as "American Indians", 23, 213
    ancestry, 214
    archaeological collecting and, 62–66
    camas fields of, 81–87
    ceremonies, 41, 118–19, 121–23, 129,
        180
    character of, 50
    diet and food practices, 70, 81–89,
        95, 96, 99, 100–101, 107–12, 127–41,
        144, 190, 195–97, 201–3, 204,
        205–6, 211, 216–17, 222–24
    dress and ornamentation, 47–48, 121,
        134–35, 190, 196–97, 206, 207
    "extinction" of, 1, 2, 19–20, 24–26,
        53–54, 60–61, 72, 142–43
    forced migration of, 60–61, 78–79, 80,
        174, 175, 181, 184, 214
    founding of Nelson and, 160–68
    historical record of, 3–4, 11–12, 19
    as "hunter-gatherers," 217
    language, 16, 30, 41, 47, 50–51, 55,

61, 70, 82, 83, 99, 202, 205, 207, 222–24
mapping of, 3–4, 26
marriages, 155–59
marriages with settlers, 163–68
naming of, 3
origins, 16, 62
personal names, 51, 52, 55–56
place names, 3–4, 8, 42–43, 53, 67–68, 70, 90–91, 95, 125–26, 136, 147, 153, 175, 180, 188, 192, 193
pronunciation of "Sinixt", 16
relations with Colville Confederated Tribes, 18, 25, 95, 111, 175
relations with settlers, 19–20, 22–24, 45, 54–60, 70–75, 83–84, 106, 130–31, 151, 156–57, 159, 194, 213
relations with Spokane Tribe, 108
reverence for nature, 128–30, 131, 214–15, 217–18
seasonal migration, 17, 23–24, 45, 55, 153, 190–91
social hierarchy, 17
spirituality, 12, 17–18, 22, 32, 50–52, 151–52, 156, 179
stories of, 127–28, 131, 147, 154, 157, 207, 210–11, 219–21
territory, 18–19, 170
women of, 17, 82, 83, 85–86, 88, 89, 95, 97–103, 137, 195–96, 201, 206, 207
Sinixt villages
archaeological evidence of, 16
Arrow Lakes, 56
Big Sheep Creek, 193
Bonnington Falls–West Arm–Salmo (map), 146–47
Brilliant, 69–75
camas and, 87
Crescent Valley, 136–37, 144
Fauquier–Castlegar (map), 67–68
Fort Shepherd, 106
in general, 82
Grohman Creek, 162
housing in, 22, 35, 49, 105, 105, 177

Inchelium, 136
Incomappleux River, 107
Kootenay River canyon, 133
Kootenay River mouth, 70–75, 84
mapped by David Thompson, 21
Nakusp, 26–27
Northport, 193
Pend d'Oreille River, 53
recorded by David Thompson, 21
Revelstoke–Fauquier (map), 42–43
Robson, 84
Rossland–Omak (map), 90–91
Slocan Lake–Slocan Pool (map), 125–26
Slocan Narrows, 17, 135
Slocan River, 144
Waneta, 104
winter life in, 45
Skaha Lake, 114
Skoyelpi. See Colville Confederated Tribes
Slade, Charlie, 38
Slade, C.J.C., 32
slavery, 18, 157
Slocan Lake, 16, 45, 94, 126, 134
Slocan Narrows, 17, 134, 135
Slocan Pool, 96, 133, 143–44
Slocan River, 94, 136
smallpox, 20, 22, 50, 52
Smith, Allan, 206
Smith, Celia, 207
Smith, Harlan, 139, 143, 147, 152, 162
snowshoe hare, 47
snowshoes, 48
soapberries, 202–3
songs, 41, 61, 122, 204, 208–9, 211
soopalallie, 202–3
Sophie Edwards (Green Blanket Feet), 154–59
South Slocan Dam, 133
spirituality, 12, 17–18, 32, 50–52, 151–52, 156, 179, 194, 205, 207, 210–11
See also burial sites
Spokane House, 171

Spokane people, 16, 53, 108, 120, 171–72, 220–23
Spokane River, 82, 83, 120, 124, 171–72
spotted knapweed, 88
Sproat, Gilbert Martin, 166
spruce, 100
Staubert Lake, 153
steelhead trout, 95, 113, 114, 116, 125–26, 132
St. Paul's Mission, 50, 52, 53, 156
St. Peter's Station, 50
Strong, William, 167
sturgeon, 41, 82, 118, 218
Sullivan, John, 217
Supreme Court of Canada, 212, 216
See also R. v. Desautel
Su-Steel, Justine, 91, 104, 163, 167
Swan, Coose, 142
Swan, Jim, 142
Swan, Yvonne, 142
sweat lodges, 18, 32, 43, 63, 95, 205
Syrett, Charles, 3
Syringa Creek, 74

Taghum, 151
tamarack, 29
Teck, 197–98
Teit, James, 24, 31, 48, 51, 71, 74, 98, 101, 102, 134, 136
thimbleberries, 201–2
Thompson, David, 19, 20, 31, 45, 64, 71, 149, 150
Thompson people, 16
Tidball, John C., 22
tiger lilies, 129, 196
Tincup Rapids, 70
Toad Mountain, 160, 165, 166, 168
Touchstones Nelson Museum, 141
Toulou, Helen, 82, 156, 181
trade, 12–15, 20, 22, 68, 70, 83, 91, 95, 104, 155, 196, 205
Trail, 198
trails, 12–15, 153, 191–92
trapping
    animals, 17, 43, 56, 57, 74, 75, 153, 204, 205, 211
    fish, 34, 39–40, 55, 94–95, 95–96, 104
    snowshoe rabbits, 47
treaties, 22, 26, 57, 118, 119–20, 187, 188
tree burials, 141
trout, 7, 9, 16, 42–43, 95, 113, 114, 116, 125–26, 130, 132, 146–47, 153, 218
Trout Lake, 16, 147, 153
Tsimshian people, 197
tule lodges, 35
Turnbull, James, 153
Turner, Nancy J., 83, 203

Universities Consortium on Columbia River Governance, 115
Upper Columbia United Tribes, 113, 115, 178
US–Canada border, 20–25, 53–54, 60–61, 76–77, 78, 163, 170–71, 172–73, 183, 190–91, 209–10, 212–13, 216
Usk, 111

vaccination, 22, 52
Vallican, 27, 142, 144
Verigin, Peter, 73–74

Waneta Dam, 104–5
war, 18
Washington Territory, 22
Watt, Robert, 27
weaving, 48, 97–103
Webber, Harold, 75
West Demars, 137
West Kootenay Power and Light, 143, 160
Whatshan, 43
White, Cull, 159
white pine, Western, 29–31, 36
Wildlife Act, 209–10, 213
Williams, Dauney, 164
Wilson Creek, 126, 203
Withered Top, Chief, 154
Wiyot people, 196
women
    as "country wives," 155–56

gender equity and diet, 196
matrilocal society and, 17, 83
war about, 18
work of, 47–48, 82, 83, 85–86, 88, 89, 95,
    97–103, 137, 139, 155, 195–96, 201, 206
Wong, Harry, 77
Wynecoop, Arnold "Judge", 108–12, 172
Wynecoop, Nancy, 32, 39, 47, 82, 107,
    108, 127, 131, 141, 204, 205, 219–21

Yakama Nation, 53, 122
yew, 29
Yurok people, 196

zoomorphic bowls, 139, 140

We would like to also take this opportunity to acknowledge the traditional territories upon which we live and work. In Calgary, Alberta, we acknowledge the Niitsítapi (Blackfoot) and the people of the Treaty 7 region in Southern Alberta, which includes the Siksika, the Piikuni, the Kainai, the Tsuut'ina, and the Stoney Nakoda First Nations, including Chiniki, Bearpaw, and Wesley First Nations. The City of Calgary is also home to Métis Nation of Alberta, Region III. In Victoria, British Columbia, we acknowledge the traditional territories of the Lkwungen (Esquimalt and Songhees), Malahat, Pacheedaht, Scia'new, T'Sou-ke, and W̱SÁNEĆ (Pauquachin, Tsartlip, Tsawout, Tseycum) peoples.

EILEEN DELEHANTY PEARKES explores landscape and the human imagination, with a focus on the history of the upper Columbia River and its tributaries. Born in the United States, educated at Stanford University (B.A., English) and the University of British Columbia (M.A., English), her work resists nationality and insists on truth. Popular on-line columns on the western Canadian landscape stress the need for reconciliation of people with land. She has spent over two decades working alongside the Sinixt tribe, to bring awareness to their story. In 2014, she curated an extensive exhibit on the history of the Upper Columbia River system in Canada for Touchstones Nelson museum and the Columbia Basin Trust. It details dramatic ecological and social changes in British Columbia, both before and after the Columbia River Treaty (1961–64), and won an award of excellence from the Canadian Museum Association. Eileen has published two books with RMB: *The Geography of Memory: Reclaiming the Cultural, Natural and Spiritual History of the Snayackstx (Sinixt) First People* and *A River Captured: The Columbia River Treaty and Catastrophic Change*. A dual citizen, Eileen divides her time between California and Nelson, British Columbia.

"It is for me to say that you white men when you came here and landed, you came on a little piece of bark, and with a few sticks tied together, and a few of you on it. You found us that day in plenty; you had nothing. You did not bring your wealth with you."

—Chief James Bernard addressing
a US congressional committee